T0381015

My 6ixties Revisited

Memoirs From St Andrew to St Andrews

MARTIN G KAVANAUGH

authorHOUSE

AuthorHouse™
1663 Liberty Drive
Bloomington, IN 47403
www.authorhouse.com
Phone: 833-262-8899

Published by AuthorHouse 01/12/2024

ISBN: 979-8-8230-1794-7 (sc)
ISBN: 979-8-8230-1793-0 (hc)
ISBN: 979-8-8230-1792-3 (e)

Library of Congress Control Number: 2023922076

Print information available on the last page.

This book is printed on acid-free paper.

Contents

Dedication

To my loving wife Ginger.
For her 48 years of love and friendship.
A great mother to our three children
and loving grandmother.

Part 1

Nineteen 6ixty

6-7 years old

It is December 31st, 1959. I do not know it today but I am about to embark on one of the most fascinating decades of the 20th Century. A decade that will play a large part in painting the mural of my life's future. A decade of family, friends, education, religion, and work that will have the greatest influence on my entire life. A decade for our country beginning in peace but heading toward war, anger, and protest. None of which I understood or cared about at the time. A decade marked by the pall of political assassinations and the fascination of achievement in space. A decade of music that paved the melodic boulevard for the rest of my life. A decade that introduced me to many sports which I dearly loved.

For now, I am a happy go lucky six-year-old first grader growing up in a loving Catholic middle-class family of eight. I have two older brothers, two younger brothers, and a younger sister. The youngest brother Patrick, three months old. We had just recently moved into a newly built four-bedroom ranch home on the northeast side of Indianapolis. This area of town was referred to as Devon Woods. The homes in the area were filled with friendly families, built on large wooded lots, and crime was something you only heard about on the news, and normally but not always, far away from where we were. Our catholic church and school, St Andrew, was the largest parish in the state. It was our good fortune to grow up as students and parishioners with many like families at St Andrew.

Our family Christmas tree is still standing in the front room from the recent holiday. Strands of C9 lights continued to be lit each evening on the artificial tree, though its days were numbered. There were a few toys still strewn about the front room floor that holds the tree, including our new Lionel train set with locomotive, three

1

box cars, and caboose. Some tinsel, originally hung with a mother's care and a child's assistance from each tree branch had haphazardly fallen to the carpet below. A few stockings still in place on our new fireplace mantel but no longer drooping with the weight of fruit, walnuts, chocolates, and gifts from Christmas morning. I am still on Christmas break for a few more days. School at St Andrew would resume on Monday January 4th. Though it is New Years' Eve, I do not recall any excitement about turning the page on the calendar from 1959 to 1960. Just another fun filled day for us as part of the holiday. And though midnight would usher in a new decade, no one would stay up to welcome it in. Oldest brother Michael was nine years old but still a few years away from being of an age to help ring in the New Year. With 6ix kids and the youngest three months old, mom and dad were not staying up until midnight. They took their rest when the opportunity presented itself.

As an active sports family, we might have interest in the New Years' Day football games, particularly the Rose Bowl featuring the Wisconsin Badgers vs. Washington's Huskies. We were not fans of either team but the Rose Bowl was already an established tradition. Mom and Dad would enjoy glimpses of the Rose Bowl Parade prior to the game on our 19th black & white Zenith TV as my two older brothers, Mike, Tim, and I, would throw the football around outdoors. The younger siblings would stay indoors playing with their new toys and be looked after as needed. January 1st 1960 was a particularly nice winter day in Indianapolis. It was dry, the sky was mostly overcast, there was a light breeze with comfortable temperatures near forty degrees. During the 6ixties it was commonplace for us to play outdoors, if not mandatory. We were life-long beneficiaries of such daily outdoor exercise. The new year was now off and running. A new decade was off and running. And even though I nor anyone else would have a clue, it would be a decade as memorable as any we might ever live through.

On Monday January 4th I was back in school at St Andrew for the second semester of Grade 1. We walked to St Andrew school every day from our new home. We walked home for lunch, back to school again, and home again at 3:00 pm. We lived a short half mile from school and it was an easy, enjoyable walk. When I saw young primary school kids while in my 60's, I cannot imagine them walking a half mile to school. They are so little. We nor our parents ever gave it a second thought. Kids in my 60's never even got on a bus in front of their home without a parent seeing them off. Unless there was serious inclement weather, I walked back and forth from school including lunch from the same location for eight straight years. Mostly uneventful, usually with a sibling or two, and classmates and neighbors. You would think walking to school for ten minutes would be a trouble-free event but you might be surprised how the temptation of throwing a stick or a snowball or jumping into a puddle of water in the middle of a near idle street could get a youngster in trouble. That is simply the way most boys are wired. One morning I was involved in a snowball throwing incident with an 8th grade patrol boy. Patrol boys stood out due to their gleaming white belt with shoulder strap they proudly wore signifying them as a safety patrol agent for the school. That is the day I met our principal, Sister Anne Imelda, in a 'business' meeting. I do not recall the verdict.

Sister Anne Timothy was my first-grade teacher. We learned to read, print, and solve minor problems in arithmetic. Art class could be difficult at times. I had problems staying inside the lines. I had the same problem in my 60's but for different reasons. In all my grade school years, I do not recall ever having much of a homework load. That is the way it should be. After school it was common to change clothes and play outdoors, weather permitting. There was a ball of some kind involved most of the time. Depending on the season it could be baseball, basketball, or football.

In February 1960, a small group of black college students began a sit-in at the F.W. Woolworth food counter in Greensboro, N.C. because the store would not serve blacks. The second day of the sit-in the group grew from 4 to 8. Day 3 brought 60 students and day 4 brought 300. The sit-ins were instrumental in an effort for equal rights. The site of the old F.W. Woolworth is now home to the International Civil Rights Center and Museum. A six-year-old first grader had no idea what was going on, but a now 60+ year old finds it extraordinary the bravery those people displayed.

On February 27th, an event happened that had no impact on me. I am certain I was not even aware it happened at the time. The US Olympic Hockey Team won their first ever Gold Medal in ice hockey at the Squaw Valley Games. Our hockey success had no immediate effect on me but later in life hockey became my avocation and vocation. I coached youth hockey teams from 1985 thru 2000. Both of our sons were stand out and all State players. Our daughter helped me run multiple tournaments. I owned a hockey equipment retail store from 1992 thru 2004. All three of our children pitched in earning a paycheck.

1960 was a year in which the nation took a Census and on April 1st it was determined that we were a country of 179 million people. In my late 60's we were double that amount, if you could find them all to count. Too many in my opinion. The world population in 1960 was 4.3 billion. In my 60's the world would top 7.5 billion but right now, I only cared about the people in my house, relatives, neighborhood, school, and a few sports heroes.

On May 11th, Adolf Eichmann was captured in Argentina. Mr. Eichmann was a key figure in the horrific holocaust of World War II and had been living in hiding in Argentina since 1950. Upon his capture he was returned to Jerusalem to face war crimes and was found guilty. He was hung for his offenses on June 1, 1962.

As late May arrived and just before Jim Rathman won one of the closest and exciting Indianapolis 500's ever, I passed Grade 1 and would enter Grade 2 in the fall of the year. The Indianapolis 500 was a major annual event for our city and everyone seemed to show an interest.

We were fortunate enough to be able to take family vacations most years. This summer dad would gas up the family wagon for twenty-five cents a gallon and we went up to northern Michigan to visit Mackinac Island. We stayed at The Grand Hotel, took horse rides, and looked forward to daily ice cream treats. There were no cars permitted on the island and that is still the way it is in my 60's.

After arriving by ferry, travel was on foot, bicycle, or horse drawn carriages. We also visited nearby Sault Ste. Marie, Michigan and we were fascinated by the Soo Locks which allow ships and boats to travel from Lake Superior to the lower Great Lakes. It is fascinating to watch and a marvel of engineering.

Labor Day was Sept 5th and it was traditional at this time to begin the school year the day following Labor Day. This year school at St Andrew started on my oldest brother Mike's tenth birthday. I wonder if that was a bummer for him? In Grade 2 I had a lay teacher, Mrs. McCann. I met a kid by the name of Joe Hagelskamp this year and my life changed for the better because of it. We became best friends throughout the 6ixties and for the next twenty years. In 1974, Joe was the best man at our wedding.

Students learned arithmetic in grade 2 by adding and subtracting two-digit figures on worksheets. Religion, Spelling, Phonics, and Music were also part of the every-day curriculum. The St. Andrew grading system was simple enough. E for Excellent, G for Very Good, S for Satisfactory, P for Poor, and F for Failure. The opposite side of the report card had boxes that could be checked for Obedience, Courtesy, Cooperation, and Punctuality. I quickly fell comfortably into the grading category of S.

This fall brought us the inaugural season of the upstart American Football League. I eventually became a big fan of the AFL as it was more offensive oriented and introduced fans to the more exciting 'vertical game.' Before decades end, AFL teams were beating their more established counterparts of the NFL. A merger agreement was made in June of 1966 at the behest of the senior league.

On September 10th, hurricane Donna blasted the Florida Keys and the southwest coast of Florida making landfall in Naples. Donna claimed 50 victims. Forty years later I purchased a condominium just up the coast in Ft. Myers and another four years after that, 2004, hurricane Charley came through with major damage on Ft. Myers beach and nearby Sanibel Island. Charley claimed 15 victims of its own. I knew nothing about hurricane Donna but in 2004 when Charley came through, the news and talk of the town was, "this is the first hurricane to hit the Ft Myers area since Donna". Old time residents of the area still remembered Donna with great recall and fear. Unfortunately, Charley seemed to spawn additional hurricanes over the next couple of decades concluding with hurricane Ian when I was 69 years old. Ian claimed over 100 lives in the Ft Myers area.

On September 26th, the first televised Presidential debate took place between John F Kennedy and Richard M Nixon. It was the first of four televised debates and 70 million viewers tuned in to watch the men in a battle of wits and vision for our country. I did not watch one bit of it. In my 60's you could not get me not to watch.

On October 13th after returning from school we rushed to our TV to watch the final innings of Game 7 of the World Series played between the Pittsburgh Pirates and our favorite, the New York Yankees. Yes, they played day games back in the day. Tied 9-9 in the bottom of the ninth, Pirate 2nd baseman Bill Mazeroski deposited a ball over Yogi Berra's head and the left field wall to take the championship. It was a walk-off before the phrase was coined. In seven games the Bronx Bombers outscored the Pirates 55-27, but the Pirates won the best of seven Fall Classic. Yankee second baseman Bobby Richardson won the Series MVP award, the first time a player from the losing team was so honored. In other sporting news earlier in the year, the Boston Celtics took out the St. Louis Hawks for the NBA title and the Montreal Canadiens beat the Toronto Maple Leafs to win the Stanley Cup. In football, Dallas and Minnesota were awarded NFL franchises. In the Rome Olympics, track star Wilma Rudolph became a household name. Boxing great Cassius Clay made his world stage debut at this same Olympiad. We would hear much more from Mr. Clay in later years.

On November 8th, John F Kennedy defeated Richard Nixon in a close Presidential race. It was the first Presidential election where all 50 States participated. Hawaii was added as a fiftieth state in 1959. The electoral results this year had one glaring difference from the map of my 60's. In 1960 the Democrat won Texas and the Republican won California. In my 60's we would expect just the opposite. However, in 1960 the Republican candidate was from

California and the Democrat Vice-Presidential candidate was from Texas. I do not know what my father thought of Kennedy but JFK was an Irish Catholic like us, so I recall his Presidency as a popular thing in my circles. All our St Andrew schools 24 classrooms would eventually have a picture of Kennedy on its walls, along with the Pope.

In 1960 entertainment, Ben Hur won the Oscar for Best Picture and Alfred Hitchcock's Psycho became a big hit. The great Clark Gable, star of 'Gone with the Wind' arguably the greatest film of all time and gets my vote, died at the age of 59. Harper Lee's 'To Kill a Mockingbird' came out in print. It would become a movie in two years and later became one of my all-time favorite films.

Nineteen 6ixty was an excellent year for me. I was always loved and looked after. If not by my parents, by neighbors or my two older brothers.

Nineteen 6ixty-one

7-8 years old

During second grade at St Andrew, I had comfortably fallen into the category of S for Satisfactory grades. We received quarterly report cards that had to be signed by a parent and returned to school. There were eleven different subjects to grade and I received thirty-eight S's out of a possible 44 for the school year. Dad occasionally referred to me as Mr. Satisfactory around our house. A lifetime of mediocre learning was on firm footing. In my 60's, I wrote my second book called, 'Mr. Satisfactory'.

Democrat John F Kennedy was sworn in as our 35th President and would usher in 'The New Frontier'. He famously said, "Ask not what your country can do for you, ask what you can do for your country." A refreshing statement like that in my 60's would place you firmly in the Republican Party and mocked by Democrats and most television news stations.

On April 12th, Yuri Gagarin, a Russian Cosmonaut, was the first man to orbit the earth beating the US in the so-called space race. A major American space event happened a few weeks later, May 5th, 1961. Every class at St Andrew school was allowed to watch TV as Alan Shepard became the first American astronaut in space. The entire school was excited. The US Space program had unthinkable accomplishments in store before this decade was over. Another event that shaped our family's life happened on this same May 5th, day. Our father struck out on his own and opened his own plumbing supply business. Before this undertaking he was a salesman for local Winthrop Supply in plumbing wholesale. In my 60's I made sales calls to Winthrop Supply as a salesman for Mueller Industries, a copper tube, and fittings manufacturer. The shingle on dad's new enterprise read, 'Kavanaugh Supply'. The bold move eventually changed the family fortunes for a generation.

A week later a band of Cuban exiles failed at their attempt to overthrow Fidel Castro's revolution in Cuba. The 'Bay of Pigs' invasion was financed and supported by President John F Kennedy and the US Government. The failed invasion led to tensions between the United States with Cuba and the Soviet Union. All the 1,300 + exile invaders were either killed or captured. This event set the stage for 1962's Cuban Missile Crisis. Children of the 6ixties became aware of nuclear threat and its danger.

On May 4th, US Freedom Riders, mostly College students, began an interstate bus ride from Washington DC to the South, to test a U.S. Supreme Court integration decision. Ten days later a Freedom Riders bus was fire-bombed in Alabama. The protesters were beaten by a mob of Ku Klux Klan members. The Alabama Governor showed indifference to the violence. Freedom Riders would continue on to Mississippi, receiving more beatings and innocent black folk were jailed. One of the young Riders was John Lewis. He became a 32-year Congressman from Georgia beginning in 1988. He was a great man in the Civil Rights movement. Attorney General Robert F Kennedy, the president's younger brother, was doing all he could to see peace prevail. There would be many more disturbances like this in the 6ixties involving race.

My 1961 summers were spent playing backyard baseball, swimming at the pool, and outdoor games with neighbors after dinner. Catching lightning bugs at night in jars was a popular pastime. My brothers and I played little baseball games in the yard such as 'hot box' or 'pepper.' Hot box was a game of 'run-down' between two bases. Pepper was a game of bunting the ball to one or two players from a short distance, the fielders continually pitching the ball back under-handed. There would be non-stop action of bunt, field, & toss. Playing these little three-man games is why I believe our generation produced better young ball players. We not only played the game, we played **at** the game.

On August 1st, Six Flags Over Texas amusement park opened near Dallas, Texas. Nine years later I visited the park as part of a Cotton Bowl trip with my dad and our family friends, the Schimschocks.

On August 13th, East Germany began construction of the Berlin Wall. This 12' high wall over 60 miles in length was built to divide West Berlin from East Berlin and East Germany. There were major political differences in Germany between the east and west. The east built the wall to 'protect their people' and to build a Socialist State. The wall stood until 1990. In my 60's, US President Donald Trump was building a wall between our southern border and Mexico. We were building a wall to keep people out as opposed to East Germany keeping people in. The United States in my 60's was having difficulty with illegal immigration.

I began Grade 3 at St Andrew in September of 1961. I had another lay teacher, this time a Mrs. Harding. Of all my teachers throughout my educational life, Mrs. Harding is the one I remember the least. I do remember that outside our classroom door and on the wall of the hallway was poster board with all the students' names carefully written. Various topics such as student academic accomplishments, attendance, or conduct were listed for recognition. Adhesive stars or dots would be affixed next to your name if it was deemed that you achieved status for such designation. It seemed like the girls always had more stars than the boys. The space next to my name had plenty of room for more stars or dots. Our school had a new principal as I entered Grade 3. Sister Anne Imelda was gone and replaced by Sister Rose Angele. I have not met the Superior Mother face to face yet.

On September 30th, The Flintstones TV show premiered becoming the first primetime animated TV show ever. Cartoons on TV were popular viewing for children in the 6ixties. Popeye or The Three Stooges were extremely popular at this time. Up until this point, all cartoons were viewed on Saturday morning, so a primetime cartoon was exciting.

My first report cards in Grade 3 showed improvement including an E for Excellent in Spelling. I must say I continued to suffer in Art class. On one project meant to take home for our parents to use in the home, my selection of colors was frightening. Our John Gnagy 'Learn to Draw' kit at home was not having a positive effect on my art skills. Mom still pretended to love my project meant to hang on a wall to hold incoming mail. I still have it at the end of my 6ixties, packed away in a box with other frivolous keepsakes.

The day before Thanksgiving mom gave birth to her 7th child. Seventh. Brian *Andrew* Kavanaugh was born on Wednesday, Nov 22nd. I wonder what happened the following day for Thanksgiving Dinner? Back in those days the mother would not have come home from the hospital for at least two days. I have no idea what we did about the holiday dinner but I will bet large money our Great Aunt Margaret was involved. My father's aunt, our Great Aunt Margaret, lived just a few miles away and she was around for all the big events. She was a life-long single lady and made time for all of us. Because of her closeness to the family, she was our most beloved relative.

In sporting news, Roger Maris broke the immortal Babe Ruth's home run record when he cracked number 61 on October 1st. The New York Yankees took care of the Cincinnati Red Legs in the World Series. The great Ty Cobb, aka the Georgia Peach died on July 17th. Mr. Cobb was a twelve-time batting champion for the Detroit Tigers and still holds the record for the highest lifetime batting average in MLB history. The Boston Celtics took out the St. Louis Hawks in consecutive years. Chicago's Blackhawks beat the Detroit Red Wings in the first all American Stanley Cup Final in eleven years. Two Canadian boys were born 8 days apart. Both would someday play professional hockey for a brief period in Indianapolis. They became hockey superstars and one became the Greatest. They were Mark Messier and Wayne Gretzky. I saw both live a couple of times but saw most of their careers on TV and they gave me much viewing pleasure. AJ Foyt won his first of four Indy 500's. AJ became arguably Indy's all-time most popular driver.

In entertainment, Disney's One Hundred and One Dalmatians movie was released. Also, the musical, West Side Story came out. The Beatles played their first gig at the Cavern Club in Liverpool, England.

Nineteen 6ixty-one was a simple year for a 7 or 8-year-old. And it was full of fun with family, friends, and neighbors.

Nineteen Sixty-Two

8-9 years old

Early in the year on January 26th, the dance 'The Twist' was declared impure and banned at all Catholic Schools. The Twist was a song and dance popularized by singer Chubby Checker. The Church was convinced it would undermine the morals of youth. I was not yet a dancer so it had no effect on me. I will be honest; I never was a dancer.

On February 20th, astronaut John Glenn orbited the earth three times in Friendship Seven. No doubt the televisions were on again in our St Andrew classrooms. The space program was dear to the heart of President Kennedy. On September 12th 1962, Kennedy delivered his "We choose to go to the Moon" speech. Kennedy considered space as the new frontier. Part of the President's speech at Rice University read: "We choose to go to the moon...We choose to go to the moon in this decade and do the other things, not because they are easy, but because they are hard." It seemed folly at the time, but we did make it to the moon and back before the decades end. John F Kennedy sadly was not around to see his dream. Looking back at the President's quote I can say that I like the idea of doing things because they are hard. I like the additional satisfaction one receives from accomplishing hard tasks.

It was traditional for my siblings and I to wear something green on St. Patrick's Day but this year mom made me wear this very large white plastic novelty bow tie with green four-leaf clovers printed on it. The tie had an elastic band that went over your head and behind your neck to keep it in place. It was terribly embarrassing but I survived it. Children do not need the ridicule or teasing from classmates but I am certain mom thought it was cute. In my 60's, teasing from fellow classmates was called bullying. A student in my 60's could be suspended for such an act.

On May 1, Target opened their first store in Minnesota. Fast on their heels was Walmart who opened their first store in Arkansas just two months later. In our 60's, my wife Ginger was a big fan of Target and I had no issue with Walmart. It seemed most everyone supported one or the other, if not both.

On May 22nd, reigning American League MVP and new home run king Roger Maris was walked five times in a nine-inning game. Four of them were intentional. How could a single batter strike that much fear in his opponent?

In September I was welcomed to 4th grade at St Andrew. I had the pleasure of being in Sister Mary Canisius' room. She was quite possibly the nicest teacher I ever had. Irene Poinsette was a classmate and the cutest girl in fourth grade and throughout most of primary school for that matter. I suppose I had a crush on Irene but like most shy young boys, did nothing about it. In later years, I sometimes wondered what ever happened to Irene after grade school as we attended different high schools. I probably saw her on occasion at Sunday Mass or some other place during our teen-age years, but it would not have been often. I did reach out to her in my 60's and we finally met up at a 50-year grade school reunion. She still looked great. We had a pleasant conversation and enjoyed each other's company much of the evening.

On October 1st, Johnny Carson took over as host of NBC's Tonight Show. He held the post for thirty years. I was not watching late night TV in nineteen-6ixty two but I saw him many times in later years. He was a legend and still the best late-night talk show host ever.

In October and November of 1962, the U.S. encountered the Soviet Union in what came to be known as the Cuban Missile Crisis. A tense situation involving nuclear missiles set up in Cuba with the support of the Soviet Union were aimed at the United States. After days of tense negotiations, cooler heads prevailed. The combatant leaders, Nikita Khrushchev of the Soviet Union, Fidel Castro of Cuba, and President John F Kennedy of the United States came to a disarming agreement. It was common in the 6ixties to see nuclear or radiation symbols in hallways or entry ways of our St Andrew grade school and church. In case of an attack, hiding under our school desk would save us from annihilation. Growing up, Nikita Khrushchev was the scariest man on earth.

On election day of 1962, the incumbent Democrat Governor of California, Pat Brown, defeated former Vice-President and 1960 Republican Presidential Nominee Richard M Nixon in the California Gubernatorial race. Mr. Nixon accused the media of favoring his opponent. In my 60's the media still overtly play favorites. In Mr. Nixon's concession speech, he said this is my "last press conference" and "you won't have Dick Nixon to kick around anymore." Six years later Richard Nixon was elected President of the United States. I liked the guy and in 1972 he is the first person I ever voted for, for President.

In the world of sports, The Toronto Maple Leafs beat the defending champion Chicago Blackhawks for The Stanley Cup. Boston's Celtics continued their dominance with a finals' series win over the L.A. Lakers. In one game during the season, Wilt Chamberlain scored a record 100 points in a single game playing for the Philadelphia Warriors. I still believe this record will someday be broken. Not because of pure talent but because of a stunt or lack of respect for the game. The Yankees took down the S.F. Giants in 7, winning the final game 1-0 behind Ralph Terry's shutout. Ralph Terry gave up the 9th inning home run to Bill Mazeroski to end the 1960 World Series. Arnold Palmer won his third green jacket at Augusta but up and comer Jack Nicklaus took Arnie down in a playoff for the U.S. Open golf title at Oakmont in Pennsylvania. Brazil won the World Cup Soccer Tournament and a young man simply known as Pele', was the star on the team. Pele' was later voted as the top soccer player of the 20th Century. Rodger Ward won the Indy 500.

'To Kill a Mockingbird' hit the big screen and 'Dr. No' starring Sean Connery became the first James Bond film in a franchise that has lasted over 50 years including more than 25 films. I have seen every one of the Bond films. Sex symbol and movie star Marilyn Monroe died at the age of 36. Even nine-year old boys knew the name Marilyn Monroe. As many as fifty years later I saw her in a 1961 movie called The Misfits. She co-starred along with Clark Gable and it was each of their last movies. The 35-year-old Marilyn looked terrific in that movie. For Clark Gable, the movie was released posthumously. The longest serving First Lady also died in 1962. Eleanor Roosevelt, wife of President Franklin D. Roosevelt passed. She was a hands-on First Lady and a major asset to Franklin's leadership.

Being 8 & 9 years old in Indianapolis was a great time. We had terrific neighbors and I enjoyed my fourth-grade schooling. Nineteen 6ixty-two was okay by me.

Nineteen 6 ixty-three

9-10 years old

As Grade 4 rolled along I was doing surprisingly well. I had become proficient at math. I was also a top speller and doing well in US Geography. I think the fact that we drove on family trips helped me in geography. It was common to have weekly spelling or math contests in the classroom. I was good at both. Oftentimes the contest would be boys versus girls. The boys might be asked to stand on the windows side of the room, the girls on the opposing locker side. There was never any hesitation. All the students knew exactly where to line up. In my 60's this might have caused confusion with some students not knowing which side of the room to stand on. Things had gotten off the rails to unthought of proportions. A fun part of grade school was changing seat assignments. This often happened at the beginning of the second semester. Usually, seating was done alphabetically but depending on the teachers' whim of choosing a left to right or front to back rotation, your seat neighbors would change.

On February 11th, the first ever cooking show was on television. In my 60's you can watch cooking shows on TV all day long. In fact, during my 60's there is a Cooking Channel with 24/7 cooking shows with various celebrity chefs. But the first was Julia Child with her version called The French Chef and she found immediate success. The series ran for ten years and won Emmy Awards.

On June 3, 1963 Pope John XXIII died. As a young boy growing up in the Catholic Church it was common knowledge knowing who the Pope was. His picture also hung on classroom walls along with our President. When Pope John XXIII died, it was major news in my circles even at the young age of nine.

A week later, Alabama Governor George Wallace made a symbolic attempt to uphold his campaign promise of segregated education. As black students Vivian Malone Jones and James Hood arrived at the University of Alabama to begin their college education, Governor Wallace stood on the steps of the doorway to block their entrance. A call was made to President Kennedy and the National Guard was brought in. After the Governor made a speech on States rights, he stepped aside to allow entrance to the first two black students at Alabama University. That evening, President Kennedy gave a national address from the Oval Office on Civil Rights. And later still that same evening in the State of Mississippi, a field secretary for the NAACP was returning home to his family from a church meeting. Just past midnight, young Medgar Evers exited his vehicle and was gunned down by Byron De La Beckwith. It took 31 years to finally convict the man. A few years after the conviction, 1996, the movie 'Ghosts of Mississippi' depicting the event and trial was out on the big screen.

Wallace ran unsuccessfully for President in 1968 as an independent and again in 1972 until he was shot five times while campaigning in Laurel, Maryland on May 15th, 1972. The shooting left Mr. Wallace paralyzed for the rest of his life. He died in 1998 at the age of 79.

In late August we took a family vacation out east. It was Mom, Dad, my two older brothers Mike, Tim, and myself. The younger half did not make the cut and I cannot explain that but have no issue with it. I was cut from a vacation years later on a 1968 trip. New York City was our final destination but our first stop along the way was Gettysburg, Pa. where a great Civil War battle took place in early July of 1863. This was the Centennial year of that battle. I love American history and the visit had quite an effect on me. I still remember a lot about this visit. It is possible that trip is what turned me on to American history. We went onward to Washington D.C. and visited The Washington Monument and Lincoln Memorial. We also visited Arlington National Cemetery and the Tomb of the Unknown Soldier. While in Washington we visited the Church of the Immaculate Conception. Mom and Dad never let a Catholic teaching moment go unfulfilled. As a ten-year old Catholic boy in every sense of the word, I was fascinated by the grandeur of the church. It was placed on the National Register of Historic Places in 2003. If I took this same trip in my 60's, the highlight of the trip might be over as I became fascinated with American history. But this was the 6ixties and my highlight was yet to come. We finally arrived in the Big Apple. Our first visit was to the observatory of the Empire State Building. I still do not like heights.

The big moment for me, and I expect my brothers too, was a Twi-night doubleheader baseball game between the New York Yankees and the Cleveland Indians. It was August 21st, 1963. We saw Yankee Stadium many times on televised games, all in black and white. We knew the lineup and batting average of every player on the New York team. Summer reading for my older brothers and I was scouring over every box score in the newspaper of the previous day's baseball games. That, and reading the back of cereal boxes. I can picture our walk up to the Stadium in my mind. It was a warm sunny day and the Longines clock outside the Stadium read 4:43. Game 1 start time was 6:02 pm. Walking out from the concourse tunnel to the box seats we were greeted by sunshine, green grass, and pinstripes. It was probably the most beautiful thing these ten-year old eyes had ever seen. We had excellent seats and enjoyed most of the pre-game warmups and batting practice.

In game one the Yankees won 3-1 in what would appear to be a normal game. We learned prior to the game that fan favorites Mickey Mantle and Roger Maris would not be playing today. I am certain it was injury related. Mickey played less than half that season and Roger played just a little more than half of the team's games. Mudcat Grant toed the rubber in game one for the Tribe. Al Downing pitched a 9 inning three hitter for the hometown Yankees and first baseman Joe Pepitone was 3 for 4 at the plate. Joe became a key figure in game 2.

Game 2 had Stan Williams as the starting pitcher for the Yankees. The Yankee lineup was Tony Kubek SS, Bobby Richardson 2B, Tom Tresh CF, Joe Pepitone 1B, Yogi Berra C, Johnny Blanchard RF, Hector Lopez LF, Phil Linz 3B, and Stan Williams P. Mostly the same lineup as game 1. The Yankees plated 2 in the bottom of the first off of a Joe Pepitone double. The Indians hit Joe Pepitone with a pitch on his next at bat in the bottom of the third. The Indians got one run back in the top of the fourth. In the bottom of the 6th, Joe Pepitone was walked with Tom Tresh on first base. The bases became loaded and the Yankees went up 3-1 on a Hector Lopez sacrifice fly. The Tribe pinch hit for their starting pitcher in the sixth and Gary Bell took the mound in the bottom of the 7th. The first batter he faced was the Yankee pitcher and he hit him with a fastball. I am certain there was a message being sent. It is not normal to put the pitcher on base in a still winnable 3-1 game. There was plenty of chatter between dugouts. Gary Bell retired the side and we went to the 8th inning, Yankees 3 Indians 1. Stan Williams struck out the leadoff batter and then put Fred Whitfield on first with a hit batsman of his own. Gary Bell was in his dugout taking mental notes. The Yankees leadoff batter in the bottom of the eighth? Joe Pepitone. Gary Bell nails him with a fastball and it is on. Both benches clear. It is the donnybrook of all donnybrooks. Arguably the greatest bench-emptying brawl in the Yankees long history. Joe Pepitone was slightly injured in the fight and required a pinch runner. Stan Williams completed the game and the Yankees took both games 3-1. Both games were under 2 hours and 30 minutes, including the ten-minute melee. In my 60's they cannot seem to get any game in in under 3 hours however at age 69, baseball changed some rules to help speed up play. Attendance at each game was just short of 26,000. We were out of the Stadium by 11:30 and on the subway for our ride back to the hotel. The entire car of the subway had been at the game and they are chanting, "we want Gary Bell, we want Gary Bell" in sing-song fashion. I thought a riot was about to break out. There is no doubt the Yankee faithful would have enjoyed seeing harm come to Gary Bell. As a ten-year old boy, I was scared. But as scary as the subway ride was, it was a thrill I will never forget. Scheduled doubleheaders in baseball went the way of the dodo bird after the 2001 season.

Other minor notes of interest from the games: 43-year-old Tribe Pitcher Early Wynn pitched 2/3 of an inning in game one and Terry Francona's (winning world series manager for the Red Sox in 2004) dad Tito was a star player for the Indians. Also, eleven years later,

Al Downing gave up the record breaking 715th home run to Hank Aaron in Atlanta.

Shortly after our return home, on August 28th of 1963, there was a peaceful protest march of some 250,000 people in front of the Lincoln Memorial in Washington D.C. that we visited only days earlier. The event was challenging inequalities faced by African Americans a full Century after Emancipation. Martin Luther King Jr. delivered his iconic "I Have a Dream" speech. Martin Luther King dreamed of a day where his children would be judged not by the color of their skin but by the content of their character. "I have a dream." I do not believe that dream can ever come 100% true for any people but I believe we got as close as possible by the turn of the century.

I was now entering 5th Grade at St Andrew with teacher Miss Kibler. I can still recall the days our Pastor Father Herold would come around and pay the lay teachers in cash. Brother Kevin was beginning first grade and oldest brother Mike was now in 8th. There were now five of us walking to and from school twice a day. I doubt we ever walked together even though classes all began at the same time. Sheaffer pens with messy ink cartridges were the popular writing instrument of the day. Being a lefty, writing could become a messy business. I was better off with the good old No. 2 pencil. In my high school years, I met up and became friends with Miss Kibler's nephew Tom. He was at my wedding in 1974.

Shortly after Grade 5 began, September 15th to be exact, four black girls were killed in a church explosion in Alabama. Four Klansman planted dynamite beneath the steps of the 16th Street Baptist Church in Birmingham, Alabama and had it set to explode with a timer. The four young girls who died were aged 11-14. A dozen more people were injured from the explosion. Though the FBI had concluded in 1965 who the alleged murderers were, it would be 1977 before the first one was prosecuted and convicted. Two others were not convicted until 2001 and 2002 and the fourth had died in the nineties before he was available for prosecution. The bombing marked a turning point in the United States during the civil rights movement and contributed to the support for passage by Congress of the Civil Rights Act of 1964.

As 5th grade merrily moved along, we looked forward to Halloween like we did every year. We seemingly went to hundreds of homes but, I will bet we would hit fifty. We wore old fashioned costumes with hard plastic masks. To store our loot of candy we would take a full-sized paper grocery bag, maybe even a pillow case. We collected more candy than any kid needs for the entire winter. And we were getting the full nickel candy bar, not the bite-sized miniatures kids got in my 60's. We had mostly good clean fun. On this night a tragedy happened in our city of Indianapolis that we were unaware of until morning. The opening night of Holiday on Ice was taking place at our Fairgrounds Coliseum with 4,000 spectators on hand. A leaky propane gas tank used to heat pre-popped popcorn exploded beneath the stands sending bodies flying and concrete falling. Sixty-five people died that evening and nine more eventually succumbed to their injuries, the last on February 7th of 1964.

The fall of fifth grade at St Andrew included a day in my life I will never forget. I am certain if you are old enough you remember it too. It is one of the few moments that happen in life when you remember exactly where you were. (I've had four such days) On this Friday afternoon on November 22nd, President John F Kennedy was assassinated in Dallas, Texas by Lee Harvey Oswald. I was in the downstairs school hallway returning from a restroom break with other classmates as the news was broadcast over the loud speaker. I was looking forward to going with my dad that evening to his Friday night church bowling league at nearby Meadows Bowl. It was customary to travel with him to the Meadows and meet up with other classmates and friends and play pinball and other games. There would be no bowling tonight. A pall fell across the nation. Lyndon Johnson was immediately sworn is as our 36th President. Did we bother to sing happy birthday to my brother Brian who turned two years old this day? I expect we got it in. As misery loves company, our family traveled to Ft. Wayne, In. two days later on Sunday to visit and commiserate with my maternal grandparents. Minutes before our arrival, Lee Harvey Oswald, Kennedy's accused assassin, was gunned down in the basement of a police station by Jack Ruby as Lee Harvey was preparing to transfer from the city jail to the county jail. Oswald died in the same Parkland Hospital that JFK died in just two days prior. On the way home from Ft. Wayne that evening, we prayed the Rosary, a family traveling tradition. In my 60's, saying the Rosary became my singular contribution to prayer and religion. Also, in my 60's and throughout my life, when the anniversary of the JFK assassination hits the news for its annual hours long run on the History Channel, I watch as if I have never seen it before. I am mesmerized to the event.

Back at St Andrew school it was common for the student body to practice fire drills occasionally. We were always notified in advance. An alarm would sound or an announcement over the loud speaker would send each room in orderly fashion out onto the parking lot or adjacent football field. In the event of the real thing, we would be ready. Other safety programs for students such as which side of the street to walk on, or ride a bike on was learned from a fictional cartoon character by the name of Herman Hoglebogle. Herman was the brainchild of Indianapolis News (local daily paper) artist Tom Johnson. Herman also taught us about crossing at stop lights and the proper safety rules near buses. A green flag would fly in front of schools who had no safety violations or student injuries.

In the world of sports, the L.A. Dodgers swept the New York Yankees with Sandy Koufax beating the great Whitey Ford twice, giving up only 3 runs in two complete games. The Toronto Maple Leafs outlasted the Detroit Red Wings in seven games. The Boston Celtics continued their winning ways handling the L.A. Lakers in six games. The Pro Football Hall of Fame opened in Canton, Ohio. Jack Nicklaus won his first of six green jackets at The Masters. The Indy 500 went to Parnelli Jones.

In entertainment, Lilies of the Field was a big hit at the movies earning Sidney Poitier the Academy Award for best male actor. In the movie, Sidney helps some Roman Catholic nuns doing odd jobs around their convent and farm and built them a chapel. As Roman

22

Catholics ourselves, it was a big hit in our family. Sidney died in 2022 when I was 68. Also, a song titled 'Dominique' by 'The Singing Nun' was released this year. It was a French tune and I believe we knew enough of the words to fake it. We just did not know what they meant. It was a catchy melody we all enjoyed.

Nineteen 6ixty-three was a good year for me. School was still good. I had more friends. We took an awesome vacation and Yankee Stadium was unforgettable. Our nation suffered racial strife and a political assassination.

Nineteen Sixty-four

10–11 years old

The year began with a State of the Union Address by our new President, Lyndon B. Johnson on Jan 8th, 1964. President Johnson was announcing his 'War on Poverty.' "Our aim is not only to relieve the symptom of poverty, but to cure it and, above all, to prevent it." I am in my 60's now and the War appears to be a futile fight and now nearly encouraged in some areas. I am convinced that some people like living the impoverished lifestyle and have no desire to make the necessary effort to change for the better. I like to use the phrase, "God helps those who help themselves".

On January 16th the 'Whisky a Go Go' opened in Hollywood, California. Johnny Rivers was the first house band at the club. A few years later The Doors were the house band until one night when things went wrong while Jim Morrison sang 'The End.' The Doors became one of my all–time favorite bands beginning in 1967.

On February 1, The Beatles hit single, 'I Want to Hold Your Hand' went to #1 on the charts. A week later the four lads from England with the mop top hairdos played on the weekly Ed Sullivan variety show on CBS on a Sunday evening. It was must see TV and we were bubbling with anticipation. Pop or Rock music became a big part of our family's lives. Even though our parents had and we listened to record albums in the house like Perry Como or The Ink Spots, I will say that this television event was the genesis of my love of music. The show drew the largest TV audience for any show in America to that time. Two months later, The Beatles held the top 5 positions on Billboards top 40 chart, an unprecedented achievement. A short month or two after that our mother and father surprised my older brothers and I by buying us two 45 RPM Beatles records. We wore those records out and started amassing our own collection of

45 RPM records and eventually LP's. It was our good fortune to grow up during the British Invasion of music and the genius of The Beatles. I am convinced The Beatles were the greatest song writing band of all time. In my 60's, I ranked my top 100 favorite Beatles songs, in order.

In the 6ixties, professional boxing was a major sport. The heavyweight division had the eyes of the sports world on it much of the time. Televised bouts were commonplace. On February 25th, 1964, upstart and 1960 light heavyweight Olympic Champion Cassius Clay was facing heavyweight champ Sonny Liston for the world heavyweight title. Liston was a 7-1 favorite. The brash Louisville Lip gave him a beating and Liston retired in the 7th round. Shortly after the fight, Clay changed his name to Muhammad Ali. Ali / Liston had a rematch on May 25, 1965 in Lewiston, Maine but Liston went down in the first round by what has come to be known as the 'phantom punch'. Muhammad Ali is largely recognized as the greatest boxer of all-time.

March 9th would be a groundbreaking date for the automobile industry. The first Ford Mustang was produced and became one of the most popular sports cars for many years to come. In 1971, brother Mike bought a red Mustang for himself. It was a sharp looking car with white interior. Later I owned two Mustangs. I had a silver Mustang with black interior in 1974 shortly after my wife Ginger and I married. Four years later we bought a Carolina blue Mustang with a white vinyl top. They were both cool cars and fun to drive. In my late 60's Ford Motor came out with an electric version of the Mustang. It was terribly ugly and a disservice to its free-roaming and powerful namesake. It reminded me of the Ford Pinto of the early 1970's. Enough said?

On March 30th, the game show Jeopardy premiered with Art Fleming as host. I watched a fair amount of Jeopardy in the late 6ixties and early seventies but then life got in the way and I did not see it much. Many years later, particularly in my 50's & 60's, I watched Jeopardy nearly every night I was home. The show was now hosted by Alex Trebek. My brother Mike and sister Mo were big Jeopardy fans and we would routinely text each other our guesses for the Final Jeopardy answer, or question if you will. My Jeopardy claim to fame was knowing the answer the night Ken Jennings, the all-time Jeopardy champion, finally lost. The answer was HR Block. I was shocked when Ken Jennings came up with the wrong answer. Ken had won 74 games straight, an amazing feat. Mr. Trebek passed away days after his final taping in November of 2020 at the age of 80. He was host for 37 seasons. While searching for a permanent replacement as host, the great Ken Jennings himself filled in as guest host for the first six weeks after Trebek's passing, and was eventually named permanent host.

In the spring of 1964, I was old enough to play my first season of organized baseball. St Andrew was such a large school that we fielded two six-team competitive leagues within the school using 5th and 6th grade for minor league, and 7th and 8th grade for major league. I loved baseball, was good at it, and we played all the time in our yard or neighbors' yard. One neighbor who did not have children, had a very large treeless back yard, and welcomed us to play ball. We had very good games on those grounds, sometimes as many as twelve kids showing up to play.

I met a new friend in 5th grade but we did not become fast friends until the baseball season started in the spring. There were three separate 5th grade class rooms and we did not rotate to different rooms. If you were in a classroom with a teacher, you had that teacher and its thirty plus students for every subject. We could have met during recess but I just do not recall. The boys' name was Steve Considine and he was on my baseball team. This was his first year in Indianapolis as his family transferred here from Minnesota. We became very good friends for many years through high school and beyond. We were born four days apart. Steve passed in 2010. As fate would have it, my final resting place (plot) is twelve feet from where Steve lies.

In May, the first major demonstrations against the war in Vietnam took place in New York's Times Square and San Francisco. They surely would not be the last. Shortly after, some young men would burn their draft cards in protest of the unpopular war.

This summer Dad had our gravel driveway paved and remodeled the garage. The asphalt driveway now made it easier when shoveling snow. As for the garage, it was turned into some type of heated play room for us kids. There was baseboard electric heat put in and a nice ping pong table purchased for our enjoyment. We had hours of fun at table tennis. I believe we still had room to bring one car in. Dad also put a basketball goal in at the end of the driveway. The half-moon backboard with rim would become home to many competitive outings.

On September 4th, the Forth Road Bridge opened in Scotland. It was the largest suspension bridge outside the U.S. at the time. The bridge carried traffic over the Firth of Forth from Edinburgh to Fife, ending ferry service for vehicular traffic. The bridge had no bearing on my life until my 60's when I crossed the bridge on multiple occasions while visiting and golfing at the Home of Golf. In my 60's, there is no place on earth I would rather be.

Golf is the true sporting pastime of the Kavanaugh family. Golf was baked into our family DNA long before my siblings and I were born. Our paternal grandparents owned and managed Lake Shore Country Club on Indy's southside in the 1940's. No longer a golf club, that property is currently home to the University of Indianapolis. Our grandmother was an avid golfer. Our father played high school golf at Indianapolis Cathedral High School, also in the forties. He was a good stick. When we were kids, there was usually a couple barrels of old golf clubs in our garage. There were mashies, niblicks, spoons, and drivers. There were even some more modern clubs with numbers on the sole of the irons. Us boys would take balls and hit them from our yard to a vacant area across the street. We would retrieve the balls and hit them again. A smashing shot might travel 100 yards. I began playing golf regularly by the mid 1970's. In my 60's, golf was my sport of choice, be it on the course or watching on TV. Brother Tim became a twelve-time champion at his local club in Carmel, Indiana. Brother Mike ran a golf league for more than twenty-five years. Brother Kevin is a member at two clubs. My brothers Tim and Brian and sister Mary all live directly on a golf course. My front door is maybe 200 yards away from the nearest fairway but not directly on the course. Nearly everyone in our family plays golf. There are many terrific golf stories you will find in the 60's section of this book, including play at St Andrews.

I was entering 6th Grade at St Andrew now. If I ranked my twelve years of schooling from 1-12 with 1 being my favorite year, 6th grade would rank a big old 12 and I do not have to think about it long. It would be easy to blame Sister Anita for my issues but the fact is we were getting into more difficult subjects for me and I was probably too embarrassed to ask questions for clarification and direction. I felt like I was in an arena where it was not safe to make a mistake in public. Better off to just be quiet. I loved U.S. History but now we were forced to learn World History and I had less interest. Then we added World Geography which was just as hard and every bit as uninteresting to me. I was even doing poorly in Religion class. We worked hard on our Penmanship in Grade 6. There was a writing training program called the Palmer Method. I worked hard at it, but the teacher was not impressed with my left-handed results. But I could still spell and I did fine in math. I am not sure I ever loved school, but I always loved being around the other kids. This year I was falling behind my classmates.

In late September the 'Gilligan's Island' TV show debuted. It became a big hit in our household. On October 14th, Martin Luther King Jr. was announced as the winner of the Nobel Peace Prize for combating racial inequality through nonviolent resistance. Unfortunately, Mr. King left our earth at an early age. Now in my 60's, we could use a man like Martin Luther King Jr. again.

During 6th grade at St Andrew, I started to enjoy the company of the opposite sex. My first 'girlfriend' was Donna Dick. She was quite an athlete and I enjoyed watching her and our classmates play other schools in kickball. She was clearly a team standout along with Julie Hurrle, Mary Anne Carriger, and others. I often met Donna on Friday nights at the Meadows Bowl as our dads both played in the Parish bowling league. One day while I was at my friend Mark Martin's house, I sang Herman's Hermits, 'Wonderful World' to Donna over the phone. So, things were going better outside of the classroom than inside. And though girlfriends do not always last long at this age, I always liked Donna and we had good times.

The 1964 November election saw Lyndon Johnson easily beating Republican Barry Goldwater. With 61% of the popular vote, Johnson received the highest percentage of vote since 1820. Goldwater could only win his native State of Arizona along with Louisiana, Mississippi, Georgia, Alabama, and South Carolina. The subsequent 89th Congress passed major legislation including Social Security Amendments and Voting Rights Act. Fifty-five years later at the age of 66, my wife and I both took advantage of our earned social security and Democrats are still crying crocodile tears about voting rights.

In early December, Rudolph the Red-Nosed Reindeer premiered on NBC. It became a traditional holiday favorite and is shown every year. I still watch it in my 60's with joy and nostalgia.

Our family drove to Miami to spend the 1964 Christmas with our paternal grandparents who now lived in Coral Gables, Fl. Can you imagine nine people in a station wagon, traveling 1,200 miles, with seven of us aged three to fourteen? I cannot and I was there. We were not driving on high-speed interstate roads most of the time. This drive was often on four lane divided US Highways. We were used to our large group and my guess is we were mostly behaved. We had games in the car that would keep us busy. Breakfast the morning after stopping overnight somewhere in Georgia would consist of eating cereal out of a variety pack box that was brought along for the trip. Dinner at restaurants was never complete until our father would do an extensive audit of the tab presented.

The big event of this trip was going to the North/South College football all-star game in the Orange Bowl on Christmas Day. This game included many players who became superstars in the National Football League. Those included Jack Snow, Dick Butkus, Gale Sayers, Roger Staubach, Bob Hayes, Fred Biletnikoff, and more.

I know some people like the idea of a white Christmas and some people just like cold weather. I do not know what their problem is but Christmas in Florida was a real treat. It would not be my last Christmas Day spent in the Sunshine State. I received a skateboard for Christmas this year and it was a smooth ride on our newly paved driveway.

In the world of sports this year the St. Louis Cardinals beat the Yankees in the World Series. The Boston Celtics took out the San Francisco Warriors. The Toronto Maple Leafs bested the Detroit Red Wings for the second year in a row. The Cleveland Browns beat the Baltimore Colts in the NFL Championship game. The Browns have not won anything since except for #1 draft picks. The Colts bolted to Indianapolis in 1984. AJ Foyt won his second Indy 500 in a race that lost two drivers, Eddie Sachs, and Dave MacDonald in a fiery crash on lap 2. Our dad attended that race.

'Mary Poppins' became a family favorite on the big screen starring Dick Van Dyke and Julie Andrews. James Bonds' 'Goldfinger' also hit the theatres in 1964. Goldfinger is one of my top 5 Bond films.

Nineteen 6ixty-four was another good year with a super ending in Florida. I was gaining some independence as I was allowed to wander away further from home unsupervised. And though school was starting to become difficult, I did enjoy my friends and the company of girls at school.

Nineteen 6ixty-five

11-12 years old

After Christmas school break and a delightful vacation in south Florida, I was back for the second half of 6th grade at St Andrew. I enjoyed my daily walks to and from school and back again for lunch. Boys would carry their books in their hand at their side. Girls carried them in front of their chest. There were no book bags back in the 6ixties. I liked walking with my friends Clara Rehs and Julie Hurrle. It became routine and it is something I think we all enjoyed. If you got back to school quick enough after lunch you could join in with other classmates for the closing minutes of recess with the majority that ate lunch at school. In my 60's I still walk a lot, now for exercise.

President Lyndon Johnson announced his 'Great Society' domestic program to eliminate poverty and racial injustice. Fifty plus years later I think at best we can call this a noble idea but still a work in progress. As I mentioned before, I think some people enjoy living the impoverished lifestyle with few responsibilities. Motivation does not come easily to everyone. As for injustice, if you are not willing to see the equalities provided by society, you are doomed to live under the conditions you accept. I thinks it is safe to say I do not feel sorry for people who make no effort. Nor would I offer them much of a lifeline. I agree with what a popular comedian and political commentator once said, "I don't mind helping the helpless, I just don't want to help the clueless."

On March 7th, a group of 600 black men and women began a peaceful 50-mile march from Selma, Al. to Montgomery, Al. to protest resistance to black voter registration. When they reached the Edmund Pettus Bridge at the county line in Selma, the march was stopped and they were brutally attacked and beaten by police who were waiting for them. The day became known as Bloody Sunday.

Two weeks later, Martin Luther King, Jr. led two thousand protesters on a similar march under the protection of the Alabama National Guard provided not by Alabama Governor George Wallace but by President Lyndon Johnson. After crossing the Edmund Pettus bridge peacefully, it took them four days to finish the trek to the State Capitol in Montgomery, Al. on U.S. 80, known in Alabama as Jefferson Davis Highway. It is currently designated a U.S. National Historic Trail. The Voting Rights Act became law on August 6th, 1965.

I did not know any black people in 1965 except for sports stars on TV like Hank Aaron, Willie Mays, & Bill Russell. While playing home run derby in a neighbors' yard we all would pick a player to be and Hank and Willie were popular picks. I do not recall my parents speaking about civil rights even though the March 7th brutal and unprovoked attack was seen by many on national TV. Beginning in the 1990's I took up movie going as a passionate hobby and pastime. In 2014 the movie 'Selma' came out. I try to put myself in the position as a white adult citizen of Alabama with a family in the 1960's. What would I do? What would I think? I do not know the answer and we will never find out but I would hope my Christian upbringing would put me on the right side of the social issue. As a senior citizen writing this history, it is hard to believe these things happened in America in my lifetime. 'Selma' was an excellent movie.

As spring approached, I was looking forward to the new baseball season. Our schools' leagues have 5th and 6th graders play together so this season would make me one of the older players in that league, and hopefully one of the better players. The St Andrew minor league diamond that I would play on had a short porch in right field while left field went forever. The short porch was due to a woods and high weeds at the property line. Our fields had no fences. Hits to right field reaching the weeds leading to trees was a ground rule double. It was wise to have some speed and leather in left or center or a guy could round the bases before the ball was ever retrieved from the hard and fast rolling ground. It was a good baseball season for me and my least favorite school year mercifully came to an end and I was thankfully promoted to Grade 7.

That summer I got to play some additional baseball on my 8th grade brother Tim's all-star team which our dad coached. I was a fifth wheel on the team but got great experience practicing with the older 7th and 8th grade boys. It was a treat wearing real uniforms with pants, stirrups, and sanitary hose. Our school baseball uniform consisted only of a numbered t-shirt. At this age the more talented boys could really whip the ball around the infield. Dad would hit infield practice and call out 'one' for go for one out or 'two' for go for a double play. After the out was made, he would call out different bases far enough in advance that the player with the ball knew where to throw it and the player receiving the ball knew to get to that base. The ball would whip around the infield and the leather was popping. This was an all-star team so errors were few and the symphony of ball, glove and the percussion of wooden bat is music to a baseball lover's ears. I saw little game action but our St Andrew school photographer, Frank Fissee, who worked for our local newspaper as a professional photographer, had excellent candid game shots of all the players. I still treasure my three 8 x 10 black and white glossies courtesy of Mr. Fissee. One photo is on the cover of this book, another on the inside. When I was 65, I crashed the 50-year St Andrew grade school reunion of the grade below me for the sole purpose of meeting up with Frank Fissee's daughter to tell her how much our family appreciated her father's work. My older brothers also have similar photos. I did meet her and she was grateful for our appreciation. Fittingly, she was taking pictures at the reunion for their class.

In July of 1965 President Lyndon Johnson signed Medicare into law. This would ensure that all people over the age of 65 would be guaranteed to have health insurance. Before Medicare only 60% of people over the age of 65 had health insurance. Coverage was unavailable or unaffordable to others. In the same month President Johnson increased the number of troops sent to Vietnam from 75,000 to 125,000. He also doubled the number of men drafted each month from 17,000 to 35,000. Protests to the war would ramp up and continue throughout the decade. Troops sent to Vietnam would also increase for the balance of the decade.

In August, full blown riots broke out in the Watts neighborhood of Los Angeles. A minor traffic violation quickly turned into an argument. The dispute then turned into fights with the police. It was reported that police had hurt a pregnant woman, and six days of unrest followed. Turmoil intensified and over 4,000 members of the National Guard were called in. Over 30,000 people participated in the Watts riots. After six days of rioting, 34 people lost their lives, over 1,000 injured, with over $40 million in property damage. It did not look like something that could happen in America but we would repeat this type of mayhem again and again. When I was 67, we had a string of nationwide riots that would make Watts look like a bad week at recess.

Grade 7 at St Andrew got off to a great start and it seemed like quite a pleasure in comparison to 6th grade. My new teacher in the fall of 6ixty-five was Sister James Michael. Sister James Michael was a classmate of my mom's when they were in grade school and high school. That sounds weird, doesn't it? She was the only nun I ever knew that did not look as old as my grandmothers. A chance at a good year seemed very possible. It was always fun to see who would be in your room with you from year to year and I was in a good class for Grade 7.

We had our first 'specialty' teacher in grade 7. A grandfatherly figure by the name of Mr. Owens. He was brought in for the sole purpose of teaching Science. I had no idea what he was talking about as he was one boring dude. Also, Julie Hurrle became my girlfriend for most of 7th and 8th grade. She was a kickball standout and a good swimmer too. She also came from a large family. She came 6th in the Hurrle family of siblings. Her family and ours both belonged to Devon Country Club where we spent many summer days at the pool. Like Irene Poinsette, Julie went to a different High School and we lost touch. It is too bad; we enjoyed each other's company. I vaguely remember this but many years later when I ran into her, she reminded me that I showed up at her high school's twenty-five-year reunion. I am sure I went for the sole purpose of reacquainting with Julie.

In October I learned of a cruel torture and murder of a teenage girl who lived a mere 4 miles from our home. Four miles back then might as well be in a different town but looking back, it was very close. It was a tragedy that a twelve-year old boy like myself should know nothing about. I would see stories on the front page of the newspaper while I was loitering in the nearby drug store. The story was in the paper every day for what seemed like a long time. I knew I should not be reading it, yet I could not take my eyes off it. I did not know the person who was killed, but it stayed with me my whole life and the dead girls name (Sylvia) has never escaped my memory. It became a national news story.

Last Christmas season, Rudolph premiered on NBC. CBS' answer was 'A Charlie Brown Christmas' which debuted on December 9th. Charlie Brown would also become an annual tradition with excellent keyboard music.

In the 1965 sports world the L.A. Dodgers took out the Twins in the World Series. It is not a broken record but again the Boston Celtics beat the L.A. Lakers. The Montreal Canadiens bested the Chicago Blackhawks. Jimmy Clark from Scotland in a green (unlucky color for racing they say) Lotus won the Indy 500. He was very popular to Indy 500 fans. Three years later he perished in a Formula 1 crash in West Germany. Jack Nicklaus won his second Masters title.

The entertainment industry thrilled millions with the nearly three-hour musical titled 'The Sound of Music' starring Christopher Plummer and Julie Andrews. The drama musical became one of my all-time favorites. Julie Andrews won Best Actress Oscar. The TV show 'I Spy' premiered on NBC featuring Bill Cosby as the first black actor to headline a television series. The show only lasted three seasons. Popular singer and jazz pianist Nat King Cole died as well as World War II stalwart Winston Churchill who was Prime Minister of England during World War II and helped lead the allies to victory.

Nineteen 6ixty-five was a great year once I was released from the hell of 6th grade. It would be the last year until retirement that I did not have a regular job.

Nineteen Sixty-six

12-13 years old

As my 7th school year was entering the 2nd semester, a new girl moved to town and she would just be getting started at St Andrew. I do not know where she moved from. I would think she might be nervous not knowing anyone. I was sitting in class at the start of the school day and I could see her in the hall, seemingly making introductions with some teachers. Possibly they were trying to figure out which of three possible classrooms to place her in. I hoped she would be in my room. She looked beautiful from my vantagepoint. Finally, after short deliberations she was placed with my class. The closer she got the more beautiful she was. Her name was Debbie Chandler. She was popular right away and we eventually became friends. Debbie was with me later in high school and we have stayed in touch throughout my 60's and beyond.

By this time, I was earning money as a paper carrier. I had various routes over the years delivering the Indianapolis Star or News. The Star was a morning route, the News an afternoon route. I followed in the footsteps of my brothers Mike and Tim. Paper routes earned money and taught responsibility. Papers were to be delivered in a timely manner, in one piece, and dry. Anything beyond proper protocol was akin to committing a venial sin. It was up to me as the carrier to collect money weekly from our subscribers. This was a door-to-door activity. The paper station (office) got their money first and I kept the balance. I do not recall how much money I made on a typical 40 home route. I can tell you from the time of my first route, I always had money in my pocket. And it was a good thing, we were not getting allowance. The hazards of paper routes for me were dogs. Our neighborhoods did not have many fences and there was no such thing in those days as an electric dog fence. It was not uncommon for dogs to roam free at all hours of the day. I am not a fan of dogs to this day and I believe it started with paper route dogs where some would terrorize or chase me away. I will never forget a large St. Bernard dog owned by the Rogers family. A scary looking animal with saliva splashing in every direction as he jogged along. The dog's name was Jingles and the family lived just one street north of our home. When you remember a dog's name over fifty years later, it is clear the animal made quite an impression on me. A negative impression. Before knocking on their door to collect for the paper I would look very hard at the bushes by the front door to see if he was there. Jingles liked to nap behind the bushes on a summer day. Only when the coast appeared to be clear did I have the courage to collect for their papers. Sometimes his hiding was better than my eyesight. He would spring to life and I would run like hell. The other hazard of morning routes was cold and darkness. More than once I might walk straight into a hanging tree limb. Moving shadows caused by wind and a bright moon on a cloudless morning could make you nervous. If I can borrow the words from a line in a song, "February made me shiver, with every paper I'd deliver." Over-all, paper routes were a great first step to learning responsibility and the power of money.

In mid-January another 15,000 troops landed in Vietnam bringing the total to 190,000. This story would not go away and it would define the 6ixties. There would be additional troops, additional dead, and scores of protests from coast to coast. A mere four months later we were up to 250,000 troops in Southeast Asia.

On February 9th the National Hockey League announced the addition of 6ix franchises, doubling the size of the league. I had a casual interest in hockey but at the time the expansion meant very little to me. Well before I had reached my 60's, hockey became and still is my favorite team sport. I coached youth hockey for fifteen seasons and both our sons were standout players. The 6ix cities awarded franchises were Pittsburgh, St. Louis, Philadelphia, Minneapolis, Oakland, and Los Angeles. All but Oakland still exists.

On March 4th an article was published stating John Lennon of the Beatles claimed, "we're more popular than Jesus now." That sparked controversy in the United States. Later in the summer John apologized for his remark, saying, "I didn't mean it as a lousy anti-religious thing."

In June of this year an important Supreme Court ruling came down that you have certainly heard on TV or in movies many times. Hopefully you have never heard it said to you. They are called the Miranda rights, named after a young convicted man in Arizona. They start out saying, "you have the right to remain silent. Anything you say can be used against you in a court of law." And so on. Like I said, hopefully no one of authority has had to say these words to you.

Many of my summer days in 1966 would have been spent playing baseball. We played untold numbers of games in various yards around the neighborhood. I might ride a bike down to the Forest Manor Park little league diamonds and meet my buddies Joe Hagelskamp, Mark Martin, and Tom Miller to play. These diamonds were nearly a mile from home. If you just showed up at Forest Manor, others would already be there or more kids would be on the way. That is the way it was in the 6ixties. You did not make plans, you just showed up and the plan came to you. Games were ongoing most of the day. A trip to Devon swimming pool to cool down would most likely follow. Devon was seemingly a daily trip. My brothers Mike, Tim, and I were oftentimes challenged by the daredevil in us to ride our bikes without peddling once a couple hundred yards from our driveway. The 6ix block trip was mostly downhill. The tricky daredevil part was needing to slow down enough to cross potentially busy four lane 46th street but not so much that you couldn't make it the rest of the way without peddling. Also, approaching 46th St. offered obstructed view because of the trees. It was somewhat dangerous yet very exciting. There were times when the traffic forced you to give up the challenge. My world at this time revolved around family, school, friends, and sports.

Another place I spent a lot of time was the Meadows. The Meadows was a modern outdoor shopping mall and it also had the nations' largest bowling alley with 64 lanes and a diner attached beyond lane 64. My dad bowled here in our church league and this is where I went with him during Friday night league play to meet up with friends. My friends and I enjoyed Saturday bowling and we continued to bowl throughout all our teen years. My brother Mike and his friend Mike Reuter might also bowl a few frames and then they would head to the diner for lunch and a few smokes. It was not uncommon to find the Mike's down at the diner. My buddies and I would hang out at the hobby store and watch the 'cool' kids race their slot cars. We also would visit The Danner's five and dime for lunch or hang out at the GC Murphy variety store. But we would always end up at the bowling alley. Besides bowling there were plenty of arcade games to play. Other places I might have spent time at in these days were Brock's Drug Store or the Dairy Queen. All these places were within walking distance or an easy bike ride from home.

In July of 1966 I was old enough for this event not to be a surprise. My little sister Mary was born on July 20th. I recall riding a bike home from a baseball game at school and someone shouted out that mom had a girl. This was sibling number seven so it really was not big news to a thirteen-year-old boy. I was probably more interested in what is for dinner and who is cooking it. I love my sister Mary. She is a great kid. In most of my 50's and half of my 60's, Mary and her husband Tony lived four blocks down the street from my wife and I in the Indianapolis suburb of Fishers.

My final year of St Andrew grade school began on September 6th, 1966. Again, the same day as my oldest brother Mike's birthday. September in Indianapolis is a wonderful time to have a birthday because the weather is fantastic but it seems like my brother got the short end of the stick more than once having a birthday on schools' opening day. Birthdays in our home were always celebrated with cake and song. Our grandparents and our Great Aunt Margaret never forgot to send each of us a birthday card including a $5 bill. My card from Aunt Margaret was always addressed to Master Martin Kavanaugh, in green ink. Adding Master on the envelope always made me feel a little special. Besides Mike's September birthday, our father, brother Patrick, and myself all have September birthdays.

Growing up Irish Catholic it was natural to root for Notre Dame in football. On November 19th top ranked Notre Dame visited number two ranked Michigan State. State took a 10-0 lead into the 2nd quarter but Notre Dame quickly came back with a touchdown of their own. It was 10-7 Michigan State at the half. The third quarter was scoreless and Notre Dame tied it up on the first play of quarter four. A defensive struggle continued and Notre Dame barely missed a 41- yard field goal later in quarter four. With 1:10 to go, Notre Dame got the ball back one last time on their own 30-yard line. Rather than risk a careless turnover, Notre Dame effectively ran out the clock while achieving one first down. The tie assured Notre Dame of the National Title in all the polls that mattered. Michigan State fans and Notre Dame detractors labeled Notre Dame coach Ara Parseghian a coward for not airing it out late in the game. In an era of no overtime games and playing on the road in a defensive struggle, he clearly did the right thing. It has popularly been labeled the "Game of the Century."

For the eighth consecutive year, I walked up Forest Manor Drive about half a mile to St Andrew school, home for lunch, back to school, and home again. Monday December 19th would be a walk to remember. I was with classmate Lily Mikels who I walked with regularly in the last two years of grade school. She lived a couple blocks north of us and I would wait for her to come by and I would join her. We were not boyfriend, girlfriend. I think we just enjoyed each other's company. About two blocks short of school, we heard a loud boom and witnessed a large plume of black smoke that appeared to be coming from the school. We ran the rest of the way to see what was going on. We always entered the school from the rear or the north and the front of the school and our classroom faced highly traveled 38th street to the south. We learned a gasoline tanker had turned over on the four-lane 38th street in front of the school and there was a massive explosion and fire. Lily and I could only see the smoke from our initial vantage point. We entered the school and were near our classroom which was the first door to our right but we were quickly turned around and sent outside as school for the day was immediately cancelled. With school cancelled, some of the kids came to my house as their parents were at work. Our mom was always home. Slowly throughout the morning my classmates were retrieved to go to their respective homes. The accident was caused when a teacher at our school, Miss Roach, was turning into the parking lot and the tanker carrying 8,100 gallons of fuel clipped her car and jackknifed, leading to the explosive fire. At least two other vehicles were involved. Miss Roach was pulled to safety but the driver of the truck, a family of three, and a gentleman in separate vehicles all perished. The blast and accident were reported that evening on the national news. We returned to school the next day but the start of Christmas break was just a short, few days away. I ran into Lily Mikels who also attended high school with me nearly forty years later and she remembered the incident in the same vivid detail as me. Like the Kennedy assassination, it is one of those days for Lily and I that can never be erased from memory.

Back to sports and you guessed it, it was the Celtics over the Lakers again. History was made in NCAA basketball as the first ever all black starting five of Texas Western (now known as University of Texas El Paso or UTEP) beat the heavily favored and all white team of the University of Kentucky for the college title. Montreal beat Detroit in the NHL and the Orioles of Baltimore beat the L.A. Dodgers for the World Series title. Jack Nicklaus repeated at Augusta for his third Masters title. The greatest golfer of all time would finish his career with a record six Masters wins. Rookie driver Graham Hill won the Indy 500 making it two wins in a row for a driver from the United Kingdom. The National Football League and the American Football League merged into the NFL as we know it today.

Walt Disney, entertainment giant and creator of Mickey Mouse and de facto founder of Orlando, Florida died at the age of 65.

Nineteen 6ixty-six was another great year and not unlike the previous year. The responsibility of a paper route was the main difference. Other than that, it was more family, school, friends, and sports. Only now with more money to spend and additional independence.

Nineteen Sixty-seven

13–14 years old

You could refer to my first semester of 8th grade as fun. Maybe I was having too much fun. Shortly after the 2nd semester started, I was awarded my own personal home room. They considered it a punishment. At the most it was an embarrassment. Apparently, I was deemed a malcontent or a distraction so when we were in home room, or when there was no class being taught, I was banished to room 3 down the hall which was currently fallow ground for fertilizing the minds of the youth at school. I do not think Sister Marie Agnese liked me much. The feeling was mutual. My talking in class, eating candy in class, and being a general smart ass had taken its toll on the good nun. At the end of our school year someone had printed up the traditional Last Will and Testament. Mine read, "I leave room 3 to the next self-conversationalist". Looking back, I would say that was a clever testament for an 8th grader to come up with. I have no idea who penned the clever epitaph. It does not sound like words I would have used at that time in my life.

A new band released their first album on January 4th of 1967. The group was called 'The Doors' and I quickly became one of their biggest fans. The album came by the same simple name, 'The Doors.' I was introduced to The Doors by my best friend Joe Hagelskamp in the summer of '67. Joe was always a step ahead of me on the music scene and his taste was impeccable. Joe and I listened to The Doors every time I was at his house that summer or when he was at my house. Jim Morrison, front man for the band, had the audacity to defy censors on The Ed Sullivan Show and use the word 'higher' in their song 'Light My Fire.' As in, "we couldn't get much higher." The censors preferred "we couldn't get much better." Jim was true to his artistry but was never asked back to perform on The Ed

Sullivan Show. Other classic vinyl albums of note released in 1967 Joe introduced me to was, The Velvet Underground & Nico, and Jimi Hendrix's 'Are You Experienced'? Also, The Beatles released two classic albums this year, Sgt. Pepper's Lonely Hearts Club Band and Magical Mystery Tour. With Beatle fan brother Mike at home, I did not need Joe to clue me in to those vinyl classics.

In January, the first ever Super Bowl was played. At the time it was referred to as the AFL-NFL World Championship Game. The NFL was considered a superior league and they proved it with the NFL Packers beating the AFL Kansas City Chiefs 35-10 on January 15th in Los Angeles. But the AFL was coming, and right soon.

Friday nights during winter months were now spent at our Fairgrounds Coliseum where many students went ice skating. We outgrew tagging along with dad to the bowling alley. A parent would volunteer to drop a group of us off and pick us up. This was considered a step up from the usual carrying-on at the bowling alley because there were more people and more places to do things you probably were not supposed to do. Like smoking, drinking, or making out. It is here at the Fairgrounds skating rink I met many future friends from outside the close-knit St Andrew circle. I met kids from nearby St Joan of Arc and Immaculate Heart schools at Friday night skates. The most popular song played during skating was 'Good Vibrations' by the Beach Boys. The song was released in October of 1966 to great success. In my 60's and well after fifteen seasons of coaching youth hockey, I still skated occasionally, usually joining our grandkids.

The Space Program that we were all so excited about a few years ago when Alan Shepard and John Glenn went into space faced tragedy on January 27th. Apollo 1 was scheduled to launch on February 21st but during a rehearsal test at Cape Kennedy, an electrical fire broke out in the cockpit immediately killing astronauts Gus Grissom, Ed White, and Roger Chaffee. Gus Grissom was a native of Indiana and went to Purdue University. He was one of the Mercury 7, a group of seven astronauts selected for the original NASA Project Mercury. Other members of the Original Seven included Alan Shepard, John

Glenn, Scott Carpenter, Gordon Cooper, Wally Schirra, and Deke Slayton. Deke Slayton's character had a small part in the 1995 hit movie, 'Apollo 13'.

As 8th grade baseball season rolled along, I toyed with the idea of pitching both left and right-handed in the same game. Dad was a coach and approved of the plan. My buddies all knew I was ambidextrous. I cannot recall how that happened. I consider myself a natural lefty in life but let's face it, we lived in a right-handed world. I do not ever remember not being able to throw effectively both ways. I owned left and right-handed gloves. I typically decided which glove to use depending on the position I played. I always played first base left-handed. I enjoyed playing first base and owned a Walter Dropo model left-handed first baseman's glove, though Walter threw right-handed. Other infield positions were always played right-handed. Outfield was anyone's guess, including mine. And if necessary, I could turn a right-handed glove over and field just as effectively with it on the other hand. It came to pass on Friday May 19th of 1967, I was the starting pitcher and went at the opposition right-handed. In the top of the fourth of the 6ix inning game, I toed the rubber throwing southpaw. I thought it was cool. What must the other team and particularly their coaches be thinking? I pulled it off. No, I did not strike out the side or throw a no-hitter but we won the game 8-4. It was the highlight of my limited team sports career. I did not choose to play high school sports.

I passed 8th grade, without honors. I really loved my years at St Andrew. I was with a great group of kids, some of whom I still see on occasion. Others I would never see again. But they have never left my memory. I wish all children could have eight years of primary education as good as I had the opportunity to receive. The subjects were broad and pivotal for a well-rounded start in life. We did not use computers or calculators. We learned by reading, figuring, and using our minds. The teachers for the most part, were kind, thoughtful, and caring. After a summer of fun, I had my sights set on Cathedral High School in the fall following in the footsteps of brothers Mike and Tim who would be Senior and Junior in the coming year. Our dad also went to Cathedral, graduating in 1946. A prophecy written at the end of my term at St Andrew portrayed me as being the future principal at Cathedral High School, such was our family's attachment to the downtown school.

On June 11th there was a shooting in Tampa, Florida of a black teen by a police officer. The nineteen-year-old allegedly robbed a photo store and was running away when the officer took aim to slow him down. News of the shooting spread throughout the community which was followed by three days of protests and rioting. I would not normally consider this a big news story from 1967. I ran across this news while doing some general research for this book. It just so happened that I found this story shortly after the infamous May 2020 George Floyd death in Minnesota. The similarity, aftermath, and citizens reaction to a death possibly caused by a police officer was such that I felt I should include it. Certain things have changed less in 50+ years than anyone might imagine.

The following day the US Supreme Court declared that prohibiting interracial marriages was unconstitutional. The case was Loving vs. The State of Virginia. Richard Loving, a white man, had married Mildred Jeter, a 'colored' woman. At the time, that went against Virginia's 'Racial Integrity Act' of 1924. When I was 63, the movie 'Loving' starring Ruth Negga and Joel Edgerton was released depicting the story. As an avid movie goer, I naturally saw the film and enjoyed it very much. What happened in Selma, Alabama in 1963 I found hard to believe happened in my lifetime, though I know it is true. This story seemed more believable. 'Loving' was a good movie.

My Summer of '67 was filled with pickup baseball games and afternoons with my girlfriend Julie Hurrle at the Devon swimming pool. It seems Julie and I spent many days together. I made money doing my paper-route and mowing a few lawns. It was 'suggested' I take a summer speed reading class to help with the upcoming high school load. I took the class given at Cathedral High School riding a city bus back and forth for each session. I believe the classes paid off. I could speed-read a book in 20% of normal time with good enough retention to pass a test.

The biggest thing that happened this summer is our family moved. I had been in the same house for eight years of grade school and now would be in another house for my four years of High School. The symmetry was not lost on me. We did not move far as we stayed in the St Andrew parish on the north eastside of Indianapolis on Denny St. We moved about six blocks and now we were nearly across the street from St Andrew church. We were literally less than a block away from the scene of the infamous gasoline tanker crash of 1966. The house was a large white colonial with limestone walls and pillars at the front. It was the biggest and coolest house we had ever seen. To us it was a mansion. It was possibly the largest house in the parish. The small front yard was protected from the quiet street by a white wooden ranch fence with swinging gate. We now had the much needed five upstairs bedrooms and two full bathrooms for our family of ten. The main floor included a kitchen with dining area, living room with fireplace, formal dining room with swinging doors to the kitchen, den, wood-paneled family room, pantry, half bathroom, and breezeway. We had a three-car garage with a driveway basketball court and a large log playhouse in the tiny backyard that included a small streamlet and 6ix foot high cinder block wall separating our property from commercial properties to the west. The entire yard was very small. So small in fact that I mowed our yard with a rotary or reel lawn mower. The house and driveway took up most of the lot. The basement had four rooms, the largest became the card playing room, pool shooting room, and psychedelic music room. It also had a fireplace. We decorated the walls with posters of bands like The Doors, Iron Butterfly, and Cream. At times we would light incense and have a blacklight. Covert burning of tobacco products was not uncommon. The other rooms included a playroom with toilet facilities, a large laundry room with sump pump, and what I will call a catch-all room that was next to the back stairway that led upstairs to the garage which came in handy for sneaking around if that became necessary. I was about to turn 14 so it did become necessary at times if you know what I mean. Dad afforded mom a cleaning lady one day a week. She kept to the basement and did the massive amounts of family laundry. You never heard a word from her unless she needed additional hangers. I lived in this home for 5 terrific years but moved out on my 19th birthday. The house was so recognizable that in 1972 some of my friends were in Florida on vacation. They sent me a postcard but did not know my address. The back of the card had my name, a description of the house, where the house was in relationship to the nearest major intersection, and the city and state name. The card was delivered. Some forty years later I wrote this poem as an homage that identified the essence of the house.

Ode To Denny

At first sight we gasped, the likes we'd never seen,
Could it be all for us, and most of us teens.
More rooms and more spaces, with two fireplaces,
We moved in right quick, it was off to the races.
Stairs aft and fore, life was never a bore,
Till it was time to cut grass, with a rotary mower.
Always walking to church, on Friday ate perch,
Then mom looked for us, on a never-ending search.
The doors left unlocked, as there was no need,
You could count on the flock, when it's time to feed.
Sumps in the basement, fans in the attic,
Eight kids in the house, you'd think it'd be frantic.
Kevin, and Pat, Mo, Mary and Brian,
Hard to keep track, in spite of the tryin'.
Smokin' and drinkin', and all kinds of parties,
Keggers and music, but it wasn't all Marty's.
Burns on the table, a right hook at the door,
It wasn't all Tim's fault, we both slept on the floor.
Mike on guitar, Linda over before prom,
Showing off his date, to both Dad and Mom.

Hamsters, goldfish, kittens, and Jenny 2,
OK by us, but who would clean the poo.
Picken' em up, and puttin' em away,
That was tough love, back in the day.
The log house or beverage house, the DQ and all,
Freedom or trouble, just a hop over the wall.
Runnin' and playin' and basketballs bangin',
The gal in the basement, wanted more things for hangin'.
The bread was a plenty, cause Margaret to care,
When she came for a visit, the day
was more than just fair.
Huntley and Brinkley near the dining room table,
I never understood, till years after cable.
I could no doubt go on, bout the best home of our lives,
But I'll stop here and now, and collect my high fives.
The house was a mansion, worth every penny,
God blessed us all, with our home on Denny.

Nationally it was called the long hot summer of 1967. Out west, the 'Summer of Love' was in full gear with the Monterey International Pop Music Festival. The festival introduced music acts to America like Jimi Hendrix, The Who, Janis Joplin, and Otis Redding. The Monterey event was the brainchild that led to Woodstock, the most popular music festival of all time, two years later.

There was no love in Buffalo, New York. A riot broke out on June 26 and lasted five days. It was not surprising. All told there were 159 race riots that swept the country during the summer of 1967. The one in Buffalo lasted a little longer and produced multiple gunshot wounds. A month later Detroit took a swing at rioting. The Detroit riot was mostly between the black community and the Detroit police department. It began with a late–night police raid of an unlicensed bar. It too lasted five days and final stats included 43 dead, 1,189 injured, and over 7,200 arrests. There were more than 2,000 Detroit city buildings destroyed. The riots of the year 2020 must have been exactly like some of these sounded. Except in 2020 the police were not shooting, they mostly stood down. If you like riots, you should check out 1967. There is really no end to them. Jersey, Milwaukee, Florida, Washington D.C., Atlanta, Boston, Cincinnati, Minnesota, etc. Later in the year Martin Luther King visited Buffalo and gave a famous speech. In the speech he said, "we are moving toward the day when we will judge a man by his character and ability instead of by the color of his skin." I felt that by the end of the century we had mostly come to that judgment.

The late summer of 1967 found me inside the hallowed halls of Cathedral High School near downtown Indianapolis with subjects taught by the 'Brothers of the Holy Cross'. My traditional route to and from High School was primarily hitchhiking, which was common in those days, or occasionally a city bus. On the odd day my brother Mike, who was a senior at Cathedral, would drive if access to the family Rambler Classic four door presented itself. It became normal for me prior to school to meet kids at a nearby restaurant for a smoke and a coke or maybe in the school cafeteria for a coke and donut. Cathedral, being an all–male school was different for me and I may not have been up to the task. I even struggled in gym class of all places. I do not believe the teacher, Mr. O'Brien, cared much for me. I was told or reminded many years later that my brother Tim also had some difficulty with Mr. O'Brien who was Tim's baseball coach. That may have helped create difficulties for me. Not that I needed the help. I was a big fan of Brother George in Algebra class and I enjoyed learning French to the point I can still make out many words in the French language today.

In October of 1967, Thurgood Marshall became the first black Justice on the Supreme Court of the United States. Justice Marshall came out of Baltimore and argued several cases in front of the Supreme Court before becoming a Justice. His most famous case being Brown vs. The Board of Education which held that racial segregation in public education is a violation of the Equal Protection Clause. He was nominated to the Court by President Lyndon Johnson and served until 1991, being replaced by another African-American, Clarence Thomas. Justice Marshall was confirmed by a vote of 69-11 with 20 not voting. Interestingly he received 89% of the Republican vote but only 58% of the Democrat vote. Let that ruminate for a while.

The Fall of 1967 brought great joy to Indianapolis which we still enjoy to this day. A new professional basketball league was started called the American Basketball Association. The Indiana Pacers became one of the nine founding members of the new ABA. Of the nine teams, only two, our Pacers and the Kentucky Colonels played all nine seasons without a relocation. The upstart league ushered in the three-point shot and the red white & blue ball. The Pacers were easily the best franchise during the leagues ten year run winning three titles with stars Mel Daniels, Bob Netolicky, Roger Brown, and Freddie Lewis. Along with head coach Bob 'Slick' Leonard, they were household names. I would listen to the end of some games in bed on my transistor radio. In 1976 the league folded and four ABA teams including our Pacers were absorbed into the senior National Basketball Association. Of the above names, only Bob Netolicky does not have his number retired in the Pacers arena. Slick's number shows his number of coaching wins. (529)

The first Christmas spent in our new home was bittersweet. Our paternal grandparents came up from Florida to spend the holiday and look at our new home. I do not remember anything about that Christmas season that might suggest anything other than the normal. Food, cookies, decorations, fun, song, laughter, and gifts. I always enjoyed making Christmas cookies with mom and decorating them with icing and sprinkles. We would cut the dough out with our molds of Santa, Christmas tree, Snowman, Reindeer, or Star. Grandpa took ill during their visit and died in our home on December 28th. I have no memory of sorrow from my dad but it must have been heavy. I do recall Grandma being heartbroken. Our Miami, Fl. cousins, aunts, and uncles raced up to partake in the funeral proceedings which took place two days later, on December 30th. It was a cold day for my first responsibility as a pallbearer and that casket is the heaviest thing I had ever held in my hands to that point in my life. I am forever thankful for being called to duty. I still visit our paternal grandparents resting place occasionally.

On the last day of nineteen 6ixty-seven, one of the great NFL games of all-time was played. The NFL Championship was a rematch of the previous year between the Dallas Cowboys and Green Bay Packers. In brutal Wisconsin conditions with temperatures reaching minus 15 degrees, the Packers scored late to win the game 21-17. The game would be immortalized as the 'Ice Bowl.'

In other sports in 1967, the Boston Celtics finally were beaten, but not in the Finals. The Finals had the Philadelphia 76ers with Wilt Chamberlain beating the San Francisco Warriors. Toronto beat Montreal for the Stanley Cup in the last championship before expansion doubled the size of the NHL. Toronto has not won or been to a title series since. The St. Louis Baseball Cardinals defeated The Boston Red Sox in the World Series. Boston's Carl Yastrzemski won baseball's Triple Crown. It was not won again until Miguel Cabrera pulled off the rare feat forty-five years later in 2012. Popular AJ Foyt won his 3rd Indy 500, beating the new revolutionary turbine powered car driven by Parnelli Jones. Parnelli's car expired while leading the race with three laps to go. Muhammad Ali refused induction into military service.

In entertainment news, actor Spencer Tracy died. Mr. Tracy won two Academy Awards for Best Actor garnering a total of nine nominations. The hit movie 'The Graduate' was released. The Beatles released two albums, Sergeant Pepper's Lonely-Hearts Club Band and Magical Mystery Tour. Sergeant Pepper won a Grammy for album of the year, the first rock LP to receive this honor. Rolling Stone Magazine printed its first copy in November of this year.

Nineteen 6ixty-seven saw strife nationally with Vietnam protests and race riots across the country. As for me, I would rate nineteen-6ixty-seven as one of the great years of my life. I graduated from grade school. I entered high school. Our family moved into a great new home. I had fun every day of the summer with baseball, my girlfriend Julie, and swimming. Music was exploding with great tunes. I had enough money in my pocket from paper routes to make daily life enjoyable. Life was good.

Nineteen 6 ixty-eight

14-15 years old

In late January of '68, NBC TV premiered Rowan & Martin's Laugh-In. 'Laugh-In' was a one-hour comedy show hosted by Dan Rowan and Dick Martin. It was must see TV and quickly became the most popular TV show in America. The show made an instant hit of Goldie Hawn along with other regulars Arte Johnson, Lily Tomlin, and Richard Dawson. The show completed 140 episodes over 6 seasons. A fellow by the name of John Carpenter was born in this same year. Thirty-one years later he was on a TV game show called, 'Who Wants to be a Millionaire'? This show debuted in August of 1999 and you had to successfully navigate fourteen consecutive multiple-choice questions to become a millionaire. The show had never produced a millionaire winner until November 19th, 1999. John had flawlessly run the gauntlet of questions to the final million-dollar question which was, "Which of these US Presidents appeared on the television series, 'Laugh-In'? His choices were Lyndon Johnson, Richard Nixon, Jimmy Carter, and Gerald Ford. John had not used a 'life-line' up to this point in the show but chose this question to use his 'call a friend' which was a call to his father. John knew the answer, as did I. John just wanted to tell his dad on national TV, he was about to become a millionaire. The answer was Richard Nixon.

I participated in something this winter that I had never done before or since. At the time it seemed clearly out of character for me. But it was some of the most team bonding fun I have ever had. I joined a nine-person troupe from our church parish and we did plays at various churches throughout the area. We competed against groups from neighboring parishes. Each parish performed a different play that I am certain had a time limit. Practices and performances covered a few months. Our troupe consisted of six guys and three girls, all of whom I knew. Our group was coached by St Andrew parishioner and teacher Mrs. Rosalyn Gale. The cast included Helen Langenbacher who was a year younger than me. Tom Scott, who was in my class and a good friend. And six players who were two grades above me including Jody Davis, Terry Scheidler, Donnie Bane, Mike Russell, Pat Brady, and my neighbor and transportation to many of the events in his struggling cargo van, Mark Adamson. All six of them were in the same class as my brother Tim during their St Andrew grade school years.

The backdrop of our play was an 1800's western saloon in the imaginary good town of Red Gulch. Red Gulch was advertised as the cleanest town in the west. We had a bartender, sheriff, and cowboys, all heeled. There was a waitress and a dance hall girl and I played the part of a poker playing cowboy. Maybe it was not out of character at all. I played a lot of poker in those days and in the coming years. I was the only actor made to look old with graying hair most likely from talcum powder. I had a five-day shadow applied to my still smooth face and wore a bandana around my neck. I was the only performer wearing a black hat. The other male actors wore white hats, some with bolo ties. Our barkeep wore a white apron, sans hat to show off his slicked back hair. One of the ladies also wore a western hat, one had heavy makeup and gaudy jewelry, and the last looked normal for the times, maybe the local school marm. I have no recollection how the characters were assigned or how any of us got involved.

I was the first speaker in the play as the curtains opened. I was sitting solo at a poker table, stage front right. I do not have the original manuscript but I believe my first words were asking the barkeep, who was behind me, for another sarsaparilla. I know I felt as if I had the leading role, but I expect lines were evenly distributed for the roughly 30-minute performance. I still have our group picture and I look at it with great fondness and nostalgia. I am sorry I do not have the manuscript. I do not recall how we fared in the competitions but I know we all had a great time.

The 1968 Winter Olympics from Grenoble, France got the year off to a fascinating start in the sporting world. U.S. skater Peggy Fleming won Gold in figure skating and was America's newest sweetheart. Frenchman Jean-Claude Killy won the downhill ski event in thrilling fashion at Chamrousse Ski Resort. I have never skied on any surface but watching Jean-Claude race down the foggy mountain was the most exciting thing I had ever seen on TV at that time in my life. Jean-Claude also captured the slalom and giant slalom titles. I was always more attracted to the winter Olympic sports and his run galvanized me to the quadrennial event.

Playing poker with friends became a common thing to do on many weekend evenings. Over the years, nickel ante became quarter ante which eventually became dollar ante. Between the ages of 14 & 30 we played in many semi-high-stakes 'friendly' poker games. I was pretty good at it and won my fair share of pots. I will never forget the first time I saw a hundred-dollar bill float into a pot. It was 1973 on a Monday night while Monday Night Football was playing in the background. Everybody wanted to get their hands on that C note.

In the second half of freshman year, I was issued a traffic ticket from a police officer for hitchhiking in the street. I was returning home from school, per usual. A few of the boys got a ticket. I guess it was OK to stand on the sidewalk to hitch a ride but we crossed the line when we stood on the street. Personally, I think the cop was being a jerk. My dad had to take me downtown one evening for my mandatory punishment which I believe was an education in traffic laws and civics. He could not have been too happy about that but I would like to think that in a private moment, he thought it funny that I got ticketed for hitchhiking.

I had a run in or two with some 'Brothers' (teachers) at Cathedral High School. One was Brother Donald whom I did not have for a class. I guess I made a remark he overheard and did not much appreciate. I became familiar with the detention room. I also did not fare too well in Brother Thomas' English class. My failing grade earned me a trip to a city High School for summer school. Somehow Greek Mythology found its way into English class and they might as well have been speaking Mandarin as far as I was concerned. A very unnecessary topic. This is the summer I was forced to miss out on the family vacation. My two-year-old sister Mary also stayed home and we were babysat by our Great Aunt Margaret. The rest of the family packed up the station wagon and headed west to the Grand Canyon.

On Sunday March 31st, President Johnson chose to address the nation this evening on national TV. The war weary President would talk about the Vietnam War and indeed spent forty minutes on the subject. In closing his address, he shocked the nation by saying, "Accordingly, I shall not seek, and I will not accept, the nomination of my party for another term as your President." This paved the way for Hubert H Humphrey to be the losing candidate on the Democrat ticket in the coming fall.

It is impossible to talk about life in the 6ixties without mentioning a large dose of Vietnam. It was the topic of the decade. Issues in the Southeast Asia country had been percolating for years but on March 8th, 1965 we sent in 3,500 troops to support South Vietnam against the North Vietnamese. These troops were joining 25,000 U.S. advisors already in place. Word from Vietnam would be in our home every night during the nightly news telecasts. And it was grim. U.S. Troops poured in more and more every year. By 1969 over 500,000 U.S. military personnel were stationed in South Vietnam. Unlike WWII where most young men volunteered to join the Army, most of the U.S. men in the Vietnam conflict were drafted. The North Vietnamese were supported by China and the USSR. The war continued through 1973 when the United States finally pulled out, effectively handing victory to the North Vietnamese. War highlights or low lights included the Tet Offensive, launched on January 30th of 1968. This was a large military campaign by the North Vietnamese. The Tet Offensive was a series of coordinated surprise attacks on over 100 towns in South Vietnam. North Vietnam thought these attacks would collapse the South Vietnam Government. The initial attacks stunned the Allies but they were able to regroup and beat them back. A Viet Cong officer was executed by a South Vietnamese police chief. The event was photographed and made headlines around the world. The photo won the Pulitzer Prize the following year and swayed U.S. opinion further against the war.

Shortly thereafter was the My Lai Massacre in March of '68 where as many as 500 unarmed South Vietnam civilians were killed by US Troops. This included men, women, and children. The incident prompted global outrage when it became public knowledge more than a year later. Twenty-six soldiers were charged with criminal offenses but only one, Lieutenant William Caffey Jr., a platoon leader, was convicted.

Overall, the dead counted in the millions with over two million Vietnam civilians dying in the war. Over 1 million North Vietnamese soldiers perished. Over 250,000 South Vietnam soldiers died along with upwards of 58,000 young men from the U.S. Other casualties for South Vietnams defense included 4,000 from South Korea and relative few from Thailand and Australia. As a boy aged 12–17, I saw this on TV nightly as my dad insisted on watching the news during many family dinners. When you watch these things on TV, some live, it did not seem real. It looks almost like a movie. But it was real and it was terrible. I would be lying to you if I said it affected me, or I cared until I reached the age of eighteen. I was never close to having to serve in the military. I was of an age that by the time I turned 18, troops were being pulled out of Vietnam and our country had seen enough suffering. Our last troops pulled out of Vietnam on March 29, 1973. The war officially ended on April 30, 1975. I never knew anyone who died in Vietnam and knew very few who served.

These few paragraphs on Vietnam do not begin to tell the story and horror. Troops came home to little or no fanfare unlike in previous wars. They never asked to go fight in the jungles of Vietnam, and they never got their due. On November 13, 1982, a memorial in Washington D.C. was dedicated to the men and women who lost their lives in Vietnam.

Prior to the end of the school year, on April 4th, 1968, civil rights leader Martin Luther King Jr. was shot to death with a single shot while standing on his balcony outside his Lorraine Motel room in Memphis, Tn. It happened the day after his "I've Been to the

Mountaintop" speech in Memphis. The lone killer was James Earl Ray who was arrested two months later in London after being on the lamb under a changed name with false passport. Martin Luther King Jr. was the standard bearer for civil rights in America. He was known for his peaceful demonstrations and smooth eloquent voice. King was a leader of the Montgomery, Al. bus boycott in the 50's which eventually ended segregation on buses. This boycott thrust MLK into the national spotlight. He was a major factor in the March on Washington in 1963 that included his "I Have a Dream" speech. He also led a march in 1965 called the Selma bridge march which began in Selma, Al. and ended at the State Capitol in Montgomery, Al. It was here he gave his "How Long, Not Long" speech. Immediately upon learning of MLK's murder, riots broke out in various cities. Washington D.C., Chicago, Baltimore, New York, Kansas City, Louisville, and others.

On the same day in my home town of Indianapolis, our citizens were fortunate to hear a different speech that evening leading to a different, peaceful outcome. Senator Robert F Kennedy of New York was in town to garner Democrat support for the Presidential nomination of his party. A rally had been planned in a mostly African-American part of town. It was thought maybe he should not give a speech for fear of an uprising based on the days' events. Senator Kennedy went ahead and gave a mostly improvised speech, not the rally speech the crowd had come to expect. Many of the people in attendance had not yet heard about the murder of MLK. It is possible they knew he had been shot, but not that he had died. He was shot after 6:00 pm and died just past 7:00 pm. Kennedy continued his speech saying he had some bad news, that Martin Luther King Jr. had been killed. The audience was visibly shaken, screaming, and gasping for breath. King was their hero. Kennedy acknowledged that many in the crowd would be filled with anger since the assassin was believed to be a white man. But he empathized with the audience referring to his own brother's assassination, also at the hands of a white man. Kennedy's most endearing remarks were, "What we need in the United States is not division, what we need in the United States is not hatred, what we need in the United States is not lawlessness, but is love and wisdom, and compassion toward one another, and a feeling of justice towards those who still suffer within our country, whether they be white or whether they be black." Kennedy asked his audience to pray for our country. The crowd exploded in applause before dispersing quietly. Those insightful words were right on the money and should be reprised during our nation's hostility during my late 60's.

RFK's speech has been listed as one of the greatest in American history. In 1994, a sculpture of Kennedy and King with outstretched arms to one another was erected at the Indianapolis location of the 1968 speech, now called Martin Luther King Jr. Park. The sculpture is called Landmark for Peace. It was in 2005 that I decided I wanted to see this landmark. I was aware of it but I was never moved to action. On a summer day in 2005 I drove down to the unassuming site, parked my car, and walked to the memorial. I do not have the exact words but it is a very moving site and worthy of your visit. In 1986, the first Martin Luther King Jr. national holiday was observed in honor of the man who preached nonviolent resistance. It falls on the third Monday of each January to closely coincide with his January 15th birthday. Sadly, two months after the King assassination, Robert F Kennedy himself was murdered following a Democrat Primary victory speech in California. Shortly after Bobby's assassination, a singer by the name of Dion released the song, "Abraham, Martin, and John" in tribute to Abraham Lincoln and the three icons assassinated in the 6ixties. In the year 2020 while in my mid-60's, mayhem destroyed cities in America from coast to coast, caused by a killing. Has anybody here seen my old friend Martin? Indeed. We could have used men like Martin Luther King Jr. and Bobby Kennedy in 2020.

Shortly after school let out for the year, I was invited to visit the USS Lexington aircraft carrier in Pensacola, Florida with my friend and grade school classmate Bob Lentz. Bob had a cousin who was stationed on the Naval Aircraft Carrier and my best recollection is they were allowed visitors for a weekend. Bob invited me to go with him. I do not recall any parents on the two-night, three-day trip, but surely there was some type of supervision. At the time, the Lexington was docked in Pensacola as a training carrier. Bob and I spent our days on the ship with full access complete with guided tours. Part of the tour included the boiler room which is still the hottest place I have ever been on earth. The ship did go out to sea far enough we could no longer see land. Aircraft went through their training exercises taking off and landing on the massive ship. It was one of the coolest things I had ever seen. Evenings were spent in town with the sailors using their day or evening pass. Sailors spent all their time on land either drinking or smoking. I do not recall how Bob and I spent our time on land but like I said, there must have been some type of supervision. Overall, it was a very cool and educational experience.

This summer the family took the vacation out west to the Grand Canyon and Pike's Peak. Due to my English class issues at Cathedral, I had to stay home to make up a grade in summer school. I was looked after by our loving and generous Great Aunt Margaret. Due to her age and naivete, I expect I had as good a time at home as my siblings did on their trip. I did eventually get to both destinations in my adult life. I was at Pike's Peak in 1991 while in Colorado Springs for a USA Hockey coaches forum. In 2008, I arrived at the Grand Canyon via chartered helicopter from Las Vegas for a champagne lunch while on an earned trip through my employer. The helicopter ride was very cool.

In August it was confirmed that I would pull out of Cathedral and enter a newer co-ed High School as a sophomore, Bishop Chatard High School. It was one of the greatest decisions my parents ever made for me. Did I thrive at Chatard? NO!! Did I enjoy Chatard? Very much and it was three of the best years of my life. So much for my grade school prophecy. It was a comfortable fit from the start as many of my old St Andrew classmates were there, plus many friends I had met in recent years that came out of other northside Catholic grade schools. The girls were pretty and the guys were friendly. For most of three years, I hitchhiked to and from Chatard high school without incident.

The Vietnam War continued to cause much unrest in the country. Riots at the Democrat Convention in Chicago now took center stage. The Democratic National Convention was held from August 26-29 in Chicago. In 1968 it seemed there were demonstrations over the Vietnam War nearly every day in some part of the country. The convention was a natural location for them all to come together. It seemed Chicago and its Mayor Richard Daley were ready. The protests were mostly over the unpopular and tiresome Vietnam War that raged on with no end in sight. Racism and poverty were also key issues. The convention closely followed the killings of Martin Luther King Jr. and Robert F Kennedy. You might say the country was ripe for unrest. On Wednesday August 28th, the Chicago streets were filled with protesters outside of the convention headquarters hotel and next to Grant Park. After some time, the cops announced a warning to clear the streets. This was repeated five or six times and finally they said, "If you don't move out of the street, my officers are going to clear the street." Then the officers did begin clearing the streets swinging clubs with all they had and beating anyone in their way. Tear gas was also used. Much of the mayhem was filmed by TV cameras. Over 1,000 protesters received medical attention and 192 police officers were injured.

The national Presidential election was held November 5th, 1968. With Lyndon Johnson and Bobby Kennedy out of the race, Richard Nixon (R) of California handily beat Hubert H Humphrey (D) of Minnesota 301 to 191 electoral votes. George Wallace of Alabama ran as an Independent carrying 5 southern States and garnering 46 electoral votes. Nixon was sworn into office on the following January 20th.

In late 1968 and in to 1969 we had a health problem with a pandemic called the Hong Kong flu. The modest estimated number of deaths was one million worldwide and over 100,000 in the US. Some estimates showed potentially four million dying globally. Most deaths were those over 65 years old. This flu had no effect on me, our family, or anyone I knew. The country took no evasive action. There were no lockdowns or closures. There were no vaccines administered to anyone I know. No one was wearing protective masks. As a sophomore in high school, I never heard it discussed or knew it was even an issue. It was business (or fun) as usual. I only bring this up because of a similar event that happened 52 years later in the year 2020. Naturally, I am referring to Covid-19.

We have not talked a lot about football through this point in the 6ixties. The fact is that football was not nearly the popular game that it became. That all changed on November 17ᵗʰ, 1968. I would say this is the day that football was recognized as the most popular sport in America. It was a cool fall evening and the upcoming holidays were on everyone's windshield. The 4:00 pm NFL game televised on NBC matched superstar Joe Namath's New York Jets against the Oakland Raiders. Pitching for the Raiders was Darryl Lamonica, the 'Mad Bomber.' You might say the Raiders invented the modern vertical game. These were two of the top teams in the AFL. As a big-time AFL fan, I was watching. That evening at 7:00 pm, NBC, the same network televising football, was scheduled to debut the highly advertised made for TV movie, 'Heidi,' a story about a little orphaned girl living in the Swiss Alps. As the unusually long football game was nearing the 7:00 pm time slot, the Jets led 32-29 with a minute to go. Dutifully, the NBC engineering crew switched to the movie at 7:00 pm on the dot. The NBC switchboard lit up with calls the likes they had never seen. The Raiders came back to win the game 43-32 including a fumble return on a kickoff for a touchdown. The football fan base was inconsolable. Many did not know the result until they read the morning paper. There was no internet or Sports Center or Google to check on such things. I believe that football overtook baseball as our national pastime on this day. Heidi was a good movie.

Christmas Day 1968 I received my first new set of golf clubs. It was a Hale Irwin set that included 2 woods, 5 irons, and a putter. Golf is the one sport that binds much of our family with a common thread. You will read much more about golf in my 60's.

The 1968 sports world, excluding the Olympics, saw Green Bay beat Oakland in Super Bowl II back in January. The Celtics beat the Lakers yet again, and Montreal beat the St. Louis Blues for the

Stanley Cup. The Detroit Tigers won the World Series over the St. Louis Cardinals. Bobby Unser won the Indy 500 in the #3 Rislone Special. To this day it is my all-time favorite race car at Indy. The red, yellow, and white color scheme with black trimming is fantastic. This is the year that three turbine cars were all favored to win the race including Joe Leonard from the pole position or 1966 winner Graham Hill from the number two slot. Rookie fan favorite from England, Mike Spence died in a practice crash driving the #30 STP Turbine. He was 31.

The motion picture rating system began this year with G PG R & X ratings. Sixty Minutes TV show aired for the first time. The U.S. population eclipsed the 200 million level.

Nineteen 6ixty-eight was a significant year nationally. Political assassinations, riots, and Vietnam ruled the news cycle. I switched High Schools which I enjoyed. It was another great year for me but the country seemed to be in upheaval.

Nineteen 6ixty-nine

15-16 years old

As an AFL football fan, this year started out great for me. Super Bowl III was played on January 12th in Miami between the AFL's New York Jets (of Heidi game fame) and the NFL powerhouse Baltimore Colts. The Colts were an 18-point favorite but I felt good about the Jets' chances. Jets quarterback Joe Namath did too as he famously guaranteed a win to some reporters three days before the game. When you hear athletes guaranteeing a win these days, Joe Namath and Super Bowl III is where it got its origins. The Jets led 16-0 in the fourth quarter thanks to multiple Colt turnovers near the Jet endzone before Johnny Unitas, injured much of the season, came off the bench to replace the NFL's MVP QB Earl Morrall. Unitas led the Colts into the end zone for their lone, late TD. The final score was 16-7. The upstart American League fairly dominated their NFL opponent for the next decade. Athletes have been copying Joe's 'Guarantee' for years, but none with the bravado or success of Broadway Joe.

I was back at Chatard High School for my second semester of sophomore year. I had some issues in Geometry class and it seemed everyone had issues with Biology class, but I was having a good time. By now, I felt like part of the group. I comfortably knew most of my new mates. I sometimes regret I was not a joiner inner. I did not try out for any sports excluding a failed attempt at baseball in my senior year. I did not play in the band or tryout for any school plays. I would never regret that many of my best friends including Joe Hagelskamp, Steve Jose, and Steve Smeehuyzen went to a rival school. I enjoyed my weekend poker games with friends from multiple schools. We also got together often for pick-up sporting events be it football, baseball, or basketball, depending on the time of year. I am not sure

I had the time, talent, or discipline for the extra-curricular activities offered at Chatard High School.

In March, Sirhan Sirhan testified that he killed Bobby Kennedy and James Earl Ray pled guilty to the murder of Dr. Martin Luther King Jr. You would never get a conviction that easily during my 60's.

In May I went to the first day of qualifications for the Indy 500. My friend Bob Kelly and I went with Bob's dad, a bucket of Kentucky Fried Chicken, and a cooler of soda pop on a cool, overcast Saturday. This story is based on how qualification rules were back in 1969. Hoosier native Jigger Sirois drew the first qualifying attempt. His average speed in the low 160's was waived off on his fourth and final lap. His crew did not feel that speed was strong enough to make the competitive field. As the second driver went out for his warmup laps, rain fell and time trials were cancelled for the remainder of the day. In the subsequent days of qualifying (there were four days) Jigger did not qualify for the race. As bad luck would have it, had Jigger accepted the checkered flag on his first attempt, he would have been the pole-sitter for the race though not the fastest car. Jigger tried unsuccessfully to qualify for the great race every year from 1970 thru 1975. He never raced in the Indy 500. Due to his hard luck in 1969, the writers and broadcasting association came up with the Jigger Award given annually to the hard luck driver of the year during qualifying.

In June, shortly after school let out, I began my 'official' working career. I had plenty of paper routes previously and mowed many lawns but this would be the first time I would punch a timeclock and receive an actual paycheck. My good friend Joe Hagelskamp was already working at the Jolly Foods grocery store when I joined up. We teamed up as bag boys, starting at 1.60 an hour plus carry-out tips. It was great receiving an actual paycheck and seeing your name on the 'Pay To' line of that check. We were living large. I worked at Jolly Foods for over six years, until shortly after I got married in May of '74, moving up from bagger, to dairy, to night stock, and assistant manager. I met my future bride at Jolly Foods in 1973. The owners, Mr. Harry Frankovitz and his adult son Joe always expected a good job done and they always treated me well. I recall the time I was directing a truck driver back to our freshly installed back doorway and new unloading dock. I did not have the door swung all the way open and flat against the outside wall. The truck hit the door, crushing it like an aluminum can as I was motioning him back. I am not sure the cement surrounding the new doorway was even cured yet. The Frankovitz boys took it well. I recall the time our Indy Mayor Richard Lugar was coming to look at the new concept in shopping with our state-of-the-art deli counter and our flagship carry-out service. I was asked by the Frankovitz's to be one of the guys to help make the store look spic and span. And I can never forget the time on Christmas Eve 1971 when I was asked to come in because they were in a pinch, servicing record sales. This after I had worked the entire previous 'night stock' shift. Finally, for an unexpected wedding gift in 1974, The Frankovitz family bought my bride and I an entire place setting of fine Wedgwood China for eight. The gesture was magnanimous. I learned a lot about work at Jolly Foods. I learned how to be on time, how to be responsible for your work, how to treat customers, and more. Three months after our wedding I left Jolly Foods for a career in the plumbing wholesale world which was our family business and my destiny.

In the music world all my three favorite bands were in the news. On January 30th, The Beatles played their last public performance on the rooftop of Apple Records on Savile Row in London. John Lennon married Yoko Ono two months later and recorded 'Give Peace A Chance.' On August 8[th,] The Beatles had their famous 'zebra crossing' photo taken on Abbey Road. The photo is arguably the most famous rock photo of all-time. In March, Jim Morrison of The Doors was convicted of indecent exposure. The Doors rarely made an average record. Though their catalog is not nearly as deep as other bands, they have the fewest bad or average songs of any group. Jim Morrison died July 3rd, 1971 at the age of 27. I was and continue to be a big fan of the Rolling Stones. Also, on July 3rd but in 1969, founding member and multi-talented musician Brian Jones died. He also was 27 years old. Jones, a known proficient swimmer, drowned in his back-yard pool. The Stones released arguably their best album, 'Let It Bleed' late in this year. The greatest band of all-time soldiered on for fifty more plus years, much to my delight.

In 1969 Congress passed the Public Health Cigarette Smoking Act which prohibited cigarette advertising on TV or radio. It also required that each pack contain a label reading, "Warning: The Surgeon General Has Determined That Cigarette Smoking Is Dangerous to Your Health." The warning label was altered from a 1965 warning that read, "Caution: Cigarette Smoking May Be Hazardous to Your Health". Advertising on billboards and sports venues continued for a while. Finally, on July 12, 1997, Camel cigarettes was forced to give up on their popular mascot 'Joe Camel' because it was thought he unfairly targeted children. A Joe Camel obituary was printed in a newspaper which I found extremely smart and comical. It read, "Joe Camel, the suave dromedary who excelled at billiards, played the saxophone, and tirelessly promoted Camel cigarettes from behind dark glasses, died Thursday at his home in North Carolina. He was 9 years old. His demise was widely anticipated after years of criticism for his not-too-subtle appeal to children and his recent emergence as a target of the federal government, including President Clinton. His health had deteriorated rapidly after the June 20 announcement that the tobacco industry would settle a bevy of lawsuits brought by 40 states. Joe's death came at the hands of his creator, RJ Reynolds Tobacco."

CHAPPAQUIDDICK – That is all you need to say to people my age to know the story. It was July 18th-19th, 1969. Chappaquiddick is a small island off the coast of Massachusetts. Senator Ted Kennedy of Massachusetts and youngest son of the prominent Kennedy family left a party and was driving a car with Mary Jo Kopechne as his companion. He was going to take her to a ferry landing for her return to Edgartown. The Senator took a wrong turn and he came upon a one lane guard-less bridge where his car slid off and submerged upside down in the shallow but deep enough water below. Kennedy escaped from the car, could not rescue Mary Jo, swam to shore, and went to his house to sleep for the night. At 10:00 am the next morning he reported the incident. The next day a diver recovered Mary Jo's body from the car. A week later Kennedy pled guilty to a charge of leaving the scene of an accident. He received a two-month suspended sentence. Suspended sentence. The incident became national news immediately and influenced Kennedy's decision not to run for President in 1972 and 1976. Ted Kennedy spent forty-seven years in the Senate from 1962 until his death in 2009. He became known as 'The Lion of the Senate.'

"One small step for man. One giant leap for mankind" Those were the words we heard late on the evening of July 20th, 1969 from astronaut Neil Armstrong after the Eagle landed, ON THE MOON. I was there looking at the grainy picture on the black and white TV set at my neighbor and friend Tom Dickmeyer's house along with friend and neighbor Tom Scott. That evening before the famous moon landing, The Toms' and I had been out carousing in Tom Dickmeyer's car. Basically, we were joy riding, smoking some cigarettes and drinking some beers. You might say it was a typical summer evening for us. The space dream of President Kennedy came true on this night. And in this decade as he had hoped. It was a remarkable achievement. Unfortunately, JFK was not around to witness it.

On August 8th and 9th there were brutal killings at the leadership and direction of Charles Manson, cult leader of the 'Manson Family'. The Manson Family brutally murdered actress Sharon Tate and four others in her home followed by the murders of Leno and Rosemary LaBianca the next day. The murders were on the orders of Charles Manson though he did not take part physically. The actual acts were committed by his 'family' members, Tex Watson, Susan Atkins, and Patricia Krenwinkel. Manson was convicted, jailed, and stayed incarcerated until his death in 2017. In 2019 the movie, 'Once Upon a Time in Hollywood' by Quentin Tarantino came out. It was largely based on the Manson Family escapades but with a much safer and happier alternative ending.

A week later, four days of peace and music were held in Bethel, New York at the farm of Max Yasgur. It would be known as the

Woodstock Rock Festival. An advance ticket for the concert would cost $18 for all four days. A crowd of 50,000 was expected to attend. Nearby residents were opposed to the event because they did not want a bunch of hippies over-running their town. Because of issues caused by the original venue being changed and time running short, a fence and ticket booths were not completed in time for the event. Eventually, it became a free concert. Creedence Clearwater became the first band to sign up for the event. Jimi Hendrix was the last to play. A total of 32 acts took part in the event held in intermittent rain. It was estimated that the audience for Woodstock peaked at 450,000 as word percolated through fandom of the rock n roll world. Traffic jams to get to Bethel were common. Singer Arlo Guthrie famously announced "The New York Thruway is closed man," but it is said the closure never really took place. Major issues such as food shortages and sanitation problems occurred. Other acts that played at the festival included Crosby, Stills, Nash, and Young, The Band, Ten Years After, The Who, Sly and the Family Stone, and Santana. Alvin Lee and 'Ten Years After's' playing of 'I'm Going Home,' made me an instant fan of that band. A documentary film of the event was released in 1970 and the promoters eventually made some money. Where was I during this festival? I was home enjoying my summer. As a near sixteen-year-old, I was too young to be expected to go. I could have seen my older brothers going, but they did not. Fact is I do not recall hearing about the event in advance but when the large crowds kept coming and coming, everyone seemed to be aware before it ended. The event was mostly peaceful. It was reported that one attendee died from an insulin overdose and another died while he was asleep in a sleeping bag under a tractor and was run over by the unassuming tractor operator. Two births occurred during the event. I wonder where those kids are now?

In late August, Junior year at high school began with great anticipation. I knew all the kids now and I really felt like an integral part of our Chatard High School class. Dad convinced me (made me) to take a class called 'Office.' He thought it would be good training for my post-school life. I suspect he did not see College as part of my future. Dad was right on. There were only two students in the class. That was considered a full class for 'Office.' I do not know how the old man heard about it but Father Knows Best. Besides myself was the very attractive Senior co-ed, Mary Quinn. The class was conducted in the office of the school and it was basically a self-taught non-paying job. It was an internship. It was also the first period of the day. Our job was to take phone calls for absentees, hand out late slips to tardy students, take doctor appointment notes and get them to the right people, and take care of other general day to day office needs such as filing during the schools' first forty-five-minute period. There was supervision but no teacher for Office. There was no grade, just school credits. With the beautiful Mary Quinn at my side, it was easily my favorite class of all-time and one of the most useful. I am certain it paid dividends for the rest of my life.

Bob Kelly was one of my best friends at Chatard HS. Neither of us played sports in school. We were together every day at school, many days after school, and weekends too. We attended many of the schools sporting events together, oftentimes sneaking in and possibly with liquor in tow. One time we snuck into a road football game by climbing on top of a low ceiling flat roof with the idea of jumping over to join the fans on the other side. We did not realize that roof was the concession stand before jumping over. But we got in. When we decided to 'cut' school or a class, we did it together. One day in May we decided to watch race cars at the Indianapolis Motor Speedway as opposed to joining our classmates at school. We had a great time. I am just not sure why we buzzed the front of the school prior to school letting out in Bob's hot Chevy Impala where all the students and teachers facing the front of the school could identify us. This act of stupidity was followed by two days labor at the school.

In late October I passed the test. After taking the requisite drivers ed class at Chatard High School during the previous summer, I got my first license to legally drive and operate a vehicle. I felt qualified and responsible enough in every way to drive a car. Now, when I see a 6ixteen year old behind the wheel I wonder what the heck our government is thinking about. I hope I am wrong but I really do feel that my generation, regardless of how many stupid things we did, was more responsible and on the ball then the youth of today.

On December 6th a 'Woodstock West' event called the Altamont Free Concert would take place at the Altamont Speedway in northern California. Billed as a free festival, nearly 300,000 people attended. Altamont was headlined by The Rolling Stones. Also playing were Santana, Jefferson Airplane, and others. The Grateful Dead were scheduled to perform but declined at the last minute due to violence occurring on the scene. Hell's Angels were hired as security around the stage. Payment for their service? Beer. They had done this in the past for Jefferson Airplane and for the Grateful Dead.

Santana was the first act and everything went very smoothly. As the day wore on, fans became agitated due to delays, some attacking each other. Occasionally they might mix it up with some of the Angels, which does not seem like a smart idea. By the time the Stones took the stage in the evening, the mood of the crowd had gotten ugly. Numerous fights had erupted amongst the crowd and with the Angels. After someone knocked over one of the Angels motorcycles, the Angels became more aggressive. As the Stones began their performance, the low stage was tightly packed with thousands of fans, many trying to get onto the stage. The Stones were forced to stop mid-song more than once waiting for some type of order in the crowd to be restored. A fight broke out between members of Hells Angels and 18-year-old music fan Meredith Hunter. Hunter was punched and chased back into the crowd but he returned for more abuse. On his return, he was seen pulling a revolver from his jacket and 'Angel' Alan Passaro charged him with a knife. Meredith was stabbed twice and killed. The Stones were aware of the skirmish' but not the killing. They completed their set fearing an all-out riot if they quit.

Altamont became the antithesis of Woodstock. Peace and Love vs. a combination of Love and Violence. A documentary called 'Altamont' also hit the big screen. I saw both Woodstock and Altamont at theaters. Altamont was the last major event of a tumultuous year and decade. 1969 was certainly a year for the record books. My decade ended with a trip to Shreveport, Louisiana with my parents and a couple siblings to visit my parent's good friends who had moved to the bayou a couple years previous. The trip included New Year's Eve and a New Year's Day trip to the Cotton Bowl game in Dallas. The University of Texas bested Notre Dame 21-17 on January 1st, 1970.

Two other deaths in 1969 made big news in America. Dwight D Eisenhower, our 34th President and 5-star General died as well as Joseph P Kennedy, father of our 35th President, John F Kennedy, and Senators Robert and Ted Kennedy.

The year in sports showed the Celtics take out the Lakers one final time in this decade. The Celtics won 9 of 10 Championships in the 6ixties. Montreal beat the expansion St. Louis Blues for the Stanley Cup in a repeat of the previous year's final. UCLA beat Purdue University for their 5th title in six years which would eventually stretch to 10 titles in a 12-year run under the guidance of native Hoosier John Wooden. Mario Andretti drank the winner's milk at the Indy 500. It would be the Andretti family's lone Indy victory suffering heartbreak on many future occasions. The decade in sports ended with the 'Amazing Mets' beating the Baltimore Orioles for the World Series title.

'Butch Cassidy and the Sundance Kid' starring Paul Newman and Robert Redford was a hit at the movie box office. The film was directed by George Roy Hill. George Roy and actor Paul Newman combined on other hits during their careers including two of my favorites: 'The Sting' and 'Slapshot.'

The most influential thing for me in the 6ixties besides family, school, and friends, had to be music. It started in 6ixty-four with the Beatles on the Ed Sullivan Show and continued through 6ixty-nine and beyond with Woodstock and Altamont. The importance of Ed Sullivan's contribution to music should not go under-stated. There were some great Vietnam Protest songs written during the decade including: 'Eve of Destruction' by Barry McGuire, 'For What It's Worth' by Buffalo Springfield, 'Fortunate Son' by Creedence Clearwater Revival, and many more.

71

Nineteen 6ixty-nine will always go down as a fascinating year for music, achievement in space, and Manson. My friends and I were getting behind the wheel of a car and more freedom was ours for the taking if we could handle the responsibility. I began working for a real paycheck for the first time. My junior year at high school was great as I had more friends and was popular at school.

Some might argue that the 6ixties was one of the most tumultuous and divisive decades of my lifetime. It was dominated by the civil rights movement, the Vietnam War, war protests and race riots. Throw in the assassination of a President, Senator, and Civil Rights Icon and you have a decade filled with friction and heartache.

As I leave the 6ixties and an educational, family-oriented, fun-filled decade for me, what would the future have in store for me and my surroundings? Would I be able to make anything of myself? And did I even care at this point in my life? I am certain it was not much of a thought. If I failed it would not be from a lack of love, support, or opportunity. All I could think about right now was friends, girls, music, work, smoking, drinking, playing and watching sports, and playing poker. And not getting caught. Being in my 60's was not something I could fathom at this time. I could not even fathom the coming of the twenty-first century, still thirty years away. I was young, carefree, and did not see a need to understand. But my 60's did come and in spite of some wild years in the early seventies, I got there in better shape than anyone could have imagined on December 31st, 1969. I also arrived with a mind, perspective, and achievements that far exceeded my papers.

1965 – Marty playing first base

Kennedy / King Memorial in Indianapolis

The Mansion

St Andrew troupe. Sitting, Jody Davis and Marty. Standing, Mark Adamson, Helen Langenbacher, Pat Brady, Tom Scott, Mike Russell, Don Bane, Terry Scheidler.

Bridge To 60

Between 1-1-1970 and my 60th birthday in 2013, a lot of developments took place as you would imagine. The country grew and changed a great deal. Some good, some bad, all subjective. Developments in innovation and technology reached unthought of heights. I married in 1974 at the young age of twenty and we are still married into our 6ixties. In all these years I was never a day without full employment. We have three well-behaved fully employed grown children (one girl and two boys) and five grand–children (four girls and one boy). I have experienced a terrific life full of family, fun, hard work, and luck. Here are some highlights of things that transpired in the 43 years until I reached age 60. Items marked with ★ were mostly of a sporting interest to me, national, or international news items. Some captivated the minds and hearts of the world. All others, I was there or directly involved.

1970   Cotton Bowl. ★Kent State massacre. ★Apollo 13.
1971   Orange Bowl. Spring Break in Panama City, Fla. Senior Prom. High School graduation. First of 16 straight Indy 500's. ★D.B. Cooper
1972   Stones STP Tour. ★Munich Olympics Massacre. ★Fischer vs Spassky.
       Kegger party on Denny St. Moved out of parent's house.
       ★Summit Series. (Canada vs USSR)
       Family Christmas Vacation in Hawaii. (Everyone made the cut)
1973   My first car, a 1970 Chevy Brookwood station wagon. Swede Savage accident at Indy 500. ★Tennis, Battle of the sexes.

1974   Married Ginger Buckheister on the same day as the 100th running of the Kentucky Derby. Left the grocery business and started career at Plumbers Supply. ★Watergate and Nixon's resignation.

1975   ★Where's Jimmy Hoffa?

1976   Vacation at Rocky Waters Motor Inn, Gatlinburg. Tn.
WHA Indy Racers, I attended most games during their Indy run.

1977   First born, Christy. ★Duel in the Sun at Turnberry. ★Tony Kiritsis.
★Roots mini-series. ★Elvis died.

1978   Bought our first home with double-digit interest rates.

1979   First of many trips to Boston Garden. ★NCAA, Magic vs. Bird.

1980   First son John born. ★1980 Olympics, "Do you believe in miracles"? ★Who shot JR? ★John Lennon murdered.

1981   ★Iran Hostage Crisis ends after 444 days.

1982   Attended ASA School of Industrial Distribution at Texas A&M.
Rock City, Tn. family vacation. Talladega 500. ★Start of bull market.

1983

1984   ★NFL Colts move to Indy. Our family moved to Indy's northside.
Second son Jason born.

1985   Another Gatlinburg family vacation. ★Ryan White / HIV/ AIDS

1986   ★Nicklaus wins 6th Masters. ★Challenger explosion. ★Red Sox blow World Series. First of 16 seasons coaching youth hockey. John scores first goal.

1987   ★Al Unser Sr. wins 4th Indy 500. ★Black Monday.
The Snowbirds Youth hockey team. I was coach.
★Baby Jessica. ★"Mr. Gorbachev, tear down this wall."

1988   Our father died. Jason scores first hockey goal as a four-year old.

Travel hockey in custom vans, first of 9 years.

*Pan Am Flight 103

1989   Ridley College summer hockey camp with John and friends.

Our Great Aunt Margaret died.

1990   Michigan National Hockey League. (Both boys eventually played in the elite league.)

1991   Earned my certificate as a USA Hockey 'Master Coach'.

My family spent Christmas in Palm Beach Gardens, Fl.

1992   I left Plumbers Supply and purchased hockey Pro Shop in Carmel, In. Due to our kids ages, this was my favorite year for our family. *Rodney King riots.

1993   *Waco massacre.

1994   Inaugural Brickyard Race, I attended the first eleven Brickyards.

Stones' Voodoo Lounge Tour in Indy. *Contract with America. *OJ Bronco chase.

1995   Family vacation in Orlando, Sonesta Suites Hotel. *OKC bombing.

Christy graduated from my alma mater, Bishop Chatard high school.

1996   *Tiger Woods, "Hello World".

1997   Coached team in Pee Wee Hockey to National Semi-finals. Jason starred at left defense.

1998   *McGwire/Sosa home run chase. Grandma Kavanaugh died. John graduated from Cathedral high school.

*Peyton Manning era begins in Indy.

1999   *Columbine shooting. Christy's wedding. First grandchild Abby born.

*Golf loses US Open Champion Payne Stewart in plane crash.

2000   Purchased Florida condo. Began work for Mueller Industries.

*Our Indiana Pacers reach NBA Finals.

*George W Bush wins disputed 'hanging chad' election.
*Y2K.

2001 *Dale Earnhardt dies in Daytona crash. *911

2002 Stones' Forty Licks Tour, Columbus, Ohio.

2003 Jason graduated high school.

2004 Moved to Fishers, In. Sold the Pro Shop.

2005 First hole in one. Jason's 21st birthday in Vegas.

2006 *Saddam Hussein killed.

2007 *Indy Colts win Super Bowl. Son Jason married Casey Chafin.

Granddaughter Kaley born. *1st I-phone introduced.

2008 *Barrack H Obama elected President.

2009 * Fort Hood shooting. *Affordable Care Act passed by Senate.

2010 John's 30th birthday in Boston. *Obamacare. My first book published. My friend Steve Considine died. *Chilean Mining Accident.

Our mother died.

2011 *Boston Bruins Win Cup. *Osama Bin Laden killed.

2012 *Sandy Hook Elementary shootings.

*Benghazi. Vacationed in Charleston, S.C.

2013 Disneyworld with granddaughter Kaley.

Part 2

60

9-19-2013 to 9-18-2014

I arrived in my 60's without a college degree but with a work ethic that could challenge the best. At 60 I considered myself an American traditionalist, mostly conservative, and with a moderating to a degree social outlook. A hard-working family man with respect for a higher being. I had my share of opportunity and luck along the way but also found the harder I worked, the luckier I got. I married at the young age of twenty. In many cases that is a recipe for disaster. Not for us. My wife and I arrived together aged 60, married 39 years, healthy and with a bit of a nest egg. Our three children and two granddaughters were nearby and everything was great.

In the 1960's I lived on the near northeast side of Indianapolis surrounded by similarly minded good Christian families. They were safe, family-oriented neighborhoods with plenty of trees but no sidewalks. At 60, my wife Ginger and I were nine years into our empty nester ranch home in the affluent northeast Indy suburb of Fishers. It is a safe, family-oriented neighborhood with sidewalks in front of every home and matching mailboxes. A good number of the homes have irrigation to water their lush lawns. I had never seen an irrigated lawn in the 1960's. Every spring sees flowers sprout up or planted on most lawns. Non-threatening dogs seem to be a part of most homes. Except for "rows of houses that are all the same" our neighborhood is possibly what 'The Monkees' had in mind when they sang the song, 'Pleasant Valley Sunday' in nineteen-6ixty-seven.

Today is September 19th, 2013. My 60th birthday. It was a beautiful day as expected. Clear morning skies opened the day with temperatures in the low 50's that would soon give way to a high of 74. September is traditionally the best weather month of the year in Indianapolis, if you like sunny skies, little breeze, low humidity, lows in the fifties, and highs in the seventies. This day was like many birthdays I have spent recently. Today was a Wednesday and I took the day off from work. A brisk two-mile walk was followed with a breakfast of circle eggs and toast. That is the name our family has adopted for poached eggs over the years. A round of golf was scheduled with friends at 11:00 am. I shot 81 at Pebble Brook which was an average score for me. In the evening we would eat dinner at Champps Restaurant which was customary not because it was my birthday but because we ate at Champps almost every Wednesday night for many years. Our son Jason was a manager there and we always got comp'd a portion of our meal. Oftentimes the tip was more than the bill presented at our table. This Wednesday was a little different however. My wife Ginger wanted to meet me there instead of driving together. There was no doubt in my mind that a surprise birthday party had been planned. And even though I knew it, I went along with the gag. When I arrived at Champps at my scheduled 7:00 pm time, I walked in and asked the girl at the front desk in a wry tone, "where are they"? We knew all the employees at Champps. She pointed me to the back area where Champps is known to host many parties. They all saw me walking in but I never looked directly in that area. Along the way in the bar area, I saw an acquaintance and we spoke briefly. At that time the party was saying, what the heck is he doing? They were all being somewhat quiet waiting for the customary, SURPRISE! When I arrived and was greeted, I was not the least bit surprised by the event that Ginger had planned but I was shocked and quite taken aback by the numbers of people who were there. All my seven brothers and sisters were there along with their spouses, except for Kevin who was working in Boston. And, of course my kids were there. Many nieces and nephews were there. My friends I played golf with today were there. Ginger had also invited friends from our hockey days in the eighties and nineties and maybe the biggest surprise was she even thought to invite our Life Insurance Agent. Truly for that time in my life, just about everyone was there that I associated with. It was a grand evening of food and drink with many gifts that were unnecessary but much appreciated.

Ginger had a custom cake made for the event. It was decorated with frosting artwork of many things from my life, like golf and hockey. So that is how I got my 60's started. I was healthy, happy, and my kids were all employed. I had 2 granddaughters and our marriage of 39 years was going great. Is it possible that the 60's could be as good as my care-free 6ixties?

I received my first I-phone at the age of 60. We have come a long way from dial telephones of the 6ixties and party lines. We have even come a long way from flip phones and Blackberry's. It took me a while to learn how to use my I-phone but I eventually got the hang of it and continued to learn new functions as time went by. I seldom watch TV without my I-phone nearby and maybe looking up someone's age or what someone's name is and where have I seen him or her before. There is nothing you cannot find and learn with an I-phone.

Two days after my 60th birthday, my nephew Zack Murphy married Angela Green at 'The Sanctuary' on North Pennsylvania St. near downtown Indianapolis. The Sanctuary is one door north of The Elbow Room bar and restaurant. The significance of The Elbow Room to our family was that our paternal grandparents opened that bar in December of 1933 immediately following the end of prohibition. When they opened the bar, it was called the Penway Tavern due to its location at the corner of Pennsylvania St. and Fort Wayne Avenue. All my brothers and sisters and their spouses gathered at The Elbow Room prior to the wedding for a bit of late lunch and some pre wedding lubricant. The early evening wedding was wonderful with an excellent reception all under the same roof. I could critique the loud music but they were not playing it for me. The entire day was flawless except for a little issue with a ceiling tile falling and hitting my niece Jessica Pigati on the foot that caused some significant swelling.

On November 22, 2013, I returned to my grade school, St. Andrew, for a visit. Why November 22nd and why the visit? It was the 50th Anniversary of President Kennedy's assassination. I simply wanted to walk the downstairs hallway, visit my 5th grade classroom, and reminisce about that fateful day 50 years prior. You might call me a bit of a romantic. St Andrew was still being run as a private school but it was a mere shadow of the burgeoning school from the 1960's that boasted the largest enrollment of any Catholic grade school in our State. Unlike back in the 6ixties where locked doors anywhere were rare, the schools' doors were locked today. I pressed a buzzer and a nice lady answered. When I told her what I wanted, she said no thanks. I could not have been less welcome had I been wearing an orange jump suit from prison. I drove around to the rear parking lot where the girls used to play kickball. I could see the classroom I was in on the historic day in question, but I could not get inside the building and I was not terribly surprised nor disappointed. I sat and looked from the comfort of my vehicle. I gave long pause to the events of that long-ago day. As always when I am near the old neighborhoods, I drove by the two homes we used to live in. Ten years later in April of 2023, St Andrew hosted an open house to recruit new students for the fall semester. I jumped at the opportunity to visit and was welcomed with open arms. I ran into a couple people that were familiar with some of my siblings. The building which looks its age from the outside looked incredibly good on the inside. It looked better than expected but just as I remembered.

The annual Kavanaugh family Christmas party which has become tradition was hosted by my brother Patrick and his wife Michelle this year. All eight siblings have been rotating this responsibility since the early nineties. Back when my older siblings and I were married with small kids, our parents always had a family Christmas dinner, oftentimes on Christmas Eve. A few years after our father passed, us kids began rotating the responsibility and this is probably Pat's third go-around. We used to have anywhere from 30-40 people but we have grown to have as many as seventy in my later 60's. This year was a brutal evening for a party. We had one of those December downpours that always comes along once or twice a month in December. We welcomed two new Kavanaugh boys to the family this year. We do not often get to say that. In fact, it had been 28 years since we have been able to say that. There is a lot of girls. My great-nephews Peter and Max were born two weeks apart in mid-summer. Their presence alone made this a very special Christmas gathering.

In 2013 sports, the Super Bowl had Baltimore over San Francisco. My Boston Bruins blew leads in nearly every game they lost losing the Stanley Cup to the Chicago Blackhawks at home in six games. My brother Kevin who works in Boston attended game 6, but inexplicably did not wait around to see the Cup paraded around the ice. The Miami Heat defended their title in basketball, this time over San Antonio and the Boston Red Sox took out the St. Louis Cardinals four games to two. Fan favorite Tony Kanaan won the Indy 500 and another fan favorite Phil Mickelson won the British Open at Muirfield in Scotland.

In the mid-nineties I began going to movie theaters as my newest pastime. In 2001 I discovered the merits of lesser-known independent movies when I saw a film called Lantana. I began averaging roughly 6ixty movies per year at the theater. In the past decade or so I became somewhat of a go-to guy in our family and even with customers in the plumbing industry for information on movies. I had a reputation. What have you seen? What should I see, etcetera? I rated every movie I saw and ranked them. For 2013 my favorite movie was Saving Mr. Banks with Tom Hanks and Emma Thompson.

Back to sports, it was January 6th of 2014 when I met a man of world-wide sports fame. I have been fortunate to meet famous people from the sporting world in my life. Bobby Orr, Gordie Howe, Johnny Bench, and Tom Watson to name a few. But I am not sure how they measure up in worldwide fame to this man. Watson, possibly. At the company I was working for, Mueller Industries, it was common to bring in a guest speaker at our annual sales meeting. Tonight's speaker was big George Foreman. Olympic star. Heavyweight Champion of the World. King of the Foreman grill. And father of multiple George Foreman's. When I shook his hand, I was not surprised at how big they were. I was shocked at how soft they were. George is a big man, entertaining, and a good speaker. He hung around for plenty of photos.

During Spring Break this year Christy, Ginger, and I took the Key West Express boat from Ft Myers to Key West. The 3 ½ hour, one-way excursion is a lot of fun. There is comfortable indoor seating and outdoor topside seating if you enjoy the breeze. A cash bar is available during the entire trip. I had never been to Key West and we only went for the day and rode the craft back that evening. I had my picture taken at the 'Southernmost Point' buoy. We made sure we hit a few bars which seemed mandatory and enjoyed some entertainment at the Sunset Pier. Going there and back makes for a long day but it is worth it and I would do it again.

Shortly after spring break in early May, Ginger and I celebrated our 40th wedding anniversary with dinner at Ruth's Chris steakhouse. I have never had a problem remembering the number of our anniversary we are celebrating because we got married on the 100th running of the Kentucky Derby. Cannonade was the winner on May 4th, 1974. We typically celebrate the first Saturday in May.

In June of 2014, son John and I left for a long awaited, much anticipated, and carefully planned golf trip to Scotland. My Dad and I had a similar trip planned in 1987 with completed itinerary. Our father had the idea to take each of his eight children on a special trip over the next few years beginning in 1987 and somehow starting with me. Dad came down with cancer and we never got to make the trip. He was never able to make any of the eight trips. I still have and treasure the itinerary of the 1987 trip that never happened. I had recently developed a similar plan for my three children. This year was John's turn.

John and I left on Friday June 20th flying out of Indy and through Philadelphia to Edinburgh, Scotland. It was our 'Trip of A Lifetime.' The flight across the ocean was my first. It was tiring, but expected. After retrieving our luggage, we met up with our travel agent from SGH Golf who accompanied us to the car rental. We then signed off for the vehicle; fittingly, a VW Golf. We loaded our grip and took a tram from the airport in to the nearby town of Edinburgh, leaving the rental car temporarily behind. We visited the spectacular Edinburgh Castle. The fortress dominates the skyline and has been the focus of many attacks over the centuries. It was a fascinating and educational visit. We followed that up with a walk down famous Princes Street and its many shops and restaurants. We had lunch and unexpectedly saw a very 'colorful' parade going through town. We saw the statue of well-known economist Adam Smith. There was an attractive young lady, entertaining passersby with her bagpipes. After some light shopping we were back on the tram to the airport to retrieve our car. Destination, Troon, Scotland.

When leaving the airport, the only thing I had on my mind was staying left. John had our pre mapped routes and he oversaw all navigation. I just needed to stay left while driving the roads of Scotland. We arrived at The Marine Hotel in Troon while only missing one minor turn on one of the many roundabouts. The Marine Hotel is adjacent to the 18th fairway of Royal Troon golf course but we did not know exactly what hole we were looking at when we saw it. We just knew it was the golf course. We checked into the hotel with Laura at the front desk. She welcomed us as if we were loving relatives she had not seen in years. She was expecting us and seemed to know who we were the minute we approached her station. We checked in and she was gracious enough to take a picture with me near the steps leading to the second floor of the three-story hotel. On our way to our room there were plenty of pictures of golfers on the walls. After unpacking, we went back down and had a much-needed relaxing drink at the hotel bar. Cheers! While sitting there I saw it. The Ailsa Craig miles out in the Firth of Clyde. The Ailsa Craig is a rock island of 240 acres standing 1,100 feet high above the water. It is here where they get material to make stones for the sport of curling. Many golfers with a keen historical sense of the game have heard of the Ailsa Craig. I knew you could see it from Turnberry, but I was not aware you could see it from as far away as Troon, 20 miles up the coast from Turnberry. The moment my eyes locked onto it, there was no doubt what I was seeing. Legend has it if you cannot see the Ailsa Craig, it is raining. If you can see it, rain is on the way. Rain must have been on the way this day but we stayed dry nearly the entire week. We visited the Troon Golf Shop next door then went for a short visit to the hotel pool and hot tub. Dinner followed and we got a well-deserved good nights' sleep.

Sunday morning came late. We slept solid until 9:00 am but were quickly refreshed after shower and breakfast. Our golfing assignment today was 2:00 pm at Turnberry. Along the way we visited Prestwick Golf & Sailing Club, home of the first British Open in 1860. Willie Park took down Old Tom Morris by two strokes. Time allowed us a visit at the Culzean Castle. President Eisenhower was given a suite of rooms at the castle as a thank you from the Scottish people. The Castle's history goes back to the late 1700's and we enjoyed every bit of that visit. But now it was down to business, Turnberry. When we arrived, it was hard to believe we were finally here. We had a light lunch upon arrival to the Club and even found time for a visit to the majestic Turnberry Hotel which sits across the street and up the hill behind the 18th green. The day was sunny and 65 degrees with the lightest of breeze. The type of day you get around these parts maybe a handful of times each year. Our caddies were Mike and Scott and we joined up with another two-ball. It was my first round ever with a caddie. After striping our first tee shots nicely, we were off. Walking toward the first fairway from the tee box was literally like walking on air. We felt like royalty. I had looked forward to a trip like this since my dad first mentioned it. Now some twenty-seven years later, it was here. John had a miracle birdie two on the 4th hole pitching in from atop a large dune some forty yards away from the cup. His caddie showed the enthusiasm of a Lee Trevino pitch-in to win the Open in the early seventies. I will call it the first family birdie in Europe. Turnberry is full of history as its fairways were used as runways during World War II. There is still one unused, somewhat crusty asphalt runway adjacent to one of the fairways. There is a majestic lighthouse near the tenth tee and WWII monuments are on parts of the course. I was playing solid enough golf today and on the Par 3 15th, I was between 5 & 6 iron. My caddie advised the 5 and I hit the ball to twenty feet right of the flag. I squeezed my putt in for my first birdie of the trip. Coming down the 18th fairway my ball was about ten yards past the Tom Watson fairway plaque commemorating the place of his approach to the green in 1977 winning the 'Duel in the Sun' vs. Jack Nicklaus. It was the first British Open played at Turnberry and no I did not hit from the same tees as Mr. Watson. Again, I felt I was between a 5 & 6 iron. This time my caddie advises the 6. I hit a nice shot and its rolling and its rolling and its rolling. I have lost sight of it as my eyes are not what I wish and with rolling terrain you can lose sight a bit easier. My caddie is saying good shot. As the ball is rolling toward the pin, one of the other caddies with a better view from the opposite side of the fairway is screaming with excitement. I thought maybe I had just made a miracle eagle. The ball stopped two feet right of the hole, level with the pin. I was just inside of Watson's clinching shot in 1977 which was 2 ½ feet left of the hole with the pin in a similar position. A birdie 3 at Turnberry's home hole, appropriately named 'Duel in the Sun'. Is there a better feeling in golf? I was about to find out tomorrow at Troon. We finished the day shooting 84 & 90. I did not know if there could be a prettier golf course in the world. Donald Trump of the US had purchased this Course and Hotel not long before our arrival. Both would undergo major renovations soon. We were back at The Marine Hotel for drinks and dinner by 9:00 pm. It was still daylight mind you and after dinner we turned in with a perfect first full day under our belts.

On Monday June 23 we ate breakfast and were off to Royal Troon for a morning tee time. This drive entailed moving our vehicle from the south parking lot of the hotel to the north parking lot of the Golf Club. About a one-minute drive. It would be another sunny day, 62 with light breeze. Arnold Palmer won at Royal Troon in the 1961 British Open and his foot print (photos) is all over the place. It is said that Arnie's win made it popular for Americans to make the annual trip to the UK to challenge for the Claret Jug. The number one fairway went straight south with the Firth of Clyde immediately to our right. Tall heather and a wind-beaten picket fence were also parallel and to our right. Bunkers dot the fairways like so many oversized catchers mitts waiting to snatch your ball. We both hit solid opening drives avoiding bunkers and we were off as a two ball with our caddies Daniel and Ben. There is nothing like playing a Championship Course with a caddie, the way golf was meant to be played. Having your son in tow enhances the pleasure immeasurably. The second tee box was literally footsteps away from the number one green. A pair of Japanese ladies played behind us and they carried their purses with them the entire round. Get to their ball, put the purse on the ground, hit the ball and pick up the purse again. We were told that the Asian people carry all their money with them and they will not let it out of their sight. As we traversed the course, planes from nearby Prestwick Airport soared low overhead during take-off. On the inward nine, particularly number 11, aptly named Railway, the high-speed rail transit moved constantly from Prestwick to Troon and onward to Glasgow. The most famous hole on the course is the Par 3 eighth. It is nicknamed the postage stamp because of the small size of the green. A score of 5 is more common than a score of 2. At 123 yards it is the shortest hole in the Open Championship Rota. If the hole was not famous already, the golfing legend Gene Sarazen put his own stamp on the hole scoring an Ace in the 1973 Open at the age of 71. A young Tiger Woods was in contention at the 1997 Troon Open until a triple bogey 6 on the short 8th did him in. As I walked up the difficult 7th, it was impossible not to sneak a peek to my right at the upcoming 8th. I was playing a good outward nine scoring birdie 4 on the long par 5 sixth. The sixth being the longest hole in the Championship Rota. After a bogey 5 on the tough 7[th,] I made my way up the hill to the 8th tee to find a finely dressed elderly Scot sitting on a bench behind the tee just taking in the air and surroundings. I assumed he was certainly a member and looked the part of possibly being a Club Captain. I selected an 8 iron today with the help of my able caddie and struck a nice shot to the green below toward the left edge of the green. A few yards further left and I might have found my grave in the coffin bunker. But this ball pitched onto the green and started rolling toward the hole. For a moment I thought the magic of the Squire (Gene Sarazen) might pay me a visit. The ball got closer and closer and ended up directly in front of the pin. With my not-so-great eyesight I thought I was just a few feet away but when we arrived on the green it was an honest eight feet. Departing the tee box, the old timer wished us well. I did make that putt for birdie 2 and it is one of the highlights of my golfing life. That and my birdie three yesterday on the 18th at Turnberry. A bigger, priceless memory from today's birdie came later in the day. As we turned to the inward nine there were a few old war planes flying overhead from the Prestwick Airport. It was a very cool surrounding. The back nine was a stiffer test as we played into a freshening breeze. I was still playing well but let a couple double bogey sixes creep onto the card. The careless error on the 18th bothered me the most. I laced a drive down the middle and had a mere 9 iron to a center flag. The Clubhouse is directly behind the green and a shot long could easily go out of bounds near the building. I thinned my nine-iron coming out of it a bit and it stayed in bounds but not stopping until it reached the rear fringe. A three putt gave me a bad bogey for a 41/44 85. John was pleased with his 88.

We lunched in the clubhouse after looking around at the many golf artifacts and artist drawings of Arnold Palmer and others. Even the Claret Jug or possibly a replica was on display in the clubhouse. As we were eating lunch, the same gentleman that watched us tee off on 8 recognized us and came up to our table for a brief chat. He congratulated me on my birdie as he unknowing to us carefully watched us finish the hole. My guess is he watches a lot of golfers from his little perch behind the 8th tee and he probably does not see many birdies there from the visiting handicappers. I must tell you it made me feel good that he noticed, he recognized me, and he took the time. Now that was a highlight.

After lunch we played Troon's more inland links course called The Portland Course. Yes, today was a 36-hole day. Wind picked up on the back nine but we shot a very respectable 84 & 87. That included the snowman I built on the 15th while John posted a seven. It was a difficult course without the notoriety of its championship neighbor and with fewer bunkers. We played with a single from Swaziland by the name of George. Back at the hotel, a pool and hot tub were beckoning. We went into town that evening for dinner and found a place called Lido's. I had excellent salmon to go along with our well-deserved drinks. Cheers! Tomorrow we would head east toward the 'Home of Golf.'

Tuesday morning June 24 we were up, and on our way to play Gleneagles Centenary Course in Auchterarder. Gleneagles would play home to the Ryder Cup three months from now. It was maybe an hour and a half drive and we arrived plenty early for our 10:30 am tee time. We took in the Pro Shop prior to play and bought souvenirs of the course and The Ryder Cup. Looking out on the first tee to the distant hills I have never seen such vibrant green in all my life. The skies were overcast today which enhanced the verdant background. We ran into occasional sprinkles with temperatures in the low to mid-sixties. We played with a husband / wife two ball and this would be the only course we used buggies on the entire trip. Gleneagles is an inland course and more like an American Resort course with a large hotel and three courses to choose from. The gentleman that joined us was not very good. His wife was a solid ball striker but very slow. I had a suspicion we were maybe playing a longer set of tees than we should have but we survived. We found the rough extremely high and I was convinced it would be cut before the Ryder Cup. Luckily for me I hit most of the fairways. When watching The Ryder Cup a few months later, I do not believe they did cut the rough. They just grew it long and punitive. The greens were a bit slow but I felt that also was on purpose in preparation for The Ryder Cup. I shot a comfortable 84 for the third time in four rounds and John came in at 92. After the round we would be headed to St Andrews but we stopped at the nearby Tullibardine Scotch distillery first, not too far up the road from Gleneagles. John drank free scotch samples for a while but since I was driving on the wrong side of the road from the wrong side of the car, I would have none of that thank you. From here to St. Andrews was about an hour and twenty-minute drive of mostly winding narrow roads lined with three-foot tall stone walls while passing sheep dotting lawns and various non-descript small towns.

As we neared St Andrews, space opened and you could see fairways, sand, and greens as far as the eye could see. We found our destination of The Scores Hotel comfortably and it was only a wedge away from the 18th green of the Old. We casually checked in and then walked over to the Old for a looksee. It was love at first sight. Our scheduled tee time here was in two days and I could not wait. I was born for this. As I gazed upon the 1st tee, I noticed the tee box was empty. I walked up to the starters box and met up with Malcolm. I asked if we could play and he apologetically said we could. He was apologetic because it was already a wee bit past 6:00 pm and he would have to charge me full price. He was fearful we might not beat darkness. I said, "so we can play"? He responds, "do you have a handicap card?" Yessir. At that point it did not matter the least what he charged me. I yell out to John, GET THE CLUBS!! He runs 100 yards up the sidewalk to retrieve the clubs from the car. At 6:20 pm we were on the Old for an unexpected bonus round of golf on the hallowed grounds of St. Andrews. With trolley in hand, we were off. We both cracked beauties off the first tee and I parred the first three holes, the second with a sand save from a deep greenside bunker. I got up and down from my first bunker on the historic course. Later in the round I snapped the perfect picture of John escaping a deep fairway bunker. I caught him in the follow through as the perfectly struck rising ball was still in the frame. As we stood on the 6th tee, we really had no idea where to hit. We knew we wanted to go west but no real idea where the fairway was as there was a perpendicular mound or dune crossing the fairway about a hundred yards ahead blocking all view of any landing area. A man on a maintenance path in a cart noticed our confusion and yelled to hit toward a certain landmark. We waived, hit nicely, and moved on. We both found unseen fairway on the other side of the hill.

I had a rudimentary understanding of the Links layout but while you are playing it for the first time, you are not thinking abouts all its vagaries, you are just excited to be there. The 7th and 11th holes crisscross, sharing the same green. The 7th is a Par 4. The 11th a very difficult Par 3, or as some have called it, the shortest Par 5 in the history of the game. As we teed off on #7 and walked toward our ball we were yelled at or cautioned by the group teeing off on #11. We were oblivious to the crisscross on our first playing of the Old. We waited for the foursome to tee off and moved on. After the ninth we caught up with a two ball. Mike and Billy were younger than John and welcomed us to join them for the inward nine. They were locals who had played the course many times. Mike was a good player who hit prodigious drives. When we got to 17, he was going to show us how it was done. The dogleg right shows you no fairway except maybe the fairway of the second hole. All you see is a 5-story hotel with its west wall looking right at you fronted by protective netting. Mike tried going high over the apex of the Hotel with a draw. He bombed it out there but forgot the draw. Reload. I hit my dependable cut but chose this time to go straight missing the unseen fairway well left in the sparse rough between the fairways of #'s 17 & # 2. John hit a nice drive and caught a piece of fairway. I could not even reach the green in two. After a desired left to right drive the long second shot requires a draw to a narrow green running from right to left with the road being in play behind the green and the deep road hole bunker in the middle of and fronting the green swallowing up any shot that is short and left. I do believe it is as hard a Par 4 as championship golf has to offer. I was 40 yards short after my second shot but hit a nice wedge over the road hole bunker onto the green leaving a fifteen-foot putt. I really wanted to par this hole. I went to local Mike for some green reading and he gave me the line. Mind you, daylight was quickly disappearing. Anyway, I drilled it to the center of the cup for what I will call a lucky par on my first effort on the road hole. We teed off on 18 at twilight and the Swilcan Bridge stares right in front of you. It is not an imposing bridge. Probably shorter than expected and certainly lower than expected. The history of the bridge is overwhelming. Even though it was now nearing dark I knew we would stop for a picture. I had to work on controlling myself or I would be overcome with emotion. It is about golf history, and thinking of my dad who was supposed to take me on this very trip in 1987 before fate took over. If it had not been for our dad, I may not be on this trip now. I composed myself enough to take some nice pictures with the gloom of lit windows in the background. We finished up at 86 & 88 and it was just a bit past 10:00 pm. The bars were still open but it was too late to order food. We did not have any lunch this day either. I brought some peanut butter crackers from home for just such an occasion. We had a couple pints with our crackers and turned in for the day. But what a day. Approaching the Swilcan Bridge for the first time is an unexplainable, near religious experience.

Wednesday June 25th was originally scheduled as an off day but I made a 12:45 tee time in Elie, Fife at the Golf House Club, built in 1875. After breakfast we did some shopping in town and walked down by the University. It was graduation week and many graduates were out enjoying the sunny morning. We saw a fellow outside practicing on his bagpipes. We investigated the Chapel and the Choir was just heading in in full dress preparing for final rehearsal. Then it was off to Elie.

After a thirty-minute drive we found the course and immediately had an issue. John was wearing shorts which is against the rules here unless you are wearing knee high socks. They were more than willing to sell John a pair and he bought two pair. They looked kind of funny but young, handsome, and fit John could pull it off. If I were wearing them, they would look like support hosiery. Lucky for me I had slacks on as usual. John was wearing a red shirt so he styled in the red knee highs. He also bought a pair of yellow knee highs which he rocked in a later round with black shorts and a black shirt trimmed in yellow. Truth is, he looked smart wearing them. The Elie course was very interesting, beginning on the first hole. The starter looks through a periscope to view the fairway below the hill to advise the players on the first tee when it is safe to play. The periscope was salvaged from HMS Excalibur in 1966 and presented to the club. Visitors are welcomed and encouraged to look. We were off and found extraordinary views of the sea along the entire way of this links. A fascinating feature of the course were the hundreds of sheep that stood on the hills surrounding the western edges of the course. You could hear the bleating sheep from nearly every corner. Another intriguing aspect of the rolling grounds was it seemed like nearly every hole after the first was uphill, yet we finished near the same spot where we started. I played well but had a disappointing bogey, bogey finish for 80, including a three putt on 18. John shot 89 and it was a great day of golf.

We took a different route back to St. Andrews and purposely went through the small town of Crail and stopped for lunch and a drink. Crail was a town that was mentioned in my dad's itinerary for my 1987 trip that never happened. We came upon the Golf Hotel Crail and had some pub food and shrimp. We toasted my old man and John's grandfather with some beers. Cheers!

After lunch we made the remaining twenty-minute drive to St. Andrews but we also stopped at Kingsbarns Golf Club which was along the route. Kingsbarns was on our itinerary to play on Saturday and we just wanted to know where it was to remove any potential moments of future travel anxiety.

After returning to our hotel, we went down by the 18th green of the Old and watched a few groups of golfers come home. It is a common pastime at St. Andrews for locals or tourists to stand by the rail behind the 18th green and applaud good shots or rounds completed. We did this on a few occasions. Later we found a nice Italian Place a couple blocks away and had dinner at Bella Italia. It was a very good meal. We ended up at One Golf Place, a bar we learned was a popular hangout for caddies. We met an old caddie who was a terrific piece of conversation. He reminded me of the Robert Shaw character in the movie 'Jaws.' Mr. Shaw was a native of the UK so I am probably close in my analogy. This caddie claimed to have looped for Arnold Palmer many years ago at the age of 16. He said he was nervous around Arnie and Mr. Palmer insisted he be called Arnie. He said Arnie was one of the nicest men he had ever met. This caddie had a lot of good stories and he loved to talk. John was in stitches. It is a shame we could only understand about half of what he said. And we wanted to believe every word of it. We never caught his name, he probably was not as old as he looked, and I took a great photo of him alongside John. We turned in about 11:00 pm.

Thursday June 24th was a day we both looked forward to with the greatest of anticipation. We had the golden ticket, aka a 10:10 tee time on The Grand Old Lady of golf. We started with breakfast as usual and as planned, we were both dressed to the nines in our plus fours. It was a bit of a cocky move for a couple of handicappers but we were well received walking into shops and milling about the 18th green awaiting our appointed tee time. Though we were fortunate enough to play The Old on Tuesday evening, this is what I would refer to as our official round, and with caddies. Before teeing off we were both asked to show our handicap cards to the starter. Our experienced loopers, Alex and Alan, were ready to go. We were paired with a couple of fellows from Wisconsin, Dan, and Ryan. For a right hander on the first at The Old, the last thing you want to do is shank one. All the audience are to the right. And by audience I do not necessarily mean they are there watching you. They are there because maybe they have a tee time coming up soon. They could be on the practice putting green. They could be going in or coming out of the caddie shed or starters office trying to get a tee time for later in the day. Whatever the reason, there is always people to your right on the opening hole. And just maybe they **were** there to watch our first shots, after all we were wearing some sharp and colorful knickers. My navy and yellow outfit looked like something from the University of Michigan. John's ensemble was complete with navy knickers topped with red Boston Red Sox polo complete with Red Sox logoed golf shoes. Before striking a ball, we could easily be mistaken as a retired Pro and his son, or a Pro and his old man. Addressing my tee ball there is plenty of room to the left and that is where I planned my cut drive to start out. Now was the time to get serious. I struck a beauty and it was time for the left–handed John to do his thing. He passed the test like a champ.

I was left with a nine iron to the welcoming opening hole. The burn in front of the 18th tee box is the same burn fronting the first green. In fact, it comes within feet of the green itself. As my crisp shot was in the air, I had no doubt it was good but I learned later that my caddie Alex was rooting my ball over the fronting burn with all he had. They say the three axioms of a caddie are show up, keep up, and shut up. At St. Andrews I learned later, the number one objective of the caddie is to get your player over the burn fronting the opening green. Alex was not comfortable my ball would cover, but I never had any doubt. We both started with a comfortable opening par though I had a fair run at a makeable birdie from fourteen feet. At the Par 5 5th, John rolled in about a 60-foot putt for birdie. He was nearly putting from the shared 13th green. Not to be outdone and happy to chalk it up to luck, I shared in his spotlight with a 20-foot birdie of my own. We were off and running. Our caddies would mention points of interest as we went along mentioning the names of the famed bunkers. Hell bunker, Shell bunker, the Strath, the Coffins, the Principals' Nose, etc. Each has their stories to tell. There are well over one hundred bunkers on the course, but none on #'s 1 & 18. On the outward nine John had a fine 37 scoring 6 pars to go along with his unexpected birdie. My equally satisfying 40 was marred by a three putt on #9, missing from three feet. After finishing the 'loop' on twelve which I also three-putt for bogey, we headed home straight into the breeze. Things got tougher for both of us. John started getting a little wild and had back-to-back-to-back-to-back double bogeys. I had a double of my own, two bogeys and a par in the stretch. Now we come to one of the most famous holes in golf, the road hole. We just played here two days ago so we knew what was in front of us but it is hard to trust hitting a fairway that you cannot see and is blocked by a brick wall doubling as a hotel. My tee shot went well left, probably closer to the #2 fairway then the 17th. Left of the #2 fairway based on the direction we were now headed is the St Andrews Links Clubhouse & Swilcan Lounge. A nice two-story restaurant with outside seating on the upper level. As John and I moved up the 17th and my ball being near the #2 fairway, we were more than noticed by the lounge patrons in our nattily attired knickers. A small crowd at the restaurant were applauding our effort at authentic links fashion. We both bogeyed the toughest Par 4 in golf. I do not know how many times I would have to play #17 to get onto that green in regulation, but I know it would take my best golf and a favorable wind. On to 18. Everyone is told the same thing. Aim for the clock on the wall of the venerable R&A behind the 18th green. With a breeze in our face, neither of us could reach Grannie Clark's Wynd that bisects the fairways on #'s 1 & 18. We crossed the Swilcan Bridge in oncoming darkness on Tuesday evening but today we would take our 'Official' trip photos. It was certainly no less emotional crossing the bridge for the second time. Yes, my eyes welled up, I am thinking about my dad, and how fortunate I am to be here with my son. If I did not know it on the first tee, I surely knew at this moment that this was the most memorable and meaningful round of golf I would ever play in my life regardless of the final tally. We took some fine photos as singles and as a pair.

My approach to #18 would take a full blast with my 4 metal such was the wind coming from ten o'clock. I aimed a good way left allowing for the wind but then I suppose I looked up and hit it right off the toe. The ball soared hard to the right heading for the line of cars parked along the road adjacent to 18. Behind the cars on the narrow road were store front windows including Old Tom Morris' shop. As my ball stayed airborne, both my caddie and I were looking to duck with embarrassment. As luck would have it, the ball struck a car at its hardest point, the door jamb area directly between the front and rear window. The solid strike spit my ball back to the fairway by about thirty yards, now just a shortish pitch from the green. We were not looking for car owners, car owners were not looking for golfers, and I really doubt that it left more than a minor mark easily buffed out. Had the ball been a few inches to either side I am confident we would have broken some glass. I played my third shot as if nothing happened. It appeared that passerby's standing behind the 18th green, were oblivious to the boner that could have been a major issue. If I can blame the poor shot on the emotional experience at the bridge and my eyes with still a bit of water in them, I will, but that would be rubbish. On the green, John made a sweet twenty-foot downhill putt for par. A generous applause from the ever-present onlookers was a good feeling. How many professional golfers over the years would have liked to sink that very putt? I made a very good 5-foot curler to save bogey. After our round, caps were doffed, hands were shaken, and caddies paid. I had brought some shot glasses from the Indianapolis Motor Speedway with me on the trip to pass out to certain starters and caddies, sort of like a souvenir bonus. The crew at St. Andrews along with others who received them looked at them as a great gesture. I thought they would be apropos since the great driver and 1965 Indy 500 champion Jimmy Clark is from Scotland as well as past Formula One champion and Indy driver Jackie Stewart and recent Indy 500 champion Dario Franchitti. The final golf score today was 40/43 83 for me. 37/48 85 for John. No one was disappointed. There is nowhere on earth we would rather be.

After our round we went to the St Andrews Links Clubhouse and Swilcan Lounge for lunch. The same two Japanese ladies we saw at Troon were eating lunch there. What were the odds? We recognized each other and briefly exchanged nods and well wishes. After lunch we visited the Old Course Hotel and spent some money shopping. Eventually we made our way to The Dunvegan Bar for additional drinks. Cheers! We spoke with the American owner Sheena, who along with her husband has owned the Dunvegan for twenty years. Sheena is a fine golfer in her own right. The walls and ceiling of her bar are filled with photos of famous people, most of them golfers, and many of them with her in the picture. It was a delight spending some time with Sheena. The bar overlooks Auchterlonies Golf Shop on Golf Place Street just a block from the 18th green of the Old and a few doors from where Old Tom Morris resided. The Dunvegan is arguably the most popular 19th hole in all of golf. It is much more than a bar; it is an experience. We ate dinner this evening at The Scores Hotel as part of our travel package. That evening we saw a wedding couple having pictures taken on the Swilcan Bridge. It is easily approachable from the street and if you are not in anyone's way, no one will bother you. I expect this couple had permission though as they spent an extended time taking important photos while ceding ground to oncoming golfers. Additional bars were frequented after dinner. I believe John tried every beer available on this trip but Guinness was his favorite. I quickly turned into a Tennents Ice Cold man. Cheers!

Friday morning, we slept in a bit. After breakfast we took in some additional shops and were off to play St. Andrews Jubilee Course at 10:56 as a two ball, sans caddies. The Old Course, New Course, and Jubilee Course all play from the same starters' hut. Their first tee boxes are all reasonably close to each other and fan out in different directions. When you see an aerial shot of the Open from St Andrews, you are seeing parts of three courses. I believe the Jubilee was part of our package because of a requirement to play a second St. Andrews Course if you are to play The Old. The Jubilee has a reputation of being the hardest course in the St. Andrews Links family of seven courses. The breeze was brisk with temperatures in the lower 60's. John went styling in his yellow knee-high socks today with his black shorts and black polo with yellow trim. I wore the usual, black slacks with yellow shirt plus an argyle sweater to complete the ensemble. The ninth was the first truly memorable hole. It was a long par three into the teeth of the wind. We came out with a 4 and a 5. The 15th hole had a large tall dune (maybe 30' high) crossing the right half of the fairway which left a blind shot in if you were middle of the fairway or right, which I was. I used a six iron which looked perfect but you could not be sure until you made your way around the mound. As I was hitting my approach on the 15th, John had snuck up behind me and took a perfect picture, catching me in my follow through with the ball in flight and true to its target. It is my version of the famous Ben Hogan one iron picture if I am allowed to have one. We found my ball on the green and it was one of my few pars on the home nine. The Jubilee is not a traditional destination course but we found it well worth our attention. I shot another 84 and John came in at 91. There were no birdies on the day. We ate lunch at the Jigger Inn which is a very small, old bar and restaurant along the 17th fairway of the Old and attached to the Old Course Hotel. You can eat or drink on the small back patio outside if you are brave enough to be in the line of wayward fire from the unseen 17th tee.

We walked around town for a bit and met up with a parade of sorts. I believe it was in conjunction with the upcoming graduation ceremony at The University. Again, we frequented the Dunvegan and the One Golf Place Bar and eventually U-turned back to The Dunvegan for dinner. Cheers! The Dunvegan is also a small hotel.

Saturday June 28th would be our last full day in Scotland. After breakfast we were off to the new and popular Kingsbarns Golf Club. Kingsbarns was built in 2000 and has already hosted professional events including the annual Dunhill Cup. It was a little cooler today with temperatures staying in the fifties. A steady breeze saw to it that we kept a jacket or sweater on all day. John wore his new St. Andrews sky blue half sleeve jacket which was nearly identical to the uniform jackets of the caddies at The Kingsbarns Club. We played with Mike from Florida and Pete out of New York. With the way John's outfit matched the caddies, we looked like a three ball with five caddies. I immediately for the first time on this trip was unimpressed with my caddie, Duncan. On the first hole he gave me my line on approach for a semi blind shot. He said hit it here as he pointed and the ball will roll straight to the hole. I proudly put my ball exactly where he pointed and then watched in dismay as the ball ran in the exact opposite direction. I should be excused for my opening 3-putt bogey. John's caddie Mike seemed to be alright. The course and views of the Firth of Forth were stunning. The sea was visible from nearly every hole. At one point our caddies pointed across the water at a town in the distance and said, "that's Carnoustie." With a little better planning and later realizing how close we were to Carnoustie, I would have put it on our trip. I am surprised our travel agent had not mentioned it. At least I do not remember them mentioning it. On with our game, we came across the shortish, downhill Par 4 sixth. John was feeling it and thought he could drive the green. He put it on the very front edge and two putted to the rear flag for a birdie three. A hole later a little rain squall came up and it was the first time we had seen rain on the trip. We donned our rain gear and opened the umbrellas and took a nice photo. It looked appropriate. The rain only lasted for two holes and we went back to our normal jacket. I had been driving the ball well today but my approaches were off and I had a few three putts on the undulating greens. I went out in 45 and John scored a very nice 40. The back nine was much of the same for me with a parade of bogeys and a double on the closing hole after popping up my drive, forcing a layup on my second shot with a chasm fronting the green and finishing it off in style with a 3 putt. I limped home with another 45 closing the trip with a 90. John's back nine did not fare much better as he came home with a 44 and a grand total of 84. John got his one win of the trip against me and I was happy for him. Our final round scores were the same as our first round at Turnberry, only in reverse. The caddies loved John and since they all were basically wearing the same gear, the five of them took a group photo after our round. We ate lunch at The Kingsbarns Club with a great view of 18. We later paid one last visit to the shops surrounding the Old and The Dunvegan. Cheers! Light rain continued off and on for the balance of the evening and we walked back to Bella Italia for dinner. We had a last drink at Golf Place and a final gaze down 1 & 18 before packing for our morning departure.

On Sunday June 29th we were off to the Airport at 7:00 am. Luggage and security took a bit of time but we arrived early and had no issues. We were wheels up as scheduled. This was truly a trip of a lifetime and John will tell stories long after I am gone. I sure hope he does. The Scottish people were the nicest group of people I have ever run across. The accommodations were first rate. We had many things to look forward to soon. The Ryder Cup later this year would be played at Gleneagles. The 2015 Open would be at St. Andrews. The 2015 Women's Open was scheduled for Turnberry. And the 2016 Open would come back to Troon. All courses we just played. And all tournaments we would look forward to watching on TV. I fell in love with Scotland and it felt like home to me. I knew I wanted to come back soon. Final note: I enjoyed nine rounds on world class venues. I lost just two balls. Hitting straight and having caddies with good eyes will never go out of style.

Back home, on August 9th 2014, racial issues brewed in the town of Ferguson, Missouri, just outside of St. Louis. Michael Brown, an

18-year-old African-American was encountered by police when things went wrong. The unarmed Mr. Brown was shot and killed and on August 10th, the riots were on. In fairness, the protests began peacefully but they never seem to stay that way. For the next few nights in Ferguson, Missouri fires broke out, glass broken, vehicles vandalized and stores looted. Police established curfews and arrived in riot gear as Molotov cocktails were lobbed in their direction. Police responded with tear gas and rubber bullets. Many arrests were made but the damage was done. Three months later after it was announced that the officer in question would not be indicted due to lack of evidence, protests started up again. Store lootings and burning of buildings was the answer from the local population. In support of the crew from St. Louis, protests broke out in other major cities including New York and Los Angeles. This type of mayhem would define my 60's much as Vietnam defined my 6ixties.

In other social news from 2014, same sex marriage bans were being declared unconstitutional in many states across the country. Many states including Indiana were all getting with the gay movement. Colorado and Washington State approved the sale of marijuana. Even with my moderating social outlook, I never could get with the legalizing of marijuana. At the end of my 60's well over half of our fifty states had legalized marijuana either recreationally or medicinally. Medicinally. I am still waiting for someone to tell me what deadly disease it cures.

On August 11th, actor Robin Williams committed suicide at the age of 63. The funnyman made his debut on an episode of the TV show Happy Days before landing a lead role as a crazy alien in the TV show Mork & Mindy in the late seventies. Robin was known for his crazy antics as an actor in a long list of comedy movies, my favorite being Mrs. Doubtfire. I also enjoyed his occasional serious roles in films such as Good Will Hunting, Insomnia, and One Hour Photo. And for fall off your seat funny, check out his stand-up comedy routine about the game of golf. He was a talented man and will be missed by his many fans.

The first year of my 60's was one for the ages starting with my surprise birthday party and topped off with my 'Trip of a Lifetime' in Scotland.

61

9-19-2014 to 9-18-2015

The day after my 61st birthday my niece Julie married Nick Vote. My oldest brother Mike and his wife Linda's youngest daughter Julie married on September 20, 2014 at The Willows, a banquet facility just north of Indianapolis in what is known as the Broad Ripple area. I believe this to be the first outdoor wedding for anyone in our family. Mike walked Julie down the infield grass to an exquisite lakeside outdoor wooden altar. The wind was blowing just hard enough to make me glance at the tall mature surrounding trees, wondering. A reception indoors at the same sight was wonderful and the music started out as if Mike or I had selected most of the songs ourselves. It sounded like channel 6 on Sirius Radio. After about an hour or so it began to sound much like the music Zack and Angela played at their wedding just a year ago. The verdict was in. I may be too old to enjoy the musical portion of these events, at least for very long anyway. It is possible I am turning into a third generation of our Great Aunt Margaret who, when hearing was not at her youthful best, sat in the distance with a bemusing smile, quietly enjoying all that surrounded her.

Julie's brother Steve was the 'Man of Honor.' I had never heard of that title before but it seemed appropriate. Steve gave the best speech I have ever heard at a wedding, and that includes movies. Some thought it was too long but when you are that good, just keep on rolling. The upset of the night, if there was one, Mike's long-standing beer of choice, Budweiser, was not one of the sudsy options.

On November 3rd, One World Trade Center, aka Freedom Tower opened in New York City. The new largest skyscraper in the United States replaces and is in the same area as the two trade towers that were destroyed by terrorists on the fateful day of September 11th, 2001.

Mike and Linda also hosted this years' family Christmas party. They had to clean out the garage to make room for everyone but we all got in and as usual, had a great time. The last time Mike and Linda were Christmas hosts, a wedding proposal broke out in the middle of the family room. There was no such surprise this year. Just food, drink, laughter, and Santa.

Champions in the 2014 sports season were Seattle over Denver in the Super Bowl. The L.A. Kings beat the N.Y. Rangers winning the Stanley Cup. The San Antonio Spurs won the NBA title. The San Francisco Giants beat the Kansas City Royals for the World Series crown. Major winners in golf included Bubba Watson at Augusta. German Martin Kaymer took the US Open at Pinehurst. Young Rory McIlroy took both the British Open and PGA titles. The Indy 500 was won by American Ryan Hunter-Reay. He was the first American winner of the great race in 8 years. The color scheme on his car (yellow with red trim) was my favorite this year. My movie of the year was St Vincent with Bill Murray and Melissa McCarthy.

On January 26th, my son Jason and his wife Casey gave birth to our 3rd granddaughter. I was surprised and very proud when I learned that they gave her the middle name of Gavin, the same as mine and her father Jason's. Kinsley Gavin Kavanaugh. The Gavin name is a mini tradition in our family. Our Great Aunt Margaret's middle name was Gavin. She and her brothers (our paternal grandfather) mother's maiden name was Gavin. Their grandparents were Gavin's who came here from Ireland in 1850 from County Galway. So, Gavin began as a surname. I was given the name Gavin after our Great Aunt Margaret and her mothers' family. We gave our second son Jason the middle name of Gavin. My sister Maureen gave her daughter Maia the middle name of Gavin. And now we have Kinsley Gavin. I think it is cool and very Irish. I hope it continues for future generations.

In early April, Ginger and I took our daughter Christy to St. Thomas, US Virgin Islands. That was her destination of choice when I promised all our kids an all-expense paid trip to basically wherever they wanted to go. John's choice was the Scotland golf trip in 2014. Jason, Casey, and Kaley took a trip to Florida including Disneyworld in 2013 just before my 60th birthday. Christy is a Caribbean type of girl. Our headquarters in St. Thomas was the Marriott Frenchman's Cove. It was everything Christy wanted. Sunshine, pools, spas, drinks, and restaurants. The entire property overlooked the beautiful blue Caribbean. On the grassy rolling grounds of the property were large Iguanas seemingly everywhere. I am not sure I have ever seen them out in the wild but they were literally everywhere. They did not bother us. One day we took a ferryboat over to neighboring St. John, the smallest of the three U.S. Virgin Islands. The entire trip was perfect.

On April 12th, Freddie Gray of Baltimore was injured while in police custody. It was mentioned that undue force was used during his arrest by 6 police officers and Freddie was not secured in the back of the van during his transport. He died on April 19th from spinal cord injuries thought to have occurred during transport. All six officers were suspended pending further investigations. On April 25th, protests of Freddie's handling turned violent, resulting in 34 arrests and injuries to 15 officers. Additional civil disorder intensified after his funeral on April 27th. Looting and burning of local businesses culminated in a state of emergency declaration by the Governor. This event along with the Ferguson, Missouri event were the first cases of major civil unrest and rioting during my 60's but it sure would not be the last. As a nation, we were losing our sense of civil decency and moral values. Our police forces were under scrutiny, and attack. I described things in America as being in a cold Civil War. There seemed to be a growing fissure in race relations and political civility. Looking back, I believe my version of the cold Civil War began on December 24th, 2009. That is the day the partisan vote for The Affordable Care Act passed through the U.S. Senate under President Barrack Obama. You may recall that as the bill where if you like your plan, you can keep your plan. If you like your doctor, you can keep your doctor. Neither was entirely true. The fatal shooting of young Trayvon Martin in 2012 also helped kick off civil unrest in our country.

Later in April our local Plumbing Heating & Cooling Association held their annual banquet dinner honoring distinguished members in our industry. The award is called esprit de corps, meaning group spirit, pride, fellowship, and loyalty. The award began about ten years ago and our father was posthumously honored as one of ten inaugural recipients. This year brother Mike was honored and he asked me to do the introduction speech. The evening went smoothly and Mike had some immediate family in attendance for the event. Several years later at the same event, I was told by some veteran association members that my introduction speech was the best they had ever heard. I do not remember what I said but it was a nice compliment.

Race Day at Indy. For a lifelong Indy resident, it still means something. Not like it used to, but still something. I went to every race from 1971 to 1986 but then other life opportunities or responsibilities got in the way. After Ginger and I bought our Fort Myers condo in 2000, we spent many Memorial Day weekends in Florida and I would watch the race on TV. It was never televised live in Indianapolis. This year I would attend the great event for the first time in 29 years. I took my 16-year-old granddaughter Abby and we sat in the Northwest Vista, aka turn 4. I do not recall how plans for the day came about. Did I ask her if she would like to go, or did she ask me to take her? I have no idea. We went and had a terrific time. In fact, we went to the next year's race, the 100th running, and again the year after that. It was a nice grandpa / granddaughter bonding.

On June 17th, there was a mass shooting at a black church in Charleston, S.C. Nine innocent people were killed at the hands of a young white supremacist during Bible study. The shooter was arrested, convicted, and sentenced to death. The shooters website had emblems associated with white supremacy and the Confederate flag. We sadly have a history of these types of shootings but nothing is ever done to stop it. I am not certain what can be done. Infamous recent shootings include Fort Hood and Sandy Hook Elementary School. Those two alone took out 41 people. In 2016 there was a shooting at an Orlando night club. In 2017 the largest shooting of all took place in Las Vegas during an outdoor concert. In 2018 a massacre at Stoneman Douglas High School in Florida. In 2019 a shooting at a Wal Mart in El Paso. Those four shootings took out 147 innocent people topped by the 58 in Vegas. Calls for gun control come up immediately after each incident and I am not convinced that would stop it, but it cannot hurt. Our political leaders fail each time to summon the courage to do the right thing. If I could, I would get the guns in question, and then some. Unfortunately, these types of acts would be repeated way too often in our country.

The shooting in Charleston however would have cause to attempt to eradicate U.S. and southern history. Confederate monuments depicting our American history were being toppled, many in the dark of night to not cause further disruption of life in daylight. In many states across the country, if there was a statue commemorating a Confederate soldier or battle, there is a good chance it was coming down, some by civil engineers, others by mob force. The main target was Robert E Lee, commander of the Confederate States Army. These statues had stood for over a hundred years but the Charleston shooting became the catalyst for their removal. Personally, I love American History and I love historical museums. History should be understood and appreciated as it happened, not from the prism of the political agenda or current day ideology that is expected or forced upon us in current times. I am all for getting the guns and much harsher sentencing. I am opposed to the removal of historic statues.

June 21st was Fathers' Day and after the annual Kavanaugh family golf outing which we have held for over twenty years, brother Mike and his wife Linda had the entire gang over for a cookout and to celebrate my recently published book, 'Mr. Satisfactory'. Someone had a cake made (most likely Ginger) to look exactly like the cover of the book. Very cool really. A handful of us took turns reading various excerpts from the book that I knew would have particular interest to some present.

The following day one of my favorite American composers died. When you saw a movie that included James Horner music, you were most likely in for a good film. He did a lot of work for director Ron Howard including Apollo 13 and A Beautiful Mind. He also worked on favorites, Field of Dreams, Braveheart, Titanic and more. I will miss his musical genius.

On July 4th of my 61st year, my favorite band, The Rolling Stones, came to town with their 'Zip Code Tour'. My brother Kevin and his wife Yolanda along with my sister Mary and her husband Tony and I went. The outdoor event was held on the lawn of The Indianapolis Motor Speedway. We had a nice piece of grass toward the back end of the front section as the seating (or standing) was arranged. The event was scheduled to begin at 9:00 pm and the first note of the 18-song set came from Jumpin' Jack Flash. It was struck precisely on time following their customary introduction of, "Ladies and Gentleman, The Rolling Stones." During this tour the fan base of each event was allowed to select one song out of a list of four by a pre-concert vote for the Stones to play. The 46201 (Indy) crowd selected 'Let It Bleed' and even Mick seemed to be surprised by that. My vote was used on 'Paint It Black,' which was one of the four options. I believe the highlight of the evening might have been when the local Butler University choir joined the boys onstage and sang background and harmony vocals on 'You Can't Always Get What You Want,' the penultimate song. The 18-song two-hour concert finished up with Satisfaction. We were all extremely Satisfied.

A short time later we took our son Jason, his wife Casey, and their two daughters to our condo for a week of relaxation. Kaley was 7 years old, Kinsley, an infant. We visited the beaches and went to the Naples Zoo. A couple rounds of putt-putt are always necessary along with daily trips to the pool. A new mini amusement park called Zoomers had recently opened and it became a must visit every time Kaley joined us in Ft Myers. I enjoyed seeing her laughter on the rides. While dining out it did not take long to figure out that Kaley loved shrimp. Also, Kilwins ice cream was a must for Kaley and me.

Being 61 was okay. Welcoming a new granddaughter, a trip to St. Thomas, USVI., getting back to the Indy 500, and seeing the Rolling Stones was quite a treat.

62

9-19-2015 to 9-18-2016

On October 9th, our son John married Rebecca Myers at a downtown Indianapolis venue called Canal 337. The wedding had a manageable number of attendees but the wedding party reversed the trend in recent years to see how many guys we can get into a tux and how many ladies we can fit for a gown and parade down the center aisle. Or how many kids we can have embarrassingly and clumsily walk to the altar with rose petals or other items. There was a bride, groom, best man, and matron of honor. That was it. I loved it. The official ceremony was completed with great dispatch and the food and drinks were perfect, including the cascade of dessert dishes. The entire event seemed to be handled smoothly and perfectly.

Every family has their own Christmas traditions. Ours is the kids and grandkids come over Christmas morning for breakfast. They get over about 9:30 and we have everything for breakfast ready to go. It gives them enough time to open gifts from Santa at home first and later have dinner with the other half of their families and we get to do whatever we want. It is a win, win. I remember dreading holidays when you ate dinner one place at 1:00 pm and hurried for another at 5:00 pm. Always rushing around. We have had years when we had everything cleaned up and off to Florida by 1:00 pm Christmas day, without rushing. One year we even had the tree undressed and taken to the dead tree lot before leaving for Florida. It is not a humbug at all. We celebrate Christmas throughout the month of December.

After breakfast we open the gifts. As usual, I ask for nothing, or just an empty box, which is an inside joke. I do have an empty box courtesy of son Jason one year. If I need something, I buy it. The kids always do get me something so this year I am standing in the kitchen area unwrapping my gift about the size of a small shirt box.

I do not notice that everyone is watching me. I guess I opened it face up because as soon as I saw the colors, I knew exactly what it was and I started to tear up. I mean, they really got me. I wondered when they had the photo taken? Who spearheaded this covert operation? It was a framed picture of my kids, Christy, John, and Jason, along with granddaughter Abby and daughter-in-law's Rebecca and Casey each wearing one of my six Original Six NHL jerseys. I have the jerseys hung neatly and covered in my closet and I guess they were afraid I might notice they had been moved or were in the wrong order. Believe me, it is one of those things I might notice. They were all replaced carefully and in order. It was an awesome gift and hangs proudly in my hockey room. Yea, I have a hockey room. The short version of the backstory is it has been well known in our family that I want my pallbearers wearing the Original Six. That is the only reason I own the jerseys. I have never worn them.

The 2015 Super Bowl was won again by Tom Brady (MVP) and the New England Patriots beating the Seattle Seahawks who threw an ill-advised pass from the Patriots 1-yard line with 26 seconds to go in the game as opposed to handing the ball off to their power runner. The pass was skillfully intercepted to seal the victory. The Chicago Blackhawks took out the Tampa Bay Lightning in 6 games to win their third Stanley Cup in 6 seasons. That is the equivalent of a modern-day dynasty. Golden States Warriors held off Lebron James and the Cleveland Cavaliers to win the NBA title and the surprising Kansas City Royals bested the New York Mets in 5 games to take the World Series crown. Major golf titles were won by Jordan Spieth (2) Zach Johnson, & Jason Day.

My favorite movie for 2015 was Bridge of Spies starring Tom Hanks. Does Hanks make bad movies?

On February 16th, 2016, my sons John and Jason along with my good friend Chuck Kelly drove over to Columbus, Ohio to watch our beloved Bruins take on the Columbus Bluejackets. It was a low scoring game but we got our money's worth. Boston took down Columbus 2-1 in overtime. On Sunday April 3rd, I went to Chicago to see the Bruins in a matinee game. Our old friend and John's teammate from his youth hockey days, John-Michael Liles, was nearing the end of an excellent pro career. He was a teammate of son John back when they played together in Indianapolis as nine to twelve-year old youth players. He was drafted by the Colorado Avalanche out of Michigan State and had seven good years there before being traded to Toronto and again a few years later to Carolina. As fate would have it, his last season and a half was with my team, the Boston Bruins. I have never mentioned John-Michael when I am asked who my favorite player is but there is no one I have enjoyed watching play as much as John-Michael. It has been nearly twenty-five years since he played with my son John but I can still recognize him on the ice by his stride alone. When he was with Colorado early on, they were a good team so we caught him on TV often. We saw him less with Toronto and even less when he went to Carolina. When he got to Boston, he was on TV a lot because Boston was on TV a fair amount of time. Back in Chicago, I went down to the glass to get John-Michaels' attention during pre-game warmups. When he finally looked up and saw me, he had this sheepish grin on his face. I am certain he was surprised to see me. Watching John-Michael succeed at the Pro level has been one of my great joys of watching the NHL. The Blackhawks took the exciting game 6-4 but my favorite Bruins (not named Liles) all put up numbers on the score sheet. Patrice Bergeron had 2 goals and 1 assist. The man is a pros pro. Brad Marchand added 1 goal and 1 assist and David Pastrnak scored a goal. Another Bruin favorite of mine, Torey Krug added 2 assists. Torey went to Indy's Cathedral High School while he was playing Junior A hockey for the Indianapolis Ice. It was a fun game.

Keeneland race track in Lexington, Kentucky was open for their Spring Meets in April and I went with some customers from Lexington. I know nothing about horse racing and possibly less about betting on horses. I am there because it beats a day of making sales calls and it is a very nice facility. The beer and food are paid for, the weather is nice, so what is not to like. My customers had some passes to get into areas not allowed through general admission. Keeneland is a bit upscale so some areas require a sport coat. I wore my seersucker sport jacket this day and we went down to the paddock looking at horses. Was I over-dressed? On two occasions I was asked if I was a horse owner. No, but thanks for asking. On the day I lost most of the modest amounts I gambled. I believe wagering is a requirement. It was a great day.

May 4th, on our 42nd wedding anniversary, the man who had no chance, Donald J Trump, became the presumptive Presidential nominee of the Republican Party. This was the day after he won the Indiana primary taking out the last standing opponent, John Kasich of Ohio.

May 29th brought about the 100th running of the Indy 500. Indianapolis always has been and is still the racing capital of the world. Attendance had suffered somewhat in recent years but the 100th brought back a crowd reminiscent of the glory days of the 20th Century. I took my granddaughter Abby to the race and we both looked forward to the event. We had been to the race the previous year but this year being the 100th would be special, including pre-race festivities. The skies were sunny, the stands were packed, and we had a nice view from the first turn. Alexander Rossi, a rookie, won the race in a battle of fuel conservation. He coasted across the finish line winning by four seconds and had to be towed to the winner's circle as he did not have enough fuel to make it around after seeing the checkered flags.

In June of my 62nd year, two all-time superstars of the sporting world died. On June 3rd 2015, Muhammad Ali passed away. Possibly the most recognized athlete in the world and unquestionably the greatest heavyweight boxer of all time. A week later, Mr. Hockey, Gordie Howe passed. Some say the best hockey player ever. He was certainly the best in what I call the black and white era. I have got him in my all-time top three and I did have the good fortune to meet him at a hockey equipment sporting goods show once in Montreal. That would have been in the nineties when I owned retail store Hockey Plus.

Just a bit later in June we took an all-family vacation to Hilton Head Island. The trip included Ginger and myself along with our 3 kids, Christy, John, & Jason. Spouses Casey and Rebecca and granddaughters Abby, Kaley, and Kinsley. The trip had been scheduled for some time and was part of the kids Christmas from the previous December. We rented a five-bedroom house with pool at 3 Osprey Street about a block away from the beach. Meals and time together at the pool or beach seemed to highlight the trip. For John, Jason, and Casey the highlight could have been the evening in the bar watching the Penguins winning the Stanley Cup. Lunch at the Salty Dog Café at South Beach Marina was a popular spot. A trip to the Harbor Town lighthouse was special and we had a great family picture taken there. Our youngest granddaughter Kinsley picked picture time to be napping in the stroller. Another highlight was watching Gregg Russell perform his folksy kid-friendly music under the Liberty Oak and within view of the famous lighthouse. The kids love him because he is fun. The parents love him because he is fun and he keeps the kids occupied. Gregg has been a mainstay under the Liberty Oak since 1976. His song, 'The Cat Came Back' was one our granddaughters really liked. The refrain went, "The cat came back, they thought he was a goner, the cat came back, the very next day." We will never forget that tune. It was an awesome vacation. The house was perfect for the occasion and everyone had a super time. John, Jason, and I played two rounds of golf and I managed to squeeze in a third round at Harbor Town Golf Links at The Seaside Resort on a blistering warm day. I acquitted myself quite nicely if I do say so myself. I came in with an 86.

On July 7th, a protest march in Dallas took place to protest a pair of killings by police officers in separate incidents of two men in Minnesota and Louisiana. Somewhere along the way a man with ill intent arrived at the protest and opened fire intentionally at police officers who were there to monitor the event. By one crazed man, five officers were killed and nine wounded. Sadly, it seemed to be the genesis of open season on police officers. The perpetrator fled inside a building, and other patrolmen had him cornered well into the night and the following morning hours of July 8th. He was eventually taken out by a remote-control bomb attached to a robot.

Late in July, my high school held our 45-year class reunion. On Friday night we observed cash bar rules at Champps Restaurant on Indy's northside. We had a great evening of outdoor relaxation and catching up. About 20 people took part in the festivities on the first night of the reunion. For the main event we partied at our high school, Bishop Chatard. Not what I would call an ideal venue but it worked out fine. Our theme for the event was 45 RPM records, a very popular way to listen to music in our youth. The event went well and there were about forty or so attendees from a graduating class of 160.

Aug 26-28 2016 I was invited to Tree Tops golf resort in Gaylord, Michigan by a customer of mine in northern Indiana. I had first heard of Tree Tops when PGA Tour Pros went up there for a televised promotional event sponsored by Tylenol at the 'Three Tops' course, a nine-hole scenic Par 3 venue. The event took place from 1999 to 2006 and included various superstars including Phil Mickelson, Lee Janzen, Lee Trevino, Fred Couples, and Fuzzy Zoeller. In 2001 Lee Trevino won a million dollars with an Ace on the seventh hole.

The Treetops Resort is all inclusive and includes hotel and restaurant along with its three championship 18-hole layouts, and the challenging Par 3 course. A good time was had by all and the weather cooperated nicely.

A family wedding and vacation, the 100th running of the Indy 500, and a class reunion all helped make my 62nd year special.

63

9-19-2016 to 9-18-2017

The NFL season is in full stride. I used to love football growing up and most of my life. But the game had become less fun or less important to me in recent years. Was it just that I was older and had better things to do? Or had the game changed? I have no doubt the game had changed. I will always believe football in the 70's and 80's was the best. Injuries have become too prevalent today. I felt the game had become too violent. Players rarely tackle. They simply bludgeon you down with brute force. There is no doubt in my mind players try to injure quarterbacks. The use of technology and coaches' challenges has destroyed the game for me. There is something wrong with a game where a coach challenges a play and hopes that his player did not catch the ball that resulted in a fumble. And when the play is overturned confirming the catch did not happen, that players' fans are cheering that he did not catch the ball. Or a touchdown is made and everyone cheers. Then it is reviewed and confirmed, and the fans cheer again. Hey, he only scored once. Some plays are reviewed and dissected like the Zapruder film from 1963. How about the replays where they need to blow up the picture X10 to see if a toe hit the chalk? Or they look at the replay for minutes on end. They have made it nearly impossible for me to spontaneously cheer during the game, knowing that most exciting plays will be reviewed. I prefer believing what I just saw with my own eyes. If the refs err, make them accountable. And why are endless replays shown between snaps? I would much rather watch the play be called and see where the players are lining up. Announcers are not always as smart as you think. While they see with their own eyes what is about to happen on the field and make their educated prediction, we are watching the fourth replay from the previous snap. Then of course you have the players that cannot seem to get off the field and need attention. Football breeds a culture of seeking attention through injury. Fantasy leagues make the game boring for me with constant statistics being scrolled at the bottom of the screen instead of scores. Commercials have gotten out of hand adding countless minutes to each game. The three-hour game that used to be commonplace, except for the Heidi game, is now an anomaly. As much rest as players get in today's game, I am surprised some two-way players have not surfaced. I think it is safe to say that the 2016 NFL season is the year that I was completely liberated from football. I would continue to watch the game occasionally. Its popularity makes it difficult to avoid altogether. It simply would never captivate me again like in the past. Give me golf any day. I realize I am in the minority.

We celebrated my birthday this year on September 25th for some reason. I did play golf that morning and shot a season's best 75. I had lunch with Ginger and the kids and grandkids after golf at Firebirds Restaurant in Carmel, In. where my son Jason now works. We had a great meal and time. Later that day the FedEx golf championship was on TV. I completely understand why people might not like to watch golf on TV but it is my favorite TV sport. I will watch any tournament including European, Seniors, or Ladies. The FedEx championship is the culmination of the PGA season so it is a big deal to me. One of my favorites, Rory McIlroy, won the event. It was a great day but one sad event also happened that day. Arnold Palmer died. I was never an Arnie fan growing up as I favored Jack Nicklaus. Well after Arnie's career was over, including his senior career, I paid more attention to the man and all he had accomplished in golf and life and all he has meant to the game. There were great documentaries of his career on Golf Channel, the channel he founded. I certainly grew to appreciate all he had done. He was a super individual. He would be on my short list as one of the greatest American men of the 20th Century. Not greatest athlete, but men. I feel a bit guilty for not being a fan of his during his career. Ten years Jack's senior, Arnie was probably a bit before my time.

The first Saturday of October was the 45-year reunion of Brebeuf High School. In my high school days, Brebeuf was an all-male Jesuit High School and athletic rival to my alma mater Chatard High School. Many of my best friends went to Brebeuf and I was invited to join their event. Close Brebeuf friends in attendance included Joe Hagelskamp, Steve Smeehuyzen, and Steve Jose. The party was upstairs at the Aristocrat Bar & Restaurant on Indy's northside. I had never been upstairs there and it was quite nice. My three buddies and I posed for a great photo. It was a good event and I was pleased to be a part of it. The four of us were together for many legendary, arguably legal nights back in the 6ixties and seventies.

On October 10th, my wife Ginger and I took a mini, 4-day, 3-night vacation to Maine. Maine is known as the Vacation State and I was about to learn why. We had an idea what we wanted to do when we got there but we did not have a fully planned out itinerary. From our base in Portland, Me., we had day trips planned to Bar Harbor, Boothbay Harbor, and Bath. We also planned on having dinner one night with my old neighbor, friend, and classmate, Clara Rehs. Clara had moved to Maine and spent most of her adult life there. On our day of arrival, we drove to Kennebunkport, home of President George Herbert Walker Bush's estate. It is a beautiful little town with plenty of shops and restaurants. I enjoyed an incredibly good bowl of clam chowder at Allison's Restaurant. The Irish shop next door was nice and there was a sports picture gallery (Stadium Gallery) with as large a collection of framed sports photos I have ever seen. We purchased a framed landscape winter picture of the town of Kennebunkport taken during a previous Christmas season. From there we drove by the Bush estate at Walker Point hard on the Atlantic and took some pictures. The President did not come out to welcome us. We heard he was out of town. The views from the rocky coastline were magnificent. The estate was originally purchased by President Bush's great-grandfather. I would also place President Bush 41 as one of the greatest American men of the 20th century, if not the greatest. That evening we enjoyed dinner at the Portland Lobster Company.

The next morning, we went up to Bar Harbor, about a two-hour drive to the north. To us this was mostly a shopping and vacation area. We had come to Maine at the tail end of touristy season so it was not very crowded at all, which was fine with us. We enjoyed an outdoor lunch in cooling but sunny fall weather and did some souvenir and Christmas shopping. I asked a cashier about Acadia National Park. I had seen signs on our drive in. I am not a hiker or an outdoors guy so I was not aware of the park. She basically said it is right across the street and if we do not go to visit, we are out of our minds. We took her up on her frank advice and she was right. As we exited Bar Harbor we crossed straight over to the park. We took the auto-route driving the approximately 20-mile scenic loop. We stopped a couple times for a better look but Ginger was slowing down physically and enjoyed the expansive vistas from the comfort of the car. Acadia was beautiful and the cashier was correct. I would not have forgiven myself had we not stopped. You could spend a day or two in there with no problem. That evening we had dinner in Portland at Gilbert's Chowder House.

The following morning, we started our day having breakfast at a well-known place called Marcy's Diner in downtown Portland. It came highly recommended to us so we were not surprised to be standing outside waiting for a table at the compact, popular restaurant. After our delicious and filling breakfast we drove up to Boothbay Harbor which was clearly nearing shutdown mode after the busy summer season. We also went into the town of Bath and ate lunch at JR Maxwell's. It was an old, cozy, and beautiful restaurant with amazing food. We continued our hot streak on restaurants. Heading back toward Portland we made a brief drive through the town of Freeport, known for its shops and home of LL Bean. We did not find the need to buy anything in Freeport. Next, we headed to the Old Head Light in Cape Elizabeth. The Old Port Head in Cape Elizabeth was on our 'to see' list. The lighthouse built in 1791 is the oldest in Maine. I do not know what it is about lighthouses but I find them fascinating if not mesmerizing. This one seemed to be as cool as any I have seen. The waves were crashing on the rocks below and there were souvenir maps for sale that showed where hundreds of boats had met their demise and docked unscheduled on the ocean's floor.

That evening we met my friend Clara at the marina for dinner at 'DiMillo's on the Water.' Clara and I went to grade school and high school together and she lived next door for most of our grade school years. We had many a walk together to and from grade school. We spent leisure time together and she was a good friend. Certainly, a better friend than I realized at the time. DiMillo's is a large dinner boat docked at the Portland harbor. I do not know if the boat ever goes out to sea but it was docked on this night and we had a fun, enjoyable evening. The food was outstanding.

On our final day in Maine, we started again at Marcy's for breakfast. This was followed by a trip to a Christmas store and another turn through Kennebunkport. I had heard about a place called Two Lights State Park from another of my old classmates (Vicki Rees nee Lane) who has enjoyed this area. The name comes from having two lighthouses. We found the popular park and its famous Two Lights Lobster Shack for lunch. I am not a lobster guy but Ginger is. We ate lunch at the Lobster Shack and Ginger had an obscenely large lobster roll. I went down above the water line on the large, smooth, flat-topped jagged edged greyish slate rocks. They looked like giant pieces of a jigsaw puzzle. You might say, "the sea was angry that day my friends." The waves crashed continuously against the large rocks. One after another. You could watch it for hours on end. I thought so much of the Old Portland Head that we went back for a second look. That evening we enjoyed a pizza and watched the Boston Bruins on TV. Very romantic, right? There are beautiful things all over this world and Maine has many of them. There was nothing we saw in Maine that was not far beyond our expectations. I recommend it to anyone who enjoys travel. It quickly became one of my very favorite States and I hope to have an opportunity at a return visit.

Earlier this month my best friend growing up, Joe Hagelskamp, invited me to join him for the October 30th Notre Dame football game vs The Miami Hurricanes in South Bend, Indiana. He had tickets through his daughter who was a Notre Dame alum. Sometime after our twenties, Joe and I seldom saw each other. He recently ran across a copy of my last book and he called me out of the blue one evening to tell me how many stories were in that book about us that he has told to many people over the years. He was glad to read that he had not been hallucinating. My stories had confirmed his memory of youth. He was also touched by some kind words I had written about his mother. A couple weeks ago he invited me to this game and there was no way I would turn that down. I was more interested in spending time with Joe, than the game itself. I drove us up and we arrived early. Joe wanted to take in the sights of the campus the same as I. He also was keen on seeing the band play before entering the stadium. I do not recall when Joe said he had last been to a game. I had not been to a game at Notre Dame since my dad took me back in the 6ixties to see Navy. I have visited the campus multiple times in recent years as my work brings me to the South Bend area a few times a year. I made it a point on many an occasion to visit the campus on my sales trips. Today's game pitted the Catholics against the Convicts but the schools were not regarded nearly as highly nationally as when they battled it out in the late eighties. This game did play out with similar excitement as the big games of the past. Notre Dame raced out to a 20-0 lead only to be tied up and then lose the lead altogether. Miami scored 27 straight points to take a 27-20 lead with just under seven minutes to go. Notre Dame tied up the game a minute later and won on a late field goal with: 30 remaining. Final score was 30-27 Notre Dame. Joe and I had a terrific day.

November 8th was an election day for the ages. Hillary Clinton was poised to become the first female President of the United States. The polls showed Hillary Clinton with a rather comfortable lead over the brash businessman Donald Trump going into the big day but the Trump camp was not buying it. The early returns showed no surprises with Trump winning both Indiana and Kentucky. Exit polls in battleground states showed something might be brewing in favor of 'The Donald.' Trump's phrases including, 'Make America Great Again,' 'Build the Wall,' 'Drain the Swamp,' and my favorite,

'What have you got to lose?', were paying large dividends against Hillary's 'Basket of Deplorables.' When states like Florida and North Carolina went for Trump, there was plenty of raw nerves at Clinton headquarters. When Ohio went Trump's way, the writing was on the wall. Other states thought to be easy wins for Clinton fell Trump's way too. Those included Wisconsin, Michigan, and Pennsylvania. It was over. The Clinton camp was in utter shock and disbelief. Trump captured 304 electoral votes to Hillary's 227 even though Clinton took the popular vote by 3 million, or plus two percentage points. The following morning the stock market began a steady climb and the impeachment process and anti-Trump protests by the hateful liberal crowd were under way. The apocalypse was upon them.

My son John and his wife Rebecca were expecting their first child and we learned on December 16th that it would be a boy. I was pumped on that news. The following week was Ginger and my turn to host the annual Kavanaugh Christmas Party. It is a big ordeal and if not planned properly, you could have some issues. It is fair to say that Ginger and I thrive on this type of project. Knowing our empty-nester home was too small to host such an event, we began plans in 2015 in search of a venue. After an exhaustive search with multiple ideas, we selected the Ambassador House in Fishers, In. We visited the house in December of 2015 and saw how it was nicely decorated for the holiday. It was the proper size and location and the price was doable. In 2015 we put down a deposit to reserve the house for December 23rd, 2016. We found a caterer from good recommendations. When you are hosting (67 was the official count) the entire family, I am always nervous that something will go wrong. The last time we hosted there was an ice storm for the ages and I was not sure anyone would make it. However, they all did. The Ambassador House had a basement so we bought coloring books and crayons and other nick knacks to keep the youngsters busy down below. We planned on having the children sing popular Christmas songs prior to serving dinner and we pulled it off and they sounded great under my direction with no rehearsing. They finished the three-song set with 'Santa Claus Is Coming to Town.'

My 17-year-old granddaughter Abby and I sang 'Amen' from the movie 'Lilies of the Field' acapella style just prior to dinner being served. The house had a large lit Christmas tree nearly ten feet tall in the living room and it was so inviting, every family took turns at taking a family photo. I got my picture with me, my sons, and nephews in our hockey jerseys. I had wanted that picture for a long time but we are seldom all together. There was a large wingback chair for Santa to do his thing. At the end of the day, the event went off as good as you could ever hope. Even the weather cooperated. I like to think it was the finest Kavanaugh Christmas party ever produced.

2016 was the 50th year for the Super Bowl. The Indy Colts great quarterback, Peyton Manning, had moved on to Denver and led Denver to a Super Bowl win over Carolina in what would be Peyton's last game of his outstanding career. Pittsburgh's Penguins won the Stanley Cup. The Cleveland Cavaliers led by Lebron James came back from a 3-1 games deficit to win the first title for the city of Cleveland since the 6ixties, 1964. And the Chicago Cubs, yes, the Chicago Cubs won the World Series. This was the first Cubs championship since 1908. In golf, Henrik Stenson of Sweden took home the Claret Jug, holding off Phil Mickelson in a thriller for the ages at Troon, Scotland. My selection for best picture in 2016 was Allied starring Brad Pitt and Marion Cotillard with Hacksaw Ridge following closely behind. Both are WWII pictures.

Nine days in to the turn of the calendar year, my employer, Mueller Industries, had their annual National Sales Meeting. This year was very different from any of my previous 17 national meetings. This year, wives or significant others were invited and it was held at the 5-star Four Seasons Hotel in Orlando, Florida. Mueller was celebrating their 100-year anniversary and they spared no expense. Ladies were guests of the in-house Spa. The golfers were treated to a round of golf at neighboring Tranquilo Golf Club. Lunches and dinners appeared to be more upscale than normal and meetings were kept to a minimum for the three-day affair. Following the main evening awards dinner, a first-class band was brought in while couples danced or just sat back and relaxed.

Two weeks after our meeting, I was back in West Palm for a customer fishing trip. My employer, Mueller, has a 63' fishing boat that is docked in West Palm for a good portion of the year and we entertain customers on a regular basis. Tiger Woods' yacht is anchored just a short distance away. It is always a 2 ½ day, 2-night trip. Again, no expense is spared when it comes to dinners and drinks. The day of arrival is normally spent so that everyone can unpack and get their bearings. We then head out for drinks followed by dinner at the most obscenely priced restaurant the Marina has to offer. The following morning, we head out early and boat captain Doug, a real pro, takes the boat out on the Atlantic where he suspects the best fishing will be. Doug is a fulltime Mueller employee and his primary job is navigating the boat and taking care of the vessel. Marlin is the prize fish we go after but plenty of Tuna and Kingfish are also reeled in. I must say I am not a fisherman. I would much rather be left on shore at a bar or a golf course and wait for the crew to return but that is not how the itinerary works. I was not even very good at playing host for our customers. I got sea sick after a few hours and it is usually about an eight-hour day on the water. I was never sick to my stomach, just a constant splitting headache. I spent plenty of time down below on a bed with my eyes closed. I just wanted the movement to stop. The boat always has 4 lines in the water and the first mate sets everything up. So that every customer can have a chance at a catch, we typically go in a pre-determined order as to who gets the first bite and so on. Once a fish is hooked, it is time to go to work. If a sailfish jumps out of the water, it is easily identifiable. The other fish are nearly the same to me but the captain and first mate identify them early on. When it was my turn to reel in a fish, I drew the unlucky white Marlin. I mean, it is a chore bringing those things in. It took at least 15 minutes. It seemed like an hour. I wanted to give up. My arms were killing me. When the leader is caught and the sailfish is tagged, it is released by law. Everyone is high fiving you and congratulating you. For what? I just had my ass kicked by a

65-pound fish and I am worn out. The Tuna and Kingfish are placed on ice and later fileted and served to us for dinner that evening at one of the marina restaurants. I do love eating fish and they will cook them up in a variety of ways so that there is something for everyone. You can taste the difference between store bought fish, fresh fish at a nice restaurant back home in Indiana, and fresh fish right out of the water earlier on the same day. It was an excellent meal. The second morning we go back out for a few hours before we all head back to the airport for home. The fish caught the second morning are fileted on the dock and packed on ice for the customers to take home. They give you enough to throw a nice party. After taking our customers to the airport for their return trip, I had a few hours to kill before my flight so I drove to nearby Seminole Golf Club. Seminole is ultra-exclusive and I called in advance to insure I would be welcome to peruse the golf shop. I was so I went in and just looked around the Pro Shop and bought a couple souvenirs. They treated me as if I was a member. They even called me by my surname after learning it. When I got home, I wrote a letter to the club thanking them for my great experience and telling them how courteous and professional their staff was to me. A few weeks later I received a hand-written reply on a Seminole stock card signed by Seminole Pro Bob Ford. Mr. Ford may be the best-known club Pro in the land. He is the Pro at two exclusive clubs. Seminole in the Winter and US Open venue Oakmont in Pennsylvania in the summer. Not a bad gig. I treasured his reply and placed it in a frame.

February 3rd and 4th, Ginger and I spent a weekend in South Haven, Michigan at their annual Winterfest. We were accompanied by brothers Mike and Brian along with their wives Linda and Robin. I have been to South Haven for a good time on many occasions but never in the winter. One of the highlights of the event was a chili cookoff. There must have been nearly 50 different people with their version of the world's best chili. We could not taste all of them but we got around to enough to place our vote for our top three. Saturday evening there was a guitar player / comedian / trivia guy, playing music in a packed bar of about 150 people. Many of his songs were from the 6ixties. We made reservations for the show and somehow, we got a table for six, right in front of the entertainer as if we were Henry Hill and Karen in Goodfella's. He might play a few notes and see who could guess the song. He might ask an obscure question about a song or artist and see who could get it right. The man was very talented for the act he was presenting. Brother Mike was a savant at answering questions. In 1966 there was a song titled, 'They're Coming to Take Me Away, Ha-Haaa!" The performer gets into the song a bit and his question became, what is on the flip side or B side of that 45 RPM record? Mike had an answer but was incorrect. No one else in the crowd seemed to have a clue. After a minute of thought Mike had an epiphany and goes full on Horshack with his hand wildly waving in the air. Mike says, "I think the flip side is the same song, only played backwards." I am telling you the artist on stage was floored. Mike was correct. I am thinking he has asked this same question many times and never gotten a correct answer. Mike knows his music and we had a great weekend, staying at a nearby Bed and Breakfast. We left for home Sunday morning and were back in plenty of time to watch Tom Brady come back from a 25-point deficit as the New England Patriots beat the Atlanta Falcons in Super Bowl LI.

On Thursday February 9th my son Jason, his wife Casey, and I were off to Boston to see our Bruins for 3 games in four days. When the schedule came out last September, this was the perfect week to go. I found inexpensive round-trip airfare and bought the plane tickets before buying any game tickets. This was Jason and Casey's 2016 Christmas gift. Our son John's old youth hockey teammate, John-Michael Liles was still playing for the Bruins. His parents (and our old friends) were also heading east for the three-game weekend. Winter weather had other plans. A major snowstorm hit Boston on February 8th and 9th. We were watching the weather reports and kept our fingers crossed. In the history of Boston's Logan Airport, they have had very few closings due to weather. Our Thursday February 9th direct flight seemed to be on again and off again. The plan was to arrive by 5:00 pm, unpack at our nearby hotel and head to game one. Finally, our flight was cancelled and now I was frantically re-booking for a Friday flight and advising the hotel of new plans. The game was played that evening but we were forced to watch on TV from home holding onto our now worthless tickets. The Bruins had a new coach behind the bench tonight too, Bruce Cassidy. The previous coach, Claude Julien, 2011 Cup winning coach for the Bruins had finally worn out his welcome as all coaches eventually do. He was the winningest coach in Boston Bruin history but was fired the previous day. Coach Cassidy won his inaugural game 6-3 against the San Jose Sharks and our friend John-Michael Liles played his usual solid, sure passing game.

We did make it out to Boston the following day and the snow was piled high on every street corner. After unpacking at the hotel where Jason was on a first name basis with the doorman from a previous visit, we headed to a nearby bar and found a nice place for dinner. We caught up with Mr. and Mrs. Liles and had a drink with them. The next morning, Saturday, we enjoyed a nice breakfast at the Marriott Long Wharf Hotel and headed out to some nearby bars to ready ourselves for the 1:00 pm matinee faceoff against the Vancouver Canucks. Come game time we learned that Liles would disappointingly be a healthy scratch today. I had seen John-Michael play on other occasions during his professional career. I saw him in one of his very first pro games in Columbus, Ohio when he was playing for Colorado. I also saw him in the Bruins final road game of last season played in Chicago on April 3rd. Today against Vancouver was a very exciting game as the Bruins beat the Canucks 4-3 with a late goal from one of our favorites, David Pastrnak. Possibly the highlight of the game was when Bruins young defenseman Colin Miller wired a shot from the point into the net. When the expansion draft came up a few months later to fill out the roster for the new Vegas Golden Knights franchise, I had little doubt they would select Colin Miller of the Bruins. And they did. After the game we did what we do best; drink, laugh, and tell stories. Later, we ended up at the same restaurant we dined at the night before. Jason liked the price of their lobstah. After dinner we caught up with the Liles, this time with John-Michael and his parents. As we were walking through Boston's North End, John-Michael would point out where different players lived. He too lived in the area which is within walking distance of the TD Boston Garden and the hotel where we were staying. As we passed a small bar, John-Michael mentioned some of the guys like to hang out there. Sure enough, three of the Bruins star players were inside having a pop and playing a competitive game of 'Gold Tee' golf. John-Michael introduced us to David Krejci, Torey Krug, and today's game winning goal scorer, David Pastrnak. We were all thrilled. Krejci just happens to be Casey's boyfriend in an alternative life. Jason was wearing a Bruin pullover and we did take a photo with him and the Bruin players. It was a great added surprise to our trip.

A bit later that evening while I was in my room, Mr. Liles called to inform me that another blast of snow was on the way and that Logan Airport was poised to be closed again. It became so bad that we had to return home the following morning and miss Sunday's 4-0 win against rival Montreal. Otherwise, we might have been stuck for an additional day and neither Jason nor Casey had the flexibility to miss any work. Sadly, I informed Jason we would be heading home Sunday morning on a 7:00 am flight. What should have been an exhilarating four-day, three-night trip with three Boston Bruin games, turned into a 1 ½ day, 2-night trip with one game. Tickets for Sunday's game also ended up in the waste bin as they were electronic and non-transferrable. It is a good thing we met the Bruin stars on Saturday night or we might have felt different about the trip. The bar meeting made it all worthwhile. And it is always good seeing our old friends, the Liles.

Late February in Indiana this year had far better weather than we normally expect. It was so good that I got in two rounds of golf. Very unusual. One evening while I was wasting time on my I-phone while watching TV I noticed that the show, 'Jersey Boys' was coming to town. Jersey Boys is a stage show and musical about Frankie Valli and The Four Seasons and included many of his hit songs from his great catalog. I wanted to see Jersey Boys while on a trip to Vegas that I won from my employer a couple years ago but the stage was 'Dark.' I looked for a single ticket for the Indy show as I did not know anyone else who wanted to go and I have no issue going by myself. I found row 3, dead center, for $50.00. It looked like a misprint and I jumped on it immediately. The seat was every bit as good as it sounds and the show was fantastic.

Our granddaughter Abby graduated from Plainfield High School on the cities' west side on May 27th. The following day I took her to the Indy 500 but not before I opened a letter from the IRS that had sat on my desk for two days. After I picked my heart up from the floor, I read the notification again. They claimed I had unreported income and owed them $10,320.00 in back taxes from 2015. Japanese star Takuma Sato won the racing thriller but 10-grand seldom left my mind. Eventually I got down to doing a deep dive into my 2015 taxes. I did some wizardry and sent them back a narrative of non-guilt. I am going to shorten this story. On August 21st, they wrote me back saying I owed $79 bucks. It is the fastest check I ever wrote in my life. I was now in the clear.

Meanwhile, on June 8th, Rebecca and John gave birth to James Henry Kavanaugh. I am certain that Rebecca did most of the heavy lifting. James is our first and only grandson. I put my Bruins jersey on and Ginger and I ran up to the hospital for our first photo with Master James.

I graduated from St Andrew grade school in early June of 1967. We had gotten a small group together to plan a fifty-year reunion. I had a collage picture of my 103 fellow graduates and with the help of classmates Bob 'Bear' Krueger and Judy Giles, we were able to place a name on every face. Finding them would be the challenge. Somehow as plans were being discussed, a few people from neighboring Catholic city grade schools got involved. These 'helpers' were also fellow high school graduates of ours. It was suggested we do a group reunion including as many as seven other northside grade schools. I was against the idea the second I heard it. But like many things in life, I was in the minority so I let it go. Finally, it was decided we would hold the reunion at the grade school that sits across the street from our high school. The date was set, August 19, 2017.

Each grade school would be responsible for their own committee and attract their own fellow students. My school found a fair number of emails or addresses but our positive response rate left a bit to be desired. There was a solar eclipse moving cross country on August 21st and one classmate said he could not attend because he was driving to Tennessee to see the eclipse from a prime viewing spot. Our 7th grade science teacher, Mr. Owens, must have had a profound impact on that young man. There were plenty of old mates I would have loved to re-connect with but I was particularly interested in two. My old girlfriend Julie Hurrle and a girl I had a crush on from a young age, Irene Poinsette. I got Irene's address through the help of my brother Mike who attends church at the same church as does Irene. I must have sent Irene four invitations with different teasers to get her to come. We received a confirmation from Julie so I was expecting her. Irene became a game day decision. I expect I volunteered so I oversaw music for the event. The music turned out awesome. I caught up with Julie while she was facing away from me in a food and beverage line. I did not recognize her from behind and she ended up seeing me first. We exchanged pleasantries and memories throughout the evening. Irene did make an appearance and she truly had not changed much at all. I do not mind saying they both looked terrific. I had a nice time catching up with Irene and I think she did too. I had my picture taken with both Julie and Irene. St Andrew ended up with a disappointing 18 attendees out of a possible 103, excluding those that had passed. St Joan of Arc had the most attendees, estimated at 30. There was no other school with more than 10. I do not think some of them ever got a committee together at all, or ever got a committee that put out much effort. Immaculate Heart, a northside school where I had a lot of friends, had three at the event. St Matthew had one. But I know Sherri of St Matthew had a good time. She spent her first seven years with me at St Andrew and we went to high school together also. Even though we only had 18 attendees, it was a good time and I still wish we had not done it as a group. The following year the St Andrew class of '68 had a reunion and they had over 50 people show up. That was over half of their class. I showed up briefly for two reasons; I wanted to see Mary Hagelskamp, my best friend Joe's good-looking sister. I also wanted to see Ruth Fissee who was the daughter of the old St Andrew sports photographer. I mentioned earlier having 3 – 8 x 10 baseball glossies from back in the day taken by Ruth's father. One of those photos is on the cover of this book, another on the inside. I wanted her to know how much our family cherished them. Ruth appreciated my sentiments. She was photographing the event for her class. And yes, Mary was there and looked good.

To finish off my 63rd year, which was a great year, a hurricane came up the southwest coast of Florida where we have our condo. Hurricane Irma seemed to do most of its damage south of us in Bonita Springs but when we went down, there was a lot of tree damage in our immediate area. Since we bought our condo in Ft. Myers there have been 5 hurricanes come through that have caused some issues. Besides Irma there was Charley, Katrina, Wilma, and Rita. Charley, Wilma, and Irma were the closest to being direct hits. None caused us any personal damage but the worst one (Ian) was still a few years away.

Maine, Boston, reunions, and a grandson. What a great year.

64

9-19-2017 to 9-18-2018

"Will you still need me, will you still feed me, when I'm 6ixty-four?" Those words were penned in song by The Beatles in nineteen 6ixty-seven, fifty years ago. I enjoyed singing along to the playful tune. Well, I'm here now. Still needed by some, fed by one. The age of 64 became a year of worldwide travel for me but I had no way of knowing that at the time of my 64th birthday. A golf trip to Ireland with three of my brothers was on the drawing board but two other trips, Canada and Mexico, just fell into place. Trips that rivaled these in my youth included 1963 when we took a family trip to Washington D.C. and New York City and in 1964 spending Christmas in Miami with our paternal grandparents and our Miami cousins. Then there was the 1972 eleven person Christmas/New Year's extravaganza vacation to Honolulu including Mom, Dad, my seven siblings, and our Great Aunt Margaret.

On October 1st, tragedy struck the country. Mass murders and shootings have become way too commonplace in our country. Calls for gun control is never ending for many in the political arena, but nothing is ever done. Personally, I do not know what can be done to completely eradicate the issue, especially if the shooter is willing to go down. But it is out of control. On this day a record 6ixty people were killed and 867 injured when a man opened fire from the 32nd floor of the Mandalay Bay Hotel on a crowd of thousands of unsuspecting people below enjoying a Route 91 Harvest Music Festival in Las Vegas. I have been to the Mandalay Bay. From the vantage point in his hotel room, it must have been like a turkey shoot. I cannot imagine the mayhem down below. It was said he fired off over 1,000 rounds before killing himself.

Early on in my 64th year my siblings and I were issued a mortality check by my brother Tim. On Oct 27th 2017, Tim underwent by-pass surgery. He was playing golf a few days earlier and was not feeling well after his round. The normally gregarious Tim eschewed his habitual pattern of heading into the club to entertain and educate any who might be present with his humor and knowledge. When entertaining a crowd, Tim casually inhales air and exhales in sentences, sometimes paragraphs. His wife Noreen insisted he go to the hospital. He went and the by-pass was scheduled for a few days out. I am happy to report that the surgery went well and it was later reported that he rather enjoyed being shaved by the prep nurse. Of course, most of his seven siblings soon thereafter went in for heart scans and treadmill testing. Tim was back on the golf course the following spring shooting his customary scratch scores.

It was my sister Maureen and her husband Brad's turn to host the Kavanaugh family Christmas party. Maureen is the only one of the eight siblings not living in the Indianapolis area. She has a nice country spread in Bloomington, Indiana, about 50 miles south of the rest of the gang. She did us all a big favor by hosting the party in Indianapolis. It would be the second year in a row that the party was not held at one of our homes. The only other times I recall having a Christmas party at a location other than one of our homes was once at an apartment complex clubhouse and when brother Brian and his wife Robin hosted at Woodland Country Club in Carmel, In. in 2012. Brad and Maureen rented out the Knights of Columbus party room on Indy's northside. It was an excellent location with plenty of room.

In 2017 sports, The Patriots won the Super Bowl with a 25-point 2nd half comeback and the first ever Super Bowl that went into overtime. The Patriots won on the first overtime possession which did not sit well with purists. The Penguins repeated as hockey champions besting the Nashville Predators. The Golden State Warriors turned the tables on Cleveland for the NBA title and the Houston Astros had to jump to the junior circuit to win their first ever World Series title over the L.A. Dodgers. A couple years later Houston was fined and lost draft picks for using technology to steal signs during that World Series. Sergio Garcia finally got in the winning major golf column securing victory at the Masters. Favorite movie in 2017? Darkest Hour with Gary Oldman and Lily James. Darkest Hour was another WWII film. I guess I like that genre.

On Jan 20th 2018, Ginger and I took our first trip to Mexico. Cabo to be exact. We were on an all expenses four-day, three-night paid trip with Plumbers Supply Co. and their customers. This is an annual trip that Plumbers Supply puts together for customers who earn a spot on the trip through purchases and includes select Plumbers Supply employees. The annual trip typically goes to a different warm weather off shore site. This year the site was Cabo. My wife Ginger and I were invited on the trip as a contributing vendor to Plumbers Supply. We stayed at the Hotel Riu Palace Cabo San Lucas at the southern tip of Mexico's Baja California peninsula. The trip to Cabo went through Houston airport and it was smooth, but like most if not all international flights, going through customs in Mexico is tedious at best. We bussed as a group from the airport to the hotel. The check-in at The Riu, controlled by the capable hands of the Plumbers Supply staff, was flawless. The coordination it took for them to handle the check-in was a lot of work I had no doubt. We were greeted by the Plumbers Supply staff who had arrived a day earlier with drink in hand, ready for us to enjoy. The Hotel accommodations at Riu were first class. Food and drink were available 24/7, and like I said, it was truly all expenses paid. The hotel sat directly on the beach. The Riu was complete with a minimum of four pools plus hot tubs and swim up bars. Restaurants seemed endless. It was an excellent property.

The trip home was arduous. Going through Houston Airport was an ordeal. We must have walked a mile from our arriving international gate to our departing gate back to Indianapolis. Ginger was wearing down. We finally made it to our gate and the rest of the trip home was fine. In my final analysis, I do not see what people see in going to Mexico. The main difference between going to Mexico or going to South Florida or Southern California or any other warm sandy American area is, it is harder. The food is not as good. Most of the limited TV stations are not in English. And in America there is no need for the passports and customs. All in all, I am glad I went. The price was more than right. The company was outstanding. But I would never go to Mexico on my own dollar. There is many more, better, and convenient places at home for my money. To each their own.

Valentine's Day brought additional grief to America. Another school shooting, the worst yet at a US High School. At Stoneman Douglas High School in Florida, a 19-year-old ex-student slaughtered 17 students and injured another 17 with a semi-automatic rifle. The killing spree was more deadly than the one I consider the genesis of school shootings, Columbine in 1999. We simply must get some of these weapons. I have never and will never buy into the mental illness excuse. I believe in mean and I believe in crazy and I can argue the difference between those behavioral patterns and mental illness. Yes, I'm certain these animals know exactly what they are doing. Calling it mental illness is like giving them an alibi. I won't do it.

Just a month after Mexico I was off on another international trip that I planned after this seasons NHL schedule came out. It was a solo trip to watch my beloved Boston Bruins and the itinerary was too good to pass up. In February of 2017 the Bruins played back-to-back games in Calgary and Edmonton and I thought about going but I never made the decision. When the schedule came out for the 2017-18 season, I immediately looked to see if they were scheduled for another back-to-back in Alberta. And they were. They would play in Calgary on February 19th and Edmonton on the 20th. Of course, I thought about it for a while and finally decided if not now, when? I left for Calgary on February 18th 2018 through Denver and arrived in frosty Alberta in the early evening. The weather for my two-day visit was dry but very cold. We are talking zero degrees, or as they say up there, minus 17 Celsius. After checking into my hotel, I went to the lobby bar and chatted up a man and his adult son wearing a Bruins jersey. They were from Montana and made the drive up for the same two games I was going to see. The next morning at breakfast I ran into more Bruin fans. This time a couple from the Boston area. They had also attended the Bruins game in Vancouver two days previous and would continue their trip to see the two Alberta games. The game on this Monday was a matinee affair. It was President's Day in the States but just another cold day in Alberta. I spent the hours before the game walking in to town and browsing in shops. Then I went to the Calgary Tower built for the 1988 Olympic Games and went up to the observation deck. There you got a magnificent view of the snow-covered Canadian Rockies. I ran into more Bruin fans at the Tower. As I walked back to the hotel I went through Olympic Plaza and its outdoor skating rink. There were only a few people skating but one young couple was outfitted in what I believe to be some of the most fashionable jerseys ever worn by NHL teams. The female was wearing the green jersey of the Hartford Whalers and her young man was wearing the blue jersey of the Quebec Nordiques. Very classy. Of course, both of those franchises are extinct but their iconic jerseys will live forever in the hearts of hockey fans. After a brief chat, I took a photo of them because of the jerseys alone.

On to the game which was a 4:00 pm start. My hotel was within walking distance to the arena (maybe six blocks) and I did not know exactly what to expect along the way but I figured it was a good bet to pass a bar or two. I did find a bar about two blocks from the arena and much to my delight at least half of the patrons were wearing Bruin gear. Obviously, I was decked out in black and gold from head to toe. I saw three young Bruin fans having some beer and asked if I could join them. I was more than welcome to join the trio from Winnipeg. They were on vacation and had been spending time in the nearby Banff area. Today's game was part of their planned trip. They were young, only twenty years old but we had an immediate bond with this thing we love called the Boston Bruins. I would regale them with my lifetime of Bruin experiences and they were impressed. Much to my surprise, they unnecessarily picked up my bar tab. I have a picture of myself with the three young men and when I look at it, it always puts a smile on my face.

After drinks it was off to Scotiabank Saddledome, home of the Calgary Flames. The arena was built in 1983 and would be the home to ice hockey and figure skating for the 1988 Olympics. The arena is now old by NHL standards but I found it quite nice. The game itself was exciting and the Bruins won in overtime with a goal by Brad Marchand.

The next day I drove up to Edmonton for the Tuesday evening game. It is a straight shot up AB-2 North. I arrived very early in time to take in some sightseeing and barhopping. The new Edmonton arena, Rogers Place, is one of the newest arenas in North America. It opened in September of 2016 and this is only the second season for the Oilers here. The arena is attached to a nice Casino. You do not even have to go outside to get from one to the other. I thought this would be right up my son Jason's alley. Inside the Casino there was a group of people playing roulette, all wearing Bruin jerseys. I watched their chips disappear beneath the table for a while before settling down in a bar across the street to mix it up with the locals.

Again, the game was great. At least it turned out great. The Bruins trailed 2-0 entering the third period but David Krejci completed the 3-2 comeback win with a goal right in front of me with about a minute to go in the game. Connor McDavid, the young Oiler superstar was very impressive. It was easy to know when he was on the ice. He was that fast and seemed that dominant. He has won two league scoring titles and one MVP award in only his first three seasons in the league. By the end of my 6ixties (he was 26) he will have five Art Ross (scoring title) trophies and three Hart (MVP) trophies. He is quite a talent and I hope he earns the honor of hoisting the Stanley Cup someday. After the game I drove back to the hotel in Calgary and it was up early the next morning to head back home. The short, three-night trip was worth every dollar and every minute.

In late April, Ginger and I planned a short trip to our Florida condo around the wedding of our nephew and Tampa resident Brandon Rich to his fiancé Sarah Whorton which took place in Tampa. The wedding was a package deal that included Sarah's two girls, Brylie and Reagan. They were married on April 28th 2018.

In the hockey world this day was game one of round two of the playoffs and my Boston Bruins were in Tampa to face-off against the Lightning, Brandon's newly adopted team. The game was a matinee just like the wedding. Ginger and I watched most of the game in a nearby bar prior to heading off to the outdoor wedding. We caught the tail end of the game on the radio before the ceremony commenced. The Bruins handily beat the Lightning in game one but the favored Tampa team was too much for the series taking four in a row after the opener.

On June 22nd 2018, my brothers Mike, Tim, Kevin, & I departed for our long-awaited golf trip to Ireland. Brother Brian had right of first refusal for the trip in lieu of Tim but after much consternation, he decided to sit it out and Tim jumped at the opportunity. Golf being a four-person game, we were looking for the trip to include only four. Tim had been to Ireland twice before. Once back in the seventies with his All-Midwest Rugby team for a series of exhibition Rugby matches. There is an iconic picture of a friend of mine and Tim's who was already in Ireland and greeted them at the airport as only this fellow could do. His name was Steve Considine, the same kid I met in 5th grade at school. Tim was also in Ireland and Northern Ireland recently with his wife Noreen, her brother, and his wife for a golf trip and a bit of sightseeing. Kevin had been to Ireland just the previous year with his wife Yolanda and friends for a sightseeing vacation but there was no golf included. Mike had never been overseas before and was froth with excitement for the long-awaited trip. I had been on a golf trip with my son John in 2014 to Scotland but had never seen the Emerald Isle. All the ground plans, tee times, hotels, etc. were set up by myself with the help of agent SGH Golf. Tim arranged air travel. Kevin, volunteered to do all the wrong side of the narrow roads driving. No one complained about that. Mike enlisted as chief navigator and lead photographer for the trip and did a splendid job. Tim and I sat in the back seat of the van and enjoyed the banter and views.

I admit to being a little nervous about the tee times and accommodations. Everything I scheduled went through SGH Golf who specializes in overseas golf vacations. I used them in 2014 when I went to Scotland with my son John and everything went smoothly on that trip. Still, some concern. You sure do not want to walk into a hotel or clubhouse, announce your presence, and they say we have no such name. You have people counting on you. But everything went as smooth as it possibly could. I might walk into a clubhouse and they look at me and say, "you must be Mr. Kavanaugh, welcome to our club." I had nothing to worry about.

Kevin left solo for Ireland from his home airport in Boston. It was reported to be the worst flight of his life thanks to his two seatmates that might have filled all three seats on their own. It sounds like they tried their best. Mike, Tim, and I left Indy at 2:15 pm for our overnight flight out of O'Hare in Chicago. We drove to Chicago and arrived at our terminal at 7:22 pm, had a small meal and a beer before boarding at the gate for our 7 ½ hour flight. We arrived in Dublin on time at 10:45 am Saturday morning and immediately met up with Kevin who had arrived two hours prior. Kevin had everything set as far as picking up our rental van. International travel always takes time and we eventually left the Dublin airport at 1:00 pm.

Our first stop was the K Club Golf Club in nearby Straffan, County Kildare. It was not our intention to play golf today after overnight travel but we wanted to see the facility. Kevin has a love affair with the Club named after the letter that our last name begins with. The Ryder Cup matches were played here in 2006 and I too looked forward to seeing the property and picking up a souvenir or two.

After dropping a few Euro at the K Club, we headed toward Kinsale, County Cork, where we would stay our first night in Ireland. A tired group from the overnight travel and now operating on adrenalin, we had two stops to make enroute to Kinsale. The first stop was the town of Naas, also of County Kildare. There we stopped at Kavanagh's Tavern for a couple of relaxing pints of Ireland's finest. Nearly every drink on this trip was toasted to a family member of generations past, the first to our Great Aunt Margaret Kavanaugh, a lady dear to all of us. Cheers! Our waitress Clare, was extremely pleasant and she took photos of us in front of the large Kavanagh sign in the open-air garden area. Was it by chance that we found a Kavanagh's Tavern on our drive from the airport to Kinsale? Absolutely not. Nearly every minute of the trip was pre-planned and mapped out for maximum benefit and pleasure. Mike had located this bar in his extensive pre-trip planning efforts of many non-golf activities. Four years later, Mike and his wife Linda visited this bar whilst vacationing in Ireland. They were pleasantly surprised if not shocked to see the picture taken this day hanging on the wall of the bar. The photo was titled, 'Kavanaugh brothers at Kavanagh's.'

After our stop at Kavanagh's, we headed further south but stopped at Matt the Millers in Kilkenny for a late lunch and of course, another toast with beer. Cheers! It was here that we rolled the dice for the week's rooming arrangements which to this point had never been discussed, but I had a plan that included dice, and rotating roomies. The die was rolled and there were no arguments. Kevin and his wife Yolanda ate lunch here during their trip to Ireland in the previous year. Kevin got a kick out of showing us a famous picture hanging on the wall that Yolanda had taken special delight in. We finally arrived in the beautiful seaside town of Kinsale at about 8:00 pm. Daylight in June goes easily to 10:00 pm so we had plenty of time to do whatever was necessary. After checking into The Trident Hotel in Kinsale, and showering up from a long night and day, we strolled to 'The White House' for dinner. Mussels and clams were a popular dinner dish for some but of course I had the good taste to stay with something a little more familiar. Mom always said I was a picky eater. We passed many a tavern on the return walk to the hotel but we were bushed and turned in for the evening. We needed our rest for tomorrow we would see the most beautiful piece of property with eighteen holes on it that we have ever seen in our lives.

Every morning in Ireland was met with a wonderful breakfast as part of our traveling package. Our leisurely breakfast complete, it was off to Old Head Links on the southernmost tip of Kinsale for our 10:45 tee time. The Links stretches two miles out to a point on the Atlantic Ocean and an elevated ocean view is present on each of its 18 holes. On arrival we found a first-class clubhouse and were met by statues of two dogs guarding the entrance door, a gracious staff, excellent caddies, and sun kissed skies with nary a breeze. After a casual warmup, it was off to challenge that which is Old Head. Mike, who was our trips appointed photographer, took many a photo including a mandatory group photo fronting the Old Head Lighthouse in the background. Every hole on this layout was spectacular and each turning corner was met with amazement. While walking down fairway number one Mike casually asked, "have the four of us ever played a round of golf together"? We have played the same course many times over the years, particularly on Father's Day but never in the same foursome. This trip promised many firsts. It would not have been unnatural to ask ourselves how we might get along together for seven days. Afterall, we were all in our 6ixties and had mapped out successful lives and idiosyncrasies of our own, one mosaic piece at a time.

The 12th hole, their signature hole, a 537-yard Par 5 dogleg left was particularly memorable. We had seen this hole prior to our arrival on paper or computer and you had to wonder how you could find land with any shot. The cliff to the left of the fairway fell 400' to the Irish Sea below. A tee shot tugged to the left would be gone. The cliff was so steep there was a sign posted requiring that a ball crossing the hazard line 'MUST BE ABANDONED'. I felt I hit my ball precisely on the line my caddy pointed out but it did not cover the required amount of land to find the safety of the fairway ahead. Tim and I both misplaced our tee shot left and settled for bogeys after our penalty. Mike and Kevin found additional issues and did not fare as well. After playing the hole, I feel there was plenty of room to the right on the drive even though that land was unseen from the tee box and would slightly lengthen the hole.

As a group we played acceptable golf and at times spectacular golf this day and I do not believe I could ever shoot better than the **81** I posted as the winning score by three on this day, including a birdie two on the third. In fact, I managed the four Par 3's in an aggregate one under par. Tim, who is by far the best player our family has, rightfully played all week from a longer set of tees, but my low score that day was unexpected and I count it as a win just the same. Our caddies, James and Killean did a fine job toting the bags. After golf we had a relaxing lunch on the veranda with the lighthouse in the distance and the 18th fairway and ocean below. Mike enjoyed a generous bowl of fresh seafood chowder. We drank beers and sat beneath the sun as if we were "the lords of all creation." There were beers and cheers for all.

Apparently some 81's look more impressive than others because it seems Kevin either never figured out how I had the lowest score or how I possibly beat Tim. Admittedly, I have never had the type of game that would impress people. I simply hit a lot of fairways, keep the ball in play, and incur very few if any penalty strokes. With each quizzical comment someone made about my score or my game today I simply responded, **81.**

After lunch we drove the easy two-hour trip to the family-owned Royal Hotel in Killarney, County Kerry. This would be home for the next three nights. The Royal is a beautiful and quaint hotel in the middle of town within a short walking distance to many shops, restaurants, ice cream stores, and bars. The rooms were spacious and elegantly appointed with welcome air-conditioning on these warm Irish days. Many hotels and restaurants do not have central air systems because it is seldom required in this part of the world. This week Ireland was amid a heat wave.

Monday morning began like every morning would during this week. An excellent breakfast with eggs, meats, potatoes, pastries, and juices. In no time we were off to our 10:50 tee time at Tralee Golf Club in County Kerry overlooking the Dingle Peninsula. Tralee was the first Arnold Palmer designed Links course in Ireland and it is a dandy, complete with a life-sized statue of Arnie behind the clubhouse. But even Arnold could not take all the credit. He is quoted as saying, "I may have designed the first nine, but surely God designed the back nine." Due to the drought the country was experiencing, we found some brown fairways yet very playable and I welcomed the additional roll. All four of us shot respectable scores and I matched my **81** from day one and was able to notch another unexpected win amongst the group. Tim came home with a disappointing 85 (from the back tees) and Mike and Kevin were at 94 & 95 respectively. I was able to continue the battle cry of **81** any time scores were debated or the winner was in question, at least for 24 more hours. Tim's game would come around, and right soon. Our caddies were Dom & Damien. All caddies in Ireland double bag while in Scotland they single bag. Many courses in the United Kingdom and Ireland name their golf holes and the uphill eleventh at Tralee was named 'Palmer's Peak.' I was fortunate to birdie the Par 5 'Palmer's Peak,' holing out an uphill right to left forty-foot putt. A leisurely lunch with beers were enjoyed after our round and before our return trip to the Royal Killarney. Cheers! Our group took advantage of the Arnold Palmer statue, surrounding it for a nice photo.

After returning to the hotel and cleaning up, I strolled to the shopping district and did a little shopping on my own. If you like Irish items, or authentic woolen materials, this is your place. The shops were plentiful and well stocked with pleasant employees to help with any of my needs.

On return through the hotel lobby, I ran into Kevin and we had a relaxing drink at the small hotel bar. Cheers! Eventually we all caught up and had a nice dinner, followed by some bar hopping into the evening. Tim, who never met a stranger, was chatting up some of the locals and Mike and Kevin joined in as well. I turned in a bit early this evening. I learned the next morning that the other boys got in past 'curfew' as the hotel doors were locked. Apparently, they had to ring the doorbell and the night manager, John, came to their rescue. John was described as some kind of character. A short rotund figure who spoke briskly and heavily in Irish Brogue. If you could understand every other word you might keep up with the conversation. My brothers could not understand every other word and the phrase 'excuse me'? was a frequent somewhat embarrassing response. I did not meet John until our departure after our three-night stay and he came exactly as advertised.

Tuesday morning, we departed for our mid-morning round at Waterville, ranked #82 in the world in a recent Golf Magazine ranking and founded in 1889. We took the northern route of The Ring of Kerry on the way to the course. We made no stops but delighted in the occasional sights we would pass. Upon arrival at the club, we were told the wind was nigh as they say but I tell you it was a two-club breeze and the windiest day of the trip. For the most part wind was not a huge factor during our rounds. Tim picked up his highly regarded game at Waterville and continued to play the excellent golf we have come to admire over these past many years. My 89 was good for second place but Tim bested me by thirteen. Mike and Kevin were in the upper nineties on this layout. We were fortunate to play six outstanding courses during our trip but to my mind, Waterville was the most 'Championship' layout we encountered during our week. The home 18th hole is spectacular running parallel to O'Grady's Beach on Ballinskelligs Bay. But I prefer to talk about the 'Mass Hole,' the Par 3 12th. This Par 3 has its tee box atop of one dune and the green atop an opposite dune that can stretch as far as 210 yards. In-between is nothing but a 100' deep hollow with shoulder high grass where errant shots will never be found, nor looked for. There is no bailout on this hole. Back when it was outlawed to practice Catholicism in Ireland under the rule of Oliver Cromwell, Catholics would secretly gather in the hollow short of the green to celebrate Mass, baptism, or weddings. They were under penalty of death if caught. Tim bogeyed the hole after finding his tee marker at 200 yards. Mike and Kevin both bogeyed the hole from our more appropriate 164 yards. I made par, on my second ball. Hitting into a two-club breeze I believe I over-swung and smothered the ball, not even coming near the 'altar' ahead. I found fringe with my second ball and pitched nicely enough that the ball was sent back my way before I could see just how close it was. My double-bogey received no penance and we were all rewarded with six additional outstanding holes. Unfortunately, our photographer (Mike) decided that this picturesque hole would make a nice place for photos on each tee ball from behind the player. A keen eye can pick up my initial tee ball in the frame on its decent to the abyss below. Our photographer did not take a mulligan. I highly recommend Waterville to any golfing visitor of Ireland. And though most of our rounds were met with good, competent caddies, Waterville's Dominic and John were by far the best. True professionals. After our round we had a group photo in front of the life-sized statue of Payne Stewart behind the eighteenth green and we included our caddies in the photo. Payne was an honorary member of the Club and would practice at Waterville when he was in the Country for the Irish Open or as a prelude to his play in what we refer to as the British Open.

We shunned the idea of lunch at the Club. Our caddies recommended a restaurant we would pass on our return trip to the Killarney Hotel via the southern route of The Ring of Kerry. As suggested, we stopped at The Blue Bull in a town called Sneem. We were not disappointed. After lunch we stopped briefly for a few roadside photos including Killarney National Park and then back to the hotel for cleanup and dinner. It was at our stop at the park where we ran into a couple of young Irish lasses who were out on a holiday of their own. Like us, they were admiring the landscape along the southern leg of the Ring of Kerry. As we struck up a conversation with the pair, the fact that we were from Indianapolis came up. They were happy to inform us that they had been in Indianapolis just a few months prior in celebration of St Patrick's Day. When asked where they visited, they said they were at a popular Irish bar near downtown Indy called the Golden Ace. Mike exclaimed that he was also at the Golden Ace on that day. After Mike wandered off for some photo opportunities of the park, one of the girls mentioned to Tim, Kevin, & I that they played in a band at the Golden Ace. Mike only heard that story after the ladies had moved on, but his curiosity was piqued. While at The Ace, Mike had taken some pictures of the band he witnessed during his short stay. The Ace rotates bands about every two hours during this all-day Irish celebration. He found the picture on his phone of the band and it was the same girl. What are the odds? The girls had left before Mike had the opportunity to show them his photo.

After hotel arrival and showering up, I did some additional shopping before heading out for dinner. We left the hotel at 7:00 pm for a night of dinner, drinks, and late-night music. This was all in town and within close walking distance to our hotel. The following morning after checking out we met up with John the night manager. Tim, Mike, and Kevin were effusive in their praise of the young man's courtesy and Irish charm. I was introduced and he was kind enough to offer to load our bags and we took a quite memorable photo with John in front of the hotel before departure. They say a picture is worth a thousand words and this picture is proof positive of that statement. Our three-night stay at the Royal Killarney was extremely pleasant.

This Wednesday morning, we were off to The Old Course at Ballybunion for our 10:00 am tee time. Traversing the narrow roadways along the way, it takes a bit of determination to reach some of these fine links. Dodging bicycle traffic adds an additional hazard. Ballybunion was recently ranked #17 in the world by Golf Magazine and founded in 1893. Ballybunion is possibly the most famous golf course name in the Country of Ireland. Like Tralee, Ballybunion also suffered from drought conditions as we found many a brown fairway, yet the turf stays firm and playable. The first hole is unique in that if you miss the fairway wide and to the right, you will find your ball, or leave your ball, in the local Killehenny graveyard. The hole is appropriately named, 'Tombstones.' Many of the greens at Ballybunion are raised with chipping areas often found front, left, and right. Tim and I both found the first green in regulation and my 20-foot downhill putt from directly behind the hole found the cup for an opening birdie. That was my highlight of the day until I found a couple of cold Smithwicks in the beautiful lounge area after the round. Tim, not to be outdone, holed his fifteen-foot putt from the left side of the hole for a matching birdie. His game was back to stay.

Ballybunion was not my favorite course, mostly because of raised greens and a few too many dog-leg left holes for my taste. But it was very scenic and enjoyable and had the never-before seen quirky finish where the 18th tee box is perpendicular to the 17th green and your drive to the uphill 18th fairway is shot directly over the preceding green. Tim shot another 76 but only bested me by eleven this day. He had had enough of my winning and his best was yet to come. Kevin bested Mike today 95 to 96. Our caddies, Mike and Maurice were thought to be in their mid to upper 6ixties if not seventies but upon our quizzical nature it was revealed they were both in their low to mid-fifties. A caddies' life overseas in the elements, cool, wind, and rain can age a man prematurely. Smoking and drinking help the aging process, but seems to be a requirement for the job. Both men were able to roll their own smokes one handed while toting our bags. Their double loop style was one bag on a trolley and one over the shoulder. They might often be quick to release the F bomb when a wayward drive would soar toward a rising hill full of brush knowing they would have to trek after it and find the little bugger. One of Kevin's unfortunate shots got a loud, almost admonishing, and reflexive F bomb from his caddy. As the ball was sailing into the abyss, we heard a quick FOOK! Kevin found the critique a bit unprofessional but it was later revealed that he tipped his man as if he shot his seasons best.

After our round we did our requisite pro shop shopping at the Club before heading upstairs for lunch and our much-earned beers in the beautiful and modern clubhouse. Cheers! The Ballybunion Gift Shop was the largest and best stocked shop of any of the clubs we visited. Outside we took a group photo in front of a bust of Tom Watson. Mr. Watson, five-time British open champion, visited here in 1981 and declared it, in his opinion, the best course in the world. The bust was erected "in recognition of his outstanding contribution to the club."

Our travels this evening would take us to the town of Lahinch, County Clare. Mike, our excellent navigator, learned of a shortcut to Lahinch on a ferry across the Mouth of Shannon. I found the ferry quite pleasing as Kevin would drive our vehicle directly onto the vessel, and we simply got out and enjoyed the 25-minute ride and the scenery. The ferry saved us well over an hours-time but also gave us a pleasant respite. Tim found it necessary to flirt with some young lasses during parts of our short boat ride. He was rewarded with simultaneous smooches on opposite cheeks from the friendly ladies. A photo of the act is forever proudly in his possession. After crossing the Shannon, we were back to the van and onward to Lahinch. Today and tomorrow promised to be one of the hottest days in the history of Ireland. They were expecting temperatures to reach the unheard heights of the lower nineties. Or as they would say, 33 or 34 Celsius. Quite a difference from the -17 Celsius I weathered in Alberta a few months earlier. Our rooms in the Lahinch Hotel in County Clare were sans air-conditioning. The evenings did cool down nicely however and it certainly was not unbearable. On arrival I quickly showered and went downstairs to a near empty hotel bar for a relaxing pint. Cheers to myself. By 7:00 pm we were off to dinner. Strolling down the street just blocks away we ran into a small group of people Kevin knew from back home. He enjoyed a short visit with the group he had not seen in a while, while the rest of us were calculating the odds of seeing someone you know on the other side of the pond. The dinner, evening, and company was outstanding. A toast at dinner to a relative of days gone by was had as was our custom which began back on our first day in the town of Naas. I did not keep track of the relatives toasted during the trip but we certainly did not leave anyone out. None of us ever lost sight of how fortunate we have been. Cheers!

Thursday morning began with a fine breakfast at Lahinch Hotel. Was it the Irish who said that breakfast is the most important meal of the day? They sure know how to serve it up. We then headed to Lahinch golf course which was less than a half mile away. Lahinch was recently ranked #35 in the world by a recent Golf Magazine ranking. I departed the van first as always to check in with the Head Pro. A pack of four yardage books, scorecards, and instructions were waiting for me on the counter as we found the service first rate at all our stops. We quickly learned that Lahinch would be hosting the 2019 Irish Open and we would certainly look forward to viewing it on TV next year. (It was won by Jon Rahm)

While we were warming up and doing our practice putting, Tim was off to make best friends with the starter or caddie-master. He had already reviewed the scorecard and the first tee area and noticed there were no blue tee or championship tee markers out. Tim went in to negotiate playing a longer course for himself than they showed available from the regular men's tees. He was in search of a course with more length befitting his golfing prowess. And rightfully so. It was agreed that Tim would be allowed to play from the 'yardarms' which are the signs that show the hole number and yardage of each hole at each tee box. The yardarms on average were twenty yards behind the tees the rest of us would play. Lahinch dissuades players from testing their skills and that is why they do not put the longer markers out daily. There was also a wager of a cold pint between Tim and the caddie-master. The club bet that Tim could not break 76 on the famed Lahinch Links from the yardage he was about to embark on. Since I had beaten Tim twice already this week, I did not have a good feel how this wager might come out. I knew Tim had the game to get the job done but none of us knew exactly what lie ahead of us for the next eighteen holes. Our caddies today were Rocky and Greg. As we all cracked our opening drives down the middle of the fairway, Rocky, Greg, four golfers, and the four bags were all moving in concert. After completion of the first hole, Rocky took us on an uphill circuitous route to the second tee box to show us what lie ahead at the unusual fourth. After playing hole 2, which upset me due to an unnecessary three putt bogey, and hole 3, we saw exactly why Rocky showed us the Par 5 fourth from a different vantage point. The fairway was about the width of a nice two-lane road. Hills or dunes rose from each side and it looked daunting to say the least. Miraculously, all our balls found the sliver of fairway and each ball was close to the next. After successfully completing our drives, we came across a large dune called Klondyke that traversed the fairway in perpendicular fashion and impeded any view of the green. On top and in the center of the mountain was a flag planted to give you direction. A first-time player without caddie might have no idea where to hit, thinking they forgot to finish the design of the hole. On this day as was custom at times, there was a forecaddie atop 'Mount Lahinch.' His main goal was to point you in the right direction should your second shot find trouble. Rest assured there was a green beyond the hill and the idea for shot number two was to go over the mountain in hopes of finding additional and more generous fairway on the other side. Elevation on shot number two was a must and I am not known to hit the highest of fairway metals but I cracked a jolly good one this time. In fact, we all hit good to reasonably good second shots on this hole. Mike ended up bogeying this peculiar yet exciting hole, Tim, and Kevin both made pars and I had a mere twelve feet for birdie. I must have been a bit nervy as my putt was perfectly on line but better suited for a putt about five feet longer. I hit the back of the cup dead on. The ball popped in the air but stayed above ground upon landing. And that is how my day went as we traversed the seaside Links along beautiful Liscannor Bay. A series of good shots, bad shots, unfortunate shots, and bad luck followed me throughout the round. At days end I shot my high round of the week, 90. I kept a good positive attitude all day and a few poor golf shots was not getting in the way of my fantastic week. Mike and Kevin both shot their low rounds of the week, 83 & 85 respectively. In fact, Mike commented that it was his lowest round in recent memory, anywhere. And how did Tim's bet come out with the caddie-master? He birdied three holes on the day including the home eighteenth on his way to a sizzling 74 from an estimated 6900 yards. I cannot say for sure whether the bet was paid off but the Club and caddies were impressed with his game. We were all impressed with his game. We enjoyed a pint or two after the round as we nourished ourselves in the clubhouse. Cheers!

Tim's daughter and our niece Colleen joined us for lunch as was pre-planned with painstaking care. The thirty-year old Colleen had been traveling the past month through much of Europe on a solo trip that I cannot tell you what kind of courage that seems to me to take. Along her travels she did meet up with some people she knew but for much of her trip, she was on her own seeking out history and adventure among old-world sights. After lunch and prior to our departure from Lahinch, the four golfers took our commemorative photo in front of the Clubs logo, a statue of a goat. Goats are free to roam the course and was incorporated as the Clubs logo in 1956. We did not see any goats during our round of play. Despite my dismal 90, I enjoyed Lahinch as much as any club we played during the week. I would welcome another crack at it.

Upon leaving Lahinch with Colleen now in the rear seat, we went to visit the Cliffs of Moher, a little better than an hours' drive away. The historic natural landmark was amazing, rising 400' above the Atlantic Ocean at Hag's Head and a full 700' to the north near O'Brien's Tower. The Cliffs is one of the most visited sights every year in Ireland and I certainly noticed a more diverse ethnic presence in the area. These people were not in search of their roots. We spent maybe two hours at the Cliffs and then headed east to Athlone where our target was Sean's Bar, Europe's oldest bar dating back to 900 A.D. according to the Guinness Book of Records. In a cramped busy end of the small town, we located the bar but parking was a treasure hunt until we found some luck of the Irish as a car exited just in front of us on our second loop around the area. A few pints of Guinness and other favorites were had in the small, low-ceilinged establishment. Cheers! Before departing Athlone, Mike fancied a bookstore two doors down and met John the owner who advertises "a small shop with thousands and thousands of books." Mike found the tagline true to its words and purchased a book from John, feeling much richer for the experience.

Today, our longest day since our inbound flight, was not near completion as we now headed further east chasing darkness toward Dublin. Portmarnock, just north of Dublin to be exact for our final two nights of our trip. We arrived at the 5 Star Portmarnock Hotel just past midnight. We checked in and Colleen took the floor in a room with Tim and Kevin who were matched up for the last two nights. Mike took our room key and hustled down to unpack but quickly returned to the lobby where I was still standing to say there was a problem with our room. Only one bed, he exclaimed. I stayed unusually calm and spoke with the manager and he would fix the situation immediately. We soon learned there were no other rooms available with two beds. We requested a rollaway and it was brought with no issue. I gladly volunteered to take the narrow and slightly less comfortable rollaway. It was very late and we were very tired and I am not really that hard to please. Because he is always the gentleman, Mike seemed to feel very guilty having the lush 'queen-sized' bed to himself after I had made all our plans. He felt I deserved better but I really had no problem with it. The next night he even insisted we switch for night #2 but I had none of it. I was good.

The next morning Mike and I went down for our hearty breakfast. We had not seen our brothers yet. We had all kinds of time as today was the only day with an afternoon tee time. As late as we got in last night, it turned out well planned. Duty would not call us to the Portmarnock Championship course until 3:00 pm. During breakfast and sitting well behind me, Mike noticed a man who asked if his ten-year old son could have his picture taken with what appeared to Mike to be a man not a part of their group. Mike wondered if this man was a person of note and asked me to turn around and see if I recognized the man who the boy was having his picture taken with. Being in Ireland and before turning around my immediate thoughts went to the great golf star Rory McIlroy. Is Rory in the house, I wondered? I glanced over but did not see anyone recognizable. We continued our meal but so did light commotion in the area behind me. A short time later the mystery was solved. Following breakfast, I went up to the luxurious and expansive lobby, took a lush seat and enjoyed the goings on. The Portmarnock resembled some 5-star American properties that I have had the good fortune to visit in my life. I noticed a few teenagers wearing jerseys of a sport I did not recognize. All of them had the same number on the back and the same unrecognizable name. My curiosity was piqued and I immediately went to my Google machine. The name on the back of the jerseys was VIRAT. I typed VIRAT into my phone and it exploded with information. Virat Kohli, Virat Kohli stats, Virat Kohli wife, and Virat Kohli net worth all popped up. Any time you Google someone and that person's wife shows up as a person of interest, you know you have hit onto someone worthy of your attention. Who is this Virat fellow? As it happens, Virat Kohli is an International Cricket star and known to be one of the world's top batsmen. He captains the Indian national cricket team that was staying in our hotel. It helps explain why there was a large menacing looking fellow who favored the look of Luca Brasi patrolling the lobby day and night. He was the security guard for the cricket players. It also explained why the hotel was on virtual 'lockdown' mode. If you did not belong in this hotel, you were not getting into this hotel. And it explained why there was a large contingent of Indian guests at the hotel. I concluded that Mr. Kohli had been downstairs eating his morning meal and obliged some young fans with a photograph. The Virat Kohli story is one of my favorite stories of our entire trip. Followed by this next story I am about to tell. About noon time, Mike, Kevin, and I walked down to the nearly full beach just behind the hotel to look around. The locals had flooded the beach on a day with some of the warmest temperatures they had experienced. We happened upon an ice cream truck parked on the beach doing a land office business. As was our custom during this entire trip, we were drawn to the ice cream like a magnet. We enjoyed a cone and the goings on of all the Irish children frolicking about on the Portmarnock beach on the Irish Sea enjoying their best and warmest day of what is typically a short summer. A young Irish lad and lass were getting ready to pony up for an ice cream and Mike decided to intervene and pay for their treats. It was a nice gesture from Mike and the kids were delighted. The kids, brother, and sister we later found out, could keep their Euros for another time. After a few minutes passed, a lady came up to us and asked if we paid for the kid's ice cream. My first thought was she might be upset, as if we were 'interfering' with her children. Friendly conversation quickly ensued and she was delighted and thanked Mike for his good deeds. After further conversation we learned that their last name was Kavanaugh. Possibly with a slightly different pronunciation taking account for the accent. A beach full of thousands of people and we met up with the Kavanaugh family. What were the odds? (I have said that before on this trip) Maybe better than I thought in County Dublin with a surname more popular than I could imagine. But it certainly was an oddity for our 'meet cute' as they say.

At 2:00 pm we were off to Portmarnock Golf Club where many Championships have been contested over the years including Irish Opens, British Amateurs, and Walker Cup Championships. Greats such as Harry Vardon, Henry Cotton, Bobby Locke, and Arnold Palmer have all played the Links. More current stars such as Tiger, Phil, Rory, and Padraig have also walked these great fairways. Upon glancing at the scorecard, I immediately felt the course was long from the traditional men's tees. Tim was comfortable from the back tees playing at 6900 yards. Mike and Kevin seemed to be comfortable from what we might call blue tees back in the States, measuring in at 6705 yards. I was here to have a good time and decided to play a hybrid set calculated from a formula some seniors use back home in our league play. My common sense shaved off 420 yards putting me in a more comfortable but still testy 6,285-yards. That was plenty for me. Our caddies today were Donncha and Harry. Kevin parred the first hole against three matching bogeys and we were off. The Portmarnock Links was similarly difficult as our other tests but lacked some of the seaside beauty, possibly due to being on lower, flatter ground. Tim posted two birdie twos enroute to a fine 77. I poured in an 84 from the shorter markers. Mike and Kevin both came in with scores in the low 90's. It was our last round on the Isle together and it was late in the day. This course had no discernable spot of fame and I am sorry that we failed to take a group photo at this venue. I went in to buy a souvenir or two before our departure but much to my dismay, the shop was closed for the day. The gentleman on sight looked for the manager with the golf shop key but the man was gone. I had missed my opportunity. On our return to the hotel to clean up for our last evenings dinner, we were greeted, or so it seemed, by hundreds of cricket fans. They were on the outskirts of the hotel property awaiting the returning bus of their victorious Indian cricket stars.

We took a cab to dinner in the nearby town of Howth. Tim's daughter Colleen was still with us and joined us for outdoor dining near the street on a fine summer evening at The Oar House. After dinner we walked around the corner to a nearby bar for late night drinks. Cheers! I only stayed for one drink and hailed a cab for the solo return trip to the hotel and some needed rest. I went to bed with a plan in mind. I would get up at a reasonable time and cab my way back to the golf course to pick up the souvenirs I had missed out on today. I did just that. As I disembarked at the Portmarnock golf shop the following morning, I had the cab wait for me as I knew I would not be long. Kevin, who had a different flight schedule than the rest of us left early with Colleen and returned the car to catch his earlier flight. I do not know exactly where Colleen was headed to continue her European adventure. I believe Manchester, England. On my return to the hotel, I went to our room to make sure my bags were in order and Mike had made an interesting discovery. We did indeed have a room with two twin beds but they were shoved together and made up with queen sheets. I found it fairly funny. After breakfast, Mike, Tim, and I were off to the Dublin Airport by cab. I paid the cab fare with the cash I had left but now at this juncture, I was officially out of Euros, which was perfect.

International travel can be very exhausting and we were all ready for the long day trip home. We arrived in Chicago via D.C. and after the drive home from O'Hare Airport I was back home at approximately 1:00 am local time on Sunday. Mind you we gained five hours on our return. Like I said, it is a long exhausting day but worth every minute of it. The thought that crossed my mind on day one was, could the four of us get along for seven straight days? I think you could say we were born for this. It was our destiny. If there was ever an argument it might be who was picking up a meal or bar tab. Kevin picked up many of the dinner tabs and my memory tells me that lunches and post round drinks were rotated on an unequal and unassuming basis. No one was keeping track in all our excitement and good fortune. Would we ever want to return? As Doc Holliday said to Johnny Ringo in his final duel, "say when."

Back home in the states in early July, Circuit Court Judge Brett Kavanaugh (no relation / not so sure) was nominated to the Supreme Court. My brothers and I had just returned from Ireland where the surname Kavanaugh, is common and nearly celebrated. Now our name was on TV every day but it was not pleasant. The Democrat leftists drug our family name into the mud daily. You might say I took it personal. Brett was wrongly accused of sexual assault allegations from as far back as his high school days. He was even accused of having a drink or two before the legal age of consumption. Oh my. I was convinced we were related. I said if you took a family photo of me and my seven siblings and tossed Brett into the picture, most people would get wrong on the question of which face did not belong. After weeks of grilling and mud-slinging, he was voted onto the Supreme Court but only by the narrowest of margins. Ultra-liberal justice Ruth Bader Ginsburg was approved nearly unanimously in 1993. The partisanship in Washington DC was not good for our country, and I did not see it ever ending in my lifetime.

My 64th year was a dream year. All family matters were in good order and three outstanding international trips were almost an embarrassment of riches. Almost.

65

9-19-2018 to 9-18-2019

My 65th birthday was celebrated not much different than many in the past eighteen years. A trip to our condo in Ft. Myers. Only this time we went down ON my birthday which was a Wednesday. A week after we returned, we attended the wedding of our niece Ana Kavanaugh to Dru Cornett. It seemed impossible that 'little Ana' (as she was so often referred) was getting married. It appears as if everyone is getting older except for me. But I know that is not true. Ana had an elaborate outdoor wedding on the estate of the owner of Lucas Oil in Carmel, Indiana. The weather was perfect. The affair was first class with cocktails, hors d'oeuvres, and dinner. A band accompanied the event. The brides' parents, my sister-in-law Yolanda, does everything first class and my brother Kevin, who I am not sure had any clue about all the details, goes along with a smile on his face.

In November I went to see a movie called Bohemian Rhapsody about a band called Queen and their lead singer Freddie Mercury. I was not a fan of Queen as I have been happily stuck in 6ixties music most of my life. In fact, I knew very little about them. I went to see the movie because seeing movies is one of the pastimes of my adult life. I average about 6ixty movies a year at theatres. I also went because of a song called, 'We Are the Champions' that played in the trailers. When I coached my sons in youth hockey back in the eighties and nineties, I had some very good teams and we won our share of tournaments. That song was played for tournament champions on a handful of occasions. I found the movie to be outstanding and considered it one of the best pictures of the year. What shocked people as I told them of the movie is, I had never heard the name Freddie Mercury before seeing this movie. That seemed to be impossible to all. Apparently, he was very well known. Rami Malek who portrayed Freddie in the movie, walked off with the Academy Award for 'best male actor in a leading role' a few months later. The girl that played his wife in the movie had a striking resemblance to my good friend Joe Hagelskamp's sister Mary.

President George HW Bush died on November 30, 2018. It was not a surprise. He had been looking very frail of late. When I read the book by George W Bush, '41: A Portrait of My Father' a couple years ago, it was my opinion that 41 may have been the greatest American of the Twentieth Century. I am not sure we deserved a man that great to be our President. His greatness began taking shape as a pilot in World War II. After the war he attended Yale University. He was a good husband and father. He was in the House of Representatives. He was a US Ambassador. He became chair of the Republican National Committee. He was Director of the CIA. He was Ronald Reagan's Vice-President for eight years before becoming our 41st President. The man was amazing. When he was sending missiles down Iraqi chimneys as President, he was beloved. When he did what needed to be done later in his presidency, raising taxes, he was reviled. George HW Bush was a military hero, family man, sportsman, and Statesman. The man was a class act. He was 94 years old.

As fall turned to winter, the annual Kavanaugh Christmas Party was just around the corner. Brother Kevin and his wife Yolanda drew the short straw this year to host the 70+ person annual event. Naturally, Yolanda put on another first-class affair in their newly remodeled home. A combination of the roomy home coupled with a sickness that was going around in the family made the event seem small. I expect as many as twenty people were missing due to illness. Final tally was just over 50 people, the smallest attendance figure in years. There was a sinful amount of food leftover. Santa Claus arrived with gifts from Mexico, Canada, Ireland, and a few from the USA. Some of the children were not there to receive them. The kids who were present lit up with delight. Santa also brought a framed collage of pictures and scorecards from the brothers' golf trip to Ireland the previous summer. It was a big hit. The collage was a gift from Santa, to Santa.

My wife Ginger, daughter Christy, and I made a late decision to go to Florida on Christmas Day after the annual Christmas breakfast at our house with immediate family members. Grandson James, all of 1½ years old was showered with lots of gifts. Christy, Ginger, and I headed south about 1:00 pm and drove as far as mid Georgia. We arrived at the condo about 2:00 pm on the 26th. Brother Kevin's family was down at his recently purchased condo at Tiburon in Naples about 30 minutes south of us. We played a round of golf on the 28th and what a pleasure it was.

In the 2018 sports season, the Philadelphia Eagles won their first Super Bowl ever beating the New England Patriots. Alex Ovechkin of the Washington Capitals won his much-needed Stanley Cup over the upstart Vegas Golden Knights. In another repeat, the Golden State Warriors took out the Cleveland Cavaliers, this time in straight sets. And the Boston Red Sox bested the L.A. Dodgers for the years' World Series title. In golf, Brooks Koepka took down both the US Open and PGA titles. Francesco Molinari stared down Tiger Woods to win The Open at Carnoustie. My favorite movie selection for 2018 was a combination of prequel and sequel similar to The Godfather Part II. Mamma Mia: Here We Go Again was a delight with Amanda Seyfried and Lily James. Cher was amazing in her brief but key and powerful appearance. Bohemian Rhapsody was a close second.

In early January the circle of life took a cruel turn. A good friend of mine in the plumbing wholesale business lost his 7-year-old granddaughter during a seemingly routine surgery that went very bad. My friend owned a vacation home about a block from the Gulf on Ft Myers Beach. We had met this sweet little girl a couple years ago as she was swimming in their backyard pool during one of our spring visits. Ginger and I would visit Jim and Mrs. Feick occasionally when our calendars placed us in Ft Myers at the same time. I could not imagine the pain from their loss. I had a memorial golf flag made in the girls' honor at the following summers plumbing golf outing in Indy. My friend has it proudly displayed in his office. A short week later my son John and daughter-in-law Rebecca announced they were expecting their second child, a girl.

The band that dominated music in the 6ixties was still relevant in my 60's. My brother Mike and I had discussed over the years about what your favorite Beatles song is and could you rank your favorite 100 Beatle songs. Mike thought this to be an impossible task, like picking his favorite child or his favorite grandchild of which he has 13. I got to work and completed my 1–100 list beginning with Eight Days A Week, followed by Penny Lane and If I Fell. Slowly but surely, I put my list in groups of 20 and whittled away at it until I was finished. If I had to do it over again it would certainly come out differently but my top 20 or so are locked in. When looking at my list it was clear I was a bigger fan of the early Beatle tunes. I once said any song with John playing harmonica is better than songs when he does not. That is not exactly true nor does it have anything to do with his singing voice. He gave up the mouthpiece in 1964 so it only meant I preferred more early songs. Also, my definition of early Beatles tunes differs from other opinions. I consider anything prior to the Apple label as early Beatles. Best album by my list? Rubber Soul. My list had 11 songs on it from Rubber Soul. Brother Mike finally completed his list just shy of three years later. Golden Slumbers headed his list.

My son Jason and his wife Casey received another trip to Boston for Christmas from Ginger and I. I accompanied them and the trip was set for February 8th 2019. Unlike the last time we scheduled a trip like this, the flights were all on time and the weather cooperated. We cruised into Boston about 5:00 pm, checked into the Marriott Long Wharf Hotel and began our siege on the bars of Boston. The following day, Saturday, the Bruins hosted the LA Kings with a 1:00 pm matinee start. We patronized The Fours Bar before the game which is nearly mandatory in Boston. Before the game started and unbeknownst to us there was a ceremony in front of the Bruins bench honoring Patrice Bergeron who two games previous had played his 1,000[th] game as a Bruin. Patrice, his wife, and three children were all down on the ice as he was showered with praise and gifts. It was well deserved. Patrice is one of our all-time favorite Bruins. He is easily one of the greatest Bruins ever. He is a gentleman. He is a leader. He is a coaches' player and a players' player. He has been a pleasure to watch.

The game commenced and there was plenty of action, including a goal by Anze Kopitar, my favorite player on the visiting Kings. Regulation ended in a 4-4 tie and poetically, Patrice Bergeron scored the game winner in OT.

Dark sets in early during Boston February's and we had plans to eat Italian at a famous North Side Restaurant but the waiting line at our restaurant of choice was already out the door by 5:00 pm. A couple doors down and across the street we noticed the Cantina Italiana. I do not know what our first choice of restaurant would have been like but the Cantina was first class in service and food selection. The owner, or manager, conversed with us and welcomed us. We enjoyed a bottle of wine that Jason ordered using his knowledge as a bartender. Simply a fantastic dinner. We hit up a couple more bars before the end of the evening and Jason and Casey stayed out well past my curfew.

The following morning, we took a cab out to Fenway Park and toured what is known as the 'Cathedral of Boston.' I rooted for the Red Sox way back in the 6ixties when they had stars such as Ken Harrelson, Jim Lonborg, and Carl Yastrzemski. My earliest memory of Red Sox baseball goes back even further when AL MVP and one of my childhood favorites, Jackie Jensen, was shagging flies for the Sawx. Our tour guide today was quite knowledgeable and after the tour we left for our second consecutive Bruin matinee start. I love the matinees on trips like this because it gives you all evening to enjoy the bar scene. The opponent for this Sunday game was the Colorado Avalanche. For some reason the Bruins had not beaten the Avs at home in over ten years. They only play them one home game a year but I still found that stat very peculiar. This was a low scoring game and again my favorite player on the visiting team, Nathan McKinnon, scored a goal. The line of McKinnon, Mikko Rantanen, and Gabriel Landaskog is the fastest, most dangerous line I have ever seen. Tied at one, this game also went into OT. Brad

Marchand lit the lamp for the game winner this time as the Bruins took back-to-back games in OT. Our seats were about twenty rows up in the end zone and the game winner was scored on our end of the arena. Naturally we were delighted and after the game we found a new bar to visit. Eventually, we found our way to the Chart House for dinner. The Chart House is the oldest building on Long Wharf and was once the office of John Hancock. Other than our excursion to Fenway, all these locations are within walking distance from our hotel. The famous Faneuil Hall and Quincy Market are directly across the street from our hotel. It is just so convenient. The next morning, we headed back to Logan Airport for our 8:00 am direct flight home. It was a perfect trip with a capital P. Hopefully, we can do it again soon.

A month later my daughters ex-husband and my oldest granddaughter Abby's father passed away. Bruce Taylor had been battling cancer for some time. It did get to the point where the end was inevitable. You just cannot ever really be ready for it when he was still so young. A few months before he passed, I wrote him a letter telling him how good a father he had been for Abby among other things. His mother Irma mentioned it to me at the funeral and said how much they all appreciated it. Bruce even called me one day telling me he wanted me to walk Abby down the aisle if that day ever came. At the time I told Bruce he would be around. What else could I say? But on March 11th, 2019 he passed. The funeral was nice and well attended. I do not know how Abby summoned the courage but she sang a beautiful song acapella style at the church. She was amazing.

In April, former vice-president Joe Biden entered the race for the 2020 Presidential election. He brought the vast and record field of contenders to twenty and immediately became the favorite to become the Democrat nominee to try to take down Donald Trump. The largest field of candidates ever would eventually reach 24. I think some of them just wanted to hear themselves talk. Biden did end up beating out a weak field. When it was down to Biden and Socialist Senator Bernie Sanders of Vermont, a man not popular with the Democrat hierarchy, it appeared the fix was in, in favor of the former VP. The 'gaffe machine' would spend much of his candidacy in hibernation to prevent further public embarrassments from his lack of physical and mental endurance or skills as an orator. And because of an upcoming virus.

On 5-24-2019 I was off on another golf trip to Scotland accompanied by my daughter Christy, who does not golf. We left for the Indianapolis Airport at 11:00 am. At 3:15 we were off to our first stop, Newark. Our transatlantic flight was delayed by one hour but we were then off without further issue. The flight was smooth and after retrieving our bags in Edinburgh, we were off to get our rental car. We took possession of the car, loaded our bags, and left it parked, the same as John and I did five years ago. We took advantage of the tram that goes from the airport in to the town of Edinburgh. It is about a twenty-minute ride. We ate lunch and did some light window shopping before getting on the return tram to the airport to drive our car to the wonder that is St. Andrews, Scotland. When you get out of the car in St Andrews, you can basically smell links golf. The seagulls screeching, the water, the salty air, the sand and turf. To a golfer, there can be no more an inspiring place. We checked into The Scores Hotel which is a wedge from the first tee of the Old. They gave us the exact same room my son John and I had when we were here in 2014. I had no golf tee time secured for this day but I did have a plan to attempt to play. After unpacking I went to the starters office to check on availability. You can play until 10:00 pm so there was time. Bruce the starter got me on the Old at 5:15 with another single Ryan who worked for Adidas plus local Mark Reed and his professor friend Kenny. Kenny has played the Old many times and he was a fast player. We were finished at 9:00 pm. The weather was gray, overcast with spitting rain. Christy met me at the 18th green and took an awesome picture with the Rusacks Hotel in the background with its lights shining through the gloaming while I was putting out. It was too late for dinner anywhere though we tried. The long overnight flight and first day was in the books.

Sunday May 26, I woke up to check the Bruins score from the previous night. It was game one of the Stanley Cup Finals and I would miss seeing the first two games. Good news. The Bruins beat St. Louis in game one 4-2. Since Christy does not play golf, we knew she would always be on a slightly different schedule than me. I went down for breakfast and was off for my 10:00 am start at Panmure Golf Club. Panmure dates to 1845 and is the club Ben Hogan practiced at prior to his 1953 British Open win at Carnoustie. The drive to Panmure was an easy 30 minutes or so. My caddie was John and he was close to me in age. I played as a single this morning. It was a nice course and I played downwind out and into the wind back. The breeze on the inward nine gave me some difficulty and I shot what I considered a respectable 87. It was a quick round. I was back at the hotel to shower by 1:30. Christy and I were off for photos and lunch at the Jigger Inn which sits alongside the 17th fairway of the Old Course. The Old is closed for play on Sunday's but you can walk parts of the course for photo opportunities. We took advantage and had our picture taken on the famous Swilcan Bridge just yards in front of the 18th tee box of the Old. Christy's siblings had no idea she was on the trip. It was her idea to keep it a secret until this very moment. In fact, the moment she texted her brothers with a picture of her and I on the bridge may have been her favorite moment of the trip. John, who has been with me on the bridge was very confused when he saw the photo. I believe he expected some photoshop mischief had taken place. After our photos we went to The Old Course Hotel to hook Christy up with some Spa treatments for the week. The Spa was part of her previous years' Christmas gift. We had a drink at Dunvegan's bar and walked through town. We stopped by the World War I Memorial, The Cathedral, and St. Rules Tower. We turned in early today and were out by 9:00 pm. Simon Pagenaud won the Indy 500 this day but we found it televised nowhere. I found that odd being we were in the home country of 1965 Indy 500 winner Jimmy Clark and recent three-time Champion Dario Franchitti.

Monday, May 27th I awoke feeling very refreshed. A solid 10 hours sleep. It was a cool morning but dry. A hearty breakfast was followed by a visit to the British Golf Museum next to the clubhouse of the Old. The museum was under construction when John and I were in town in 2014 so I was looking forward to seeing what it had to offer. It was educational, enjoyable, but not what I would call spectacular. Some minor shopping was then followed by a visit to the Rusack's Hotel and additional photo opportunities of golfing landscape, paintings, and memorabilia on the hotel walls. The Rusack's is adjacent to the Old's 18th fairway.

I left town at 11:30 for my long awaited 1:30 tee time at famed Carnoustie. Some argue the hardest Links course the world has to offer. I arrived in plenty of time and just found the visual of the property awe inspiring. I picked up a couple of souvenirs and met up with Sean Bissett, one of the hosts of SGH Golf who made all my hotel and golf arrangements. Sean was pleased to hear that everything was going well. My caddie was Jim and I played with three brothers from Idaho. It was a great pairing. They were about the same age as my sons and nephews. They gave each other the needle and I felt comfortable enough with them to chime in on occasion. It was truly like playing with my kids and a nephew. On the first tee my caddie said, "don't go left and you'll do fine here." He was not referring to hole #1, but the entire course. That was music to my ears as I seldom visit the left half of a course when I am playing my best. The sixth hole is named Hogan's Alley because of the way the great man played the hole with precision drives in the 1953 Open. It is a par 5 with out of bounds fencing all the way down the left side. A trio of bunkers angled in the middle of the fairway make the opening between the fence and bunkers quite narrow. But it also shortens the hole if you have the nerve and skill to pull it off. Most players opt for the passage to the right of the bunkers but not Ben Hogan. Hard as I tried to hit Hogan's Alley, my downwind drive veered right, but still in the fairway. My second shot was pin high and right but somehow managed to escape a pair of bunkers right of the green. I was able to use putter for my third shot from off the green but could not get it up and down for birdie. I settled for a tap in par. The course was magnificent. The Barry Burn serpentines its way about the course.

I had a nice round going but found the burn with my approach on the 10th ('South America') after blistering a drive down the middle. I think I must call my easy second shot a semi shank. That led to an unforced error double bogey. I made another par 5 on the classy 14th ('Spectacles'). The Par 3 16th ('Barry Burn') was 212 yards into the wind to an elevated green. Tom Watson made four 4's on this hole enroute to victory in the 1975 British Open and called it the hardest Par 3 in the world. I had to hit driver and was exactly pin high but down the slope left of the pin. I used putter and got it to three feet before holing out for par. The 17th ('Island') may be as tough a par 4 as there is in golf. I believe it to be the near equal of the Road Hole at St Andrews. Most players do not hit driver because of the way the Barry Burn intertwines its way through the fairway. I should have hit driver; it is my best club. The caddy talked me out of it and I think it cost me a stroke. I believe driver would have still left me short of the burn. The caddy would have been correct for many players. Due to my laying up, I was unable to reach the green in two and put my second shot into a front bunker. Bogey 5. Who goes to Carnoustie without thinking of the debacle that was Jean Van De Velde on Carnoustie's ('Home') hole of the 1999 British Open? With a three-shot lead on the final hole, he made triple bogey in spectacular fashion after some bad luck and bad choices, eventually losing in a playoff. The 18th tee looks directly toward the fabulous Carnoustie Hotel. It is a majestic site. I hit a nice drive against the wind and was in light wispy rough, but a good lie. I did not feel I could carry the burn fronting the green so I laid up, perfectly I might add. My sand wedge to the green from about 50 yards was clipped with perfection. It was the best fairway sand wedge shot I believe I have ever hit in my life. The ball looked to be 'gimme' range from my view before taking one of my favorite photos ever on the Barry Burn bridge and before arriving at the green. The only thing that could make the picture better is family. I arrived on the green finding my ball to be five or six feet above the hole. I was going to have to earn this par. I now recalled Sergio Garcia with a nearly identical putt to win the 2007 British Open. His putt stayed left. My putt would stay agonizingly to the right. I would have loved to par the ('Home') hole at Carnoustie but I was delighted with my effort and the round. 86.

I returned to our hotel at 6:50 and Christy and I had dinner at The Scores feasting on chicken and Sea Bass. After dinner we walked over to The Rusack's for a nightcap or two. Cheers! I must stay at The Rusack's on a future visit. It was built in 1887 and has an awesome look and feel to it and looks right out at the Old's 18th fairway. (In 2021 the Rusack's was renovated and increased their number of rooms and bars).

Tuesday morning it was breakfast and off to Crail Golfing Society and the Balcomie Links. It was about a thirty-minute drive and I stopped at Kingsbarns on the way just to have a nostalgic look around. Son John and I played the picturesque Kingsbarns on our 2014 trip. Balcomie was a little shorter course with a Par of 69 but the views were beautiful and I really enjoyed it. The Firth of Forth or Fife Ness as it is referred to here is within view on every hole. It was originally laid out by Old Tom Morris in 1894. I shot 78 alongside my caddie Jim. It was the first time I broke 80 in Europe and even though it was a shorter course, I will take it with pride.

On my return to The Scores Hotel, I stopped at the newest link in the St. Andrews chain of courses, The Castle Course. I just wanted to get a glimpse and I must say this course looks like it should also be on a future visit. So many courses yet only so much time. Without a doubt I could spend a month in Scotland alone. I could probably spend the whole summer. Christy was spending her day at the Spa at The Old Course Hotel and she was still there when I returned. When Christy is at a Spa with a drink nearby, she is in her element. Eventually we caught up and had a drink at The Dunvegan. Cheers! This was followed by one of the great pastimes of St Andrews, watching golfers coming home on the 18th. Though Christy doesn't golf, she understands its significance to me and our family. She can appreciate the history of where we stood. We eventually drove north to the town of Dundee for dinner. We did not have a reservation but we knew we would find something good. It was nice to experience a different city on the trip. We settled on Italian at Tony Macaroni. It was great food and a welcoming property.

Wednesday May 29th I was up early for a quick breakfast. Today would be a more robust drive to play Royal Aberdeen. It was a 1:45 hour drive north and with my trusty GPS, I never missed a turn. Much of the drive was US quality highway. Aberdeen is a port city in northeast Scotland. From the clubhouse you could see many ships anchored out in the water. I expect waiting to come to shore for loading or unloading. Aberdeen is also known as the 'Granite City' for its many grey-stone buildings. My tee time was 10:00 am and upon arrival I met up with the assistant pro who was quite gracious and showed me around the clubhouse, the locker facilities, restaurant and how to go through all the keypad coded doors. My caddy was a young lad named Paul, probably about twenty years old. The first tee at Royal Aberdeen is just steps from the clubhouse. I had a solid day of ball striking and today was the best weather day of the week. Wind picked up on the inward half but I posted a more than respectable 43/39 82. The highlights of my round both came on Par 3's. I was playing as a single again today and did not catch a foursome until the Par 3 11th. I teed off after the group ahead left the green for the nearby slightly higher ground 12th tee. I put my tee ball pin high about twelve feet right of the flag. The group ahead noticed and seemed to be impressed. They were going to allow me to pass after I putted out so they waited to watch and see if I could hole the birdie putt. It was a good effort but I could not find the bottom of the cup. We thanked the fourball and moved on. On the 17th hole par 3 I was playing directly into a three-club wind and threw a lawn dart directly at the flag but about ten feet short. As simple a birdie putt as you could have but again, I came up wanting. My two par 3's on the inward nine played a large role in my solid score. After my 2 ½ hour round I had a leisurely lunch and drink enjoying the club's facilities. Christy was spending the day where else, at the Spa. I had no doubt she was enjoying her peace and pampering. She works very hard in her regional managers role back home and does a lot of travel for work. I know her preference is probably a warm spot in the US Virgin Islands but The Old Course Hotel is a very special place. I was back at our hotel by 3:30. I showered and went to Uncle Ken's house. Ken is not our family's uncle. He is a real–life character in a book I read called 'An American Caddie in St Andrews.' If you love golf, you should give this book a read. If you have played golf at St Andrews, it should be considered a must read. While reading the book you fall in love with this elderly character. Uncle Ken was the American author's great uncle whom with he had a special relationship. Not unlike our family's relationship with our Great Aunt Margaret. His St. Andrews address was mentioned in the book and I knew it was close so I took a walk over just to see. After seeing Ken's front door, I went back to the Old to watch more golfers. I probably could have played again but Christy and I had dinner plans and it was her vacation too. I met up with Christy at 6:00 pm and we went to the top floor (5th) of The Old Course Hotel for some drinks and watch golfers down below heading in on the 17th fairway. Cheers! Dinner at The Rusack's Hotel included Surf & Turf tonight. We followed that up with a drink at Golf Hotel & Bar. This is the known caddie hangout that John and I had an unforgettable couple of drinks at back in 2014 with an interesting caddie. Christy liked the music and stole a Tennents beer glass for me to have as a souvenir. She would steal another one a couple days later. I am sure she figured I had to have a matching set. I had no problem with the petty theft.

On Thursday May 30 we were up, had breakfast, and faced a sad part of the trip for me. Checking out and leaving St. Andrews. If you are a golfer and have any sense of the history of the game, it is a very special town. It is truly the Mecca of golf. It has a homey feel to it for me. Our eventual destination today had us crossing the Forth Road Bridge to the coastal town of North Berwick about two hours away. We planned a stop at historic Muirfield Golf Course, aka The Honourable Company of Edinburgh Golfers. Muirfield, established in 1744, is in Gullane, East Lothian, Scotland, overlooking the Firth of Forth and just up the road from North Berwick. Muirfield is part of the British Open rotation and its list of champions is golfing majesty. Its most recent champion is Phil Mickelson preceded by

Ernie Els, Nick Faldo, Tom Watson, Lee Trevino, Jack Nicklaus, and Gary Player. Not a bad list. Muirfield is one of the most private clubs in all of Scotland and I did not anticipate getting through the gates to see much. I was not disappointed nor did I make much of an effort. I took a photo out by the gate and moved on. A few miles down the road we checked into the Nether Abbey Hotel in North Berwick. We found it to be a gorgeous little hotel with a great restaurant and bar. It only has 12 rooms as it was originally a stately stone home. We went in to town for lunch and found the Ship Inn to have excellent food. The portions were very generous and we could have easily split something after ordering an appetizer. I had a 2:32 tee time at Gullane Golf Club today which sits just between North Berwick and Muirfield. I played with three guys from Switzerland, mostly in drizzle and rain. And wind of course. Today was the full Scottish experience. The rain suit went on before the beginning of play. My caddie was Des and he had also caddied for Scottish LPGA star Catriona Matthew who is from this area. I did not find the course special but I expect I might have had a different opinion if the sun was out and I had a chance to look around more. No matter. I shot an excellent 83 including pars on the last two holes when I was my wettest.

Though our hotel was small, it has a reputation for terrific dining facilities and townspeople do come in to dine in the ample restaurant that belies the property. We ate a light meal in the generous and packed dining room and I enjoyed a bottle of wine with dinner. Cheers! This was a magnificent little hotel.

On Friday May 31 we had breakfast and went in to town for a bit of sightseeing. My tee time at North Berwick (founded in 1832) today was 2:00 pm. About a mile off shore is Bass Rock. Gannets migrate here every year. The rock is known to be black in the winter but come spring and summer it is white. (Full of the large Gannet birds) There were many thousands of them on the rock today. Christy bought a ticket to take a tour boat out to the rock while I was playing golf. The shops in town were traditional touristy shops and I do not believe we spent much if any money. Christy and I eventually split up and I went to the car to grab my golf bag.

Our foursome at North Berwick happened to be four singles. The other three were all about forty years old. We seemed to all have similar games and it was a comfortable pairing. I did not have a caddy today so I went with a trolley. Two of my four-some had a caddy so I was able to glean a bit of information from them. I found North Berwick to be an excellent Links Course and I would rate it as one of my favorite courses ever played in Scotland or Ireland. There were a few holes with blind tee shots and they placed these large, tall 'lollipops' in the distance for directional help. Another peculiar hole was the 13th which has a three-foot stone wall fronting the green diagonally from left to right. It is said not to argue with the stone wall because it has been there longer than you. If you cannot get your ball air born, you are not getting to the green unless you knock it around croquet style until you find the four-foot wide opening the golfers use for arrival to the green. There were multiple places along the course for good photos and the Bass Rock was ever present in the distance. Earlier I mentioned Catriona Matthew. I have been a fan of hers for a long time. She has a home next to the 18th tee of North Berwick. She also captained the 2019 Solheim Cup team to victory at Gleneagles in Scotland. The 18th might have been my favorite hole though I enjoyed my birdie 2 at the 10th. The clubhouse is directly behind the 18th green and it was arranged for Christy to meet me there for a drink after my round. Walking up the 18th fairway is a beautiful sight with the clubhouse and the town in the distance. Christy was getting a head start in the clubhouse on the 2nd floor and saw me walking up the 18th. She said she could recognize me by the way I was walking. I get it. We had a couple of beers and Christy helped herself to my second Tennents beer glass. Cheers! My golf in Scotland on this trip was over and we headed toward the Edinburgh Airport to stay at the adjacent Hampton Inn. It was a nice new hotel with a good bar and restaurant and we could walk to the airport if we did not have a car to return. It was that convenient.

On Saturday June 1 we started the long journey home. It took two grueling hours to get through customs in DC. We did arrive home on schedule and I was there in time to watch the Bruins in Game 3 of The Stanley Cup Final. They won game three but eventually lost the Cup in seven games on home ice. It was a disappointing end to a great hockey season. I have cheered for The Blues occasionally over the years and even owned a Blues jersey once. It was their first championship in 53 years of trying and I thought, "good on them".

On September 2nd, Labor Day, I played golf at an Indianapolis city course I used to play many times as a young man but had not been there in 40 years. I had heard from some of my local golf community that the course was in great shape and one guy said it had the fastest greens in town. It had my interest. I made efforts to get guys there over the past year or two but it never happened. It happened today with my old golfing group. I played a solid round and had more greenside up and downs than I usually get in a round. I had three birdies which is at least two more than normal. My final tally at Pleasant Run Golf Course was 73, my all-time low score. It was the icing on top of a great year.

My 65th year was a beauty. When you can get Boston hockey and Scotland golf together in one year, there will be no complaints. It was nice having Christy with me on the trip.

66

9-19-2019 to 9-18-2020

September 19th, 2019. There comes a time in life when you can no longer deny that you are getting old, regardless of how well you feel or think you look. The birth certificate reveals the facts and today is that day. The twilight of life. With some luck, I am only in the late fall of life. Next month our government will make a deposit into our checking account simply for being an aged American who worked for a living. I decided to start collecting Social Security at 66. They do not pay that to young people. Like everyone who gets to this age I did the math and the answer came up, why wait? And they will deposit that amount every month as long as I or my spouse stay alive. I realize it is my money to start with. People are concerned about the future financial stability of Social Security. Can it sustain itself? Politicians don't seem to want to touch the issue. I swear I could fix it in no time at all. Another oddity of late that I have noticed is young and middle-aged men sometimes open the door for me, or allow me to enter a building first. What the hell? I'm reasonably fit, walk upright, and have most of my brown hair. Other people are seeing something in me that I have yet to recognize.

A week later I was in South Bend to play the Warren Golf Course at Notre Dame. There is a contractor up there that I met a few years ago and we have played every year for the past four years. I arranged for him to play with me today. He is about a five handicap. I have never beaten him and he is fun to play with. I beat him this day and broke 80 at the Warren for the first time with a sizzling 75. I had three birdies on the round and an unfortunate but not unaccustomed three 3 putts. I shot 73 earlier in the month at an Indy city course but this 75 I say is the best round of golf in my life. I handily beat my friend Jeff and he was impressed. I was impressed.

A week after that I was at Notre Dame again. This time with brothers Mike and Brian and my nephew Steve, Mike's son. We drove up to watch the Irish play football against Virginia. We received the tickets free from our cousin Patty Kavanaugh who lives in Chicago. I do not know where she got the tickets but it was nice of her to think of us and the seats were excellent. We arrived early and took in a bit of the campus. We watched the marching band come into the stadium which was nice to see. Brian stole (borrowed) a flugelhorn for our group photo with the golden dome in the distance. Seeing a game on Notre Dame's campus is more than just about football. It is truly an experience. Virginia led 17-14 at half and had some talented, speedy players. A strong second half by the Irish secured a 35-20 win. We had a swell time.

On November 2nd, a well-planned mini family reunion trip to Ft. Wayne, In. organized by myself and our cousin Michelle took place amongst the Indianapolis Kavanaugh's and our cousins, the Ft. Wayne Early's. All four of the Early's were there with their spouses and six of the Kavanaugh siblings made the trip including Mike, Tim, Kevin, Brian, Mary, and myself. All our spouses were also present and my daughter Christy and my granddaughter Abby also joined us. The Early's are the children of our moms' youngest brother Richard and we do not see them as often as we would like. They are good company. The truth is everyone is busy with growing families and it is difficult to arrange. We met at Salvatori's Restaurant in Ft. Wayne for lunch and had a relaxing and delightful time. I believe it had been five years since we last met up together. The day turned out perfect.

The following day on November 3rd, our newest granddaughter Kennedy was baptized at Christ the King Church in Indianapolis. She is the daughter of my son John. The event following Mass included three baptisms. All the families of the baptized children had front row seats reserved in each of the three sections of the Church. Kennedy's entourage included twelve people. The family to our right must have had at least 50 in attendance. Again, to their right was a family with about forty. It was a nice event and Kennedy was the only baby of the three that behaved for the entire event.

On November 13th, the impeachment of President Trump began in earnest and it was finished off in record time by a partisan Democrat vote on December 19th. That same December day, Ginger and I took my son Jason, his wife Casey and their girls Kaley and Kinsley downtown for dinner and the annual Yuletide Celebration in downtown Indianapolis at the Hilbert Center. Yuletide is an annual Christmas holiday song and dance event presented by the Indianapolis Symphony Orchestra complete with dancing Santa's. Dinner before the show was enjoyed at Iaria's Italian Restaurant. The famous restaurant has been serving fine Italian food at the same location in Indy since 1933. This Yuletide / dinner event has become somewhat tradition in recent years. Our seats were three rows from the front. When the host hit the stage in front of us, he immediately pointed, smiled, and waved at our young 5-year-old granddaughter Kinsley. Her eyes lit up and she had a huge smile. It was worth the price of admission and made my night.

The next evening some of my old classmates got together for a bit of holiday cheer. This has also become somewhat of an annual event in recent years but unfortunately, we never get too big of a crowd. The ones that do show up (the usual suspects) always have a good evening. Tonight's faithful attendees other than myself was Debbie Mitchell nee Chandler, Tim O'Brian, Mike Bussell, Rita Welch, and Bob Krueger. Molly Akard nee O'Hara made a surprise visit tonight and I always enjoy seeing my friend Molly. We go all the way back to grade school. Also arriving fashionably late was Suzanne Teegarden nee Epaves. An enjoyable evening at Flynn's Restaurant was had by all.

Christmas traditions in our household have also included Christmas dinner at an upscale restaurant since the early 2000's. Usually planned for the 23rd or 24th with my wife Ginger and our immediate family. With a restless two-year old grandson this year and his 5-month-old sister, it was thought best to do it as a luncheon this season. We celebrated our Christmas lunch this year on December

21st which happened to be granddaughter Kaley's 12th birthday. We dined at Maggiano's and the timing, location, and meal worked to everyone's benefit. Kaley was showered with a few birthday gifts. It almost seems unfair to have a birthday so close to the big holiday but Jason and Casey always see that Kaley has her special day.

The Kavanaugh family Christmas dinner this year was again hosted by brother Patrick. It has only been six years since he last hosted but a few years back, he swapped dates with sister Mary and now we are back on the correct rotation. Santa Claus was making his 17th straight appearance at the Kavanaugh Christmas jubilee. The first time Santa showed up was at Pat's house when he lived nearer to downtown Indy back in 2003. Santa has arrived in different outfits and with various facial disguises over the years. The disguises could not fool all of them. Santa has also brought in some accomplices over the years including The Elf, The Grinch, and one year a sexy female Santa helper. There was a rumor this year that this might be Santa's last hurrah. Maybe he was getting too old or maybe the family had grown too much. The gift theme this year seemed to be U.S.A. sports as Santa's bag was full of red, white, and blue balls for a variety of sports. Footballs, basketballs, kickballs, and soccer balls. As usual, the entire affair was well done and enjoyed by all. Gifts for other lucky recipients always seemed to find their way into Santa's bag. Santa started this gift giving jubilee at Pat's house and 16 years later it will end here as well. This was indeed this version of Santa's last visit.

Christmas morning at our house was like previous years, breakfast with the kids and grandkids. There was not as much under the tree this year. Christy got a plane ticket to Ireland. John and Rebecca got a swing set for the kids to be delivered to their home in the spring. Jason and Casey received another trip to Boston to see the Bruins. The hockey schedule did us no favors this year so they were only able to see one game. You used to be able to bank on the Bruins home on Thursday night with a Saturday matinee. It seems added teams to the league have made scheduling a bigger challenge and less predictable. They did get to see the Bruins play their 2nd favorite team. Possibly favorite for Casey. The Pittsburgh Penguins with Sid

Crosby and Evgeny Malkin. Due to my own scheduling conflicts, I would not join them on this trip. When I made the arrangements, I prayed the weather would cooperate. We have had weather issues with winter travel in the past.

My favorite gift under our tree was a pair of CCM hockey skates for our 2 ½ year old grandson James. My boys started skating between three and four years old but I thought Master James just might be ready. Two days after Christmas we took James to the rink. He had no problem standing up on his skates in the lobby. He walked around with them on like he was born to wear skates. But I have no miracle to tell you about. He struggled on the ice and never did get in a hands-free stride. He was able to move about with adult hand in clutch or slowly pushing a traffic cone. I had no doubt with continued efforts he would be skating proudly in no time. Four years later at six years old he would sign up for his first hockey season.

Sports champions in 2019 were New England's Patriots once again in football. The St. Louis Blues broke my heart beating the Boston Bruins in seven games for the Stanley Cup. The Toronto Raptors won the NBA crown and the Washington Nationals won the World Series. In golf, Tiger Woods resurrected his game enough to fend off Xander Schauffele, Brooks Koepka, and Dustin Johnson all by one stroke to win the Masters. It was Tigers' first Major since 2008. Irishman Shane Lowry won the British Open at Portrush in Northern Ireland and had a proper celebration later that day in a bar singing 'Fields of Athenry' with the jubilant hometown crowd. I have since fallen in love with the Irish anthem and somewhat sad song. The best movie (for me) in 2019 was Ford vs Ferrari with Matt Damon and Christian Bale.

Most of us celebrate the incoming new year. Today, Jan 1st, 2020 would be no different. But today no one could forecast the hell coming our way in the year ahead.

On Wednesday January 15th, Jason and Casey departed for their Boston trip to see the Bruins play on Thursday evening at the Boston Garden. It had been a mild Indianapolis winter to this point. In fact, it hit sixty degrees on Christmas Day. As it turned out, weather on the 15th was perfect for flying. The kids had a great time visiting their favorite pubs and the game was terrific. One of their favorite players, Sidney Crosby of the Penguins had missed the two previous months due to injury but returned to the lineup just the game before at a Pittsburgh home game. In the Garden on the 16th, Sid opened the scoring: 24 seconds into the game. It looked like it could be a long night as the strong Bruin team was facing the hottest team in the league over the previous six weeks. The Bruins potted two goals themselves in Period 1 with much needed help from the 2nd and 3rd lines. There was no scoring in Period 2 but there was a nice fight involving two non-traditional fighters. Boston's Torey Krug vs Patric Hornqvist. The home crowd was delighted. In Period 3, superstar Patrice Bergeron scored an insurance goal as the B's went up 3-1 and Brad Marchand popped in an empty netter from Pastrnak to seal the deal and fill the streets and bars with happy Bruin fans. The final score was 4-1. All four Bruin goals were scored on the end of the ice that Jason and Casey were sitting. I must say that I got as much enjoyment knowing how much fun they had, as if I was on the trip with them.

During their trip, on January 15th House Speaker Nancy Pelosi finally found the courage to deliver the Houses' Articles of Impeachment to the Senate. This 'urgent matter of National Security,' an emergency according to Speaker Pelosi, only took a little less than a month to move the business on to the Senate. I felt safer immediately. On February 5th, the day after Speaker Pelosi deliberately and disrespectfully tore President Trump's State of the Union speech in half on national TV standing behind the President, the Senate acquitted President Trump.

Earlier this winter, brother Kevin invited me down to his place in Naples to join him for an annual golf tournament held at his club, Tiburon. I accepted with pleasure. The tournament ran from March 12-14, 2020. I have never played in an 'Official' tournament in my life so I thought I might be a bit nervous. I finished off last season strong with my all-time low score and another round I consider the best of my life. My handicap was at an all-time low and I went into the tournament with no recent rounds under my belt. Winter up north had been mild so I was able to hit a few buckets of balls for practice. I flew down to Kevin and his wife Yolanda's place on March 11th. The format for the event worked like this: We would play a two-man best ball with handicap against another two-man team. There were six two-man teams in each flight and we were placed in flight three of six. After an 18-hole practice round, you played against each team in your flight in a 9-hole match. The first 9-hole match was played on Thursday the 12th following our 18-hole practice round. There would be two additional 9-hole matches on Friday and Saturday with a huge spread for lunch served in between rounds, drinks included. Kevin and I matched our outfits for Friday's play. We both wore black slacks with a yellow Boston Bruin polo. We were easily the best dressed two-ball. We got waxed pretty good in a couple of matches but the other three were very competitive. I played solid enough golf from tee to green but the greens confused me all week. I never could get the speed of the greens down. I do not think I did a good job reading the grain, which on Bermuda greens is very important. I would run 30 and 40-foot putts ten feet long. Twice, I putted my ball off the green. That just never happens up north on bent grass greens. I **was** able to squeeze out a win on a closest to the pin hole. That earned me a nice gift card to the pro shop. We had very comfortable pairings in every match. It seems like we played against a lot of folks from the Boston area which is where Kevin makes his living. I am a big Boston sports fan so things were very comfortable with our opponents. One of the fellows in our last match was from Scotland and was a member at a course I played last spring. We exchanged contact information and he welcomed me to his North Berwick Club the next time I am overseas. I must say all the participants I met were very friendly and The Tiburon staff was outstanding, insuring all a good time.

Every player in the tournament was a big winner. As part of the event, besides lunches being served with drinks, dinner was also served each night. One night as part of dinner they had an open Bourbon Bar and a gentleman hand rolling cigars for our relaxing pleasure. Each player received a $200 gift card to the Pro Shop with merchandise discounted at 30%. Also, each player received a nice Calloway sand wedge. There was some grumbling about not having enough left-handed wedges such as the type my brother Kevin would need. I did notice an inordinate number of lefties in our flight. Friday evening, we skipped dinner at the club as I wanted to host Kevin and Yolanda in town for a meal. We ate at The City Dock in Naples. I also skipped the final banquet meal on Saturday evening as I headed home a very fortunate man. This event was as first class as they come.

The End of Liberty and the Pursuit of Happiness?

That is the way I interpreted it shortly after it all went down. On Thursday evening March 12th while I was in Naples, Fl., President Trump gave his Coronavirus speech. Coronavirus or COVID-19 was a new virus detected that had its origins in Wuhan, China and had turned into a worldwide pandemic. It did not put a pall on our golf event but it sure messed up life for everyone with a life in the foreseeable future. The PGA 'Players' professional golf tournament at TPC Sawgrass which played its first round on March 12th in northeast Florida was immediately cancelled and the dominos fell into place. No NBA, no NHL, no PGA Golf, Spring Training baseball halted, no restaurants or movie theaters. Life in general was coming to a screeching halt. This was coast to coast. The President called it a national emergency. Churches were shuttered, as well as schools from Kindergarten through University. Besides schools now being closed, all school sports, proms, and graduations were cancelled. International travel was cancelled which affected an upcoming trip of mine. Eventually, The Masters golf tournament was cancelled and the Indy 500. Life was over as we knew it. Or was it just freedom taking a hiatus? Any way you look at it, the pursuit of unlimited happiness was no longer an option. How could this happen in America? I was certain the liberal leftists would come out quickly to protest but I soon realized I read the situation wrong. Maybe the good citizens of New Hampshire would take a stand. Afterall, their state motto is, "Live Free or Die." But no, they were mute.

The new words in our daily vocabulary were Coronavirus, COVID-19, mitigation, masks, Zoom, shelter in place, and social distancing. Handshakes and high fives would become a thing of the past, replaced with fist pumps and elbow bumps. Plexiglas went up at every cash register in the country to safely separate workers from customers at grocery stores. Indiana, like most states, shuttered restaurants, and bars. Indiana's Governor Holcomb came out on March 23rd to shut everything else down. Work was all done from home, if you were lucky enough to keep your job. Unemployment soared during the next months.

It did not take long for Coronavirus to be christened with a middle name at my house. The same middle name that NY Yankees' Bucky Dent and Aaron Boone earned years ago. With all bars and restaurants closed due to the national virus shutdown, all traditional St. Patrick's Day celebrations were canceled. A group of family members headed over to brother Tim's house to enjoy a minor St Pat's celebration. Tim and his wife Noreen, brother Mike and wife Linda, brother Brian and wife Robin, sister Mary and husband Tony, and myself enjoyed some beer and light snacks during a sort of St. Patrick's Day light festivity.

I was against the country's Coronavirus lockdown measures of safety from the very beginning. We have had many viruses and illnesses over the past century without shutting the economy down. If you looked at past viruses or had any idea how many people die every day from various maladies, I believe I could convince you how overboard our government had gone. And the longer it went, the more I felt I was right. As a nation we have been through many diseases over the decades. Typhoid Fever, Smallpox, Asian Flu, Whooping Cough, Polio, Measles, Ebola, SARS, AIDS, and others. No shutdowns, forge ahead. Find a cure or vaccine and forge ahead. In 1968–69 there was a pandemic called the Hong Kong flu. Over 100,000 Americans died and over 1 million worldwide. No shutdowns. After three years we would eclipse the one million dead mark in the U.S. from or with Covid-19 but there is also an additional 125 million of us in the U.S. today. I do not know how many of those deaths were from the virus alone. It attacked the aged the most and people with comorbidities. The average age of people who died from the virus was 78 years old. Many of these people also had underlying conditions. Leave the rest of us to live our lives. What happened to personal responsibility? More people were dying from other issues during this same period led by smoking and heart disease.

Did I believe there was a virus? Yes. Did I believe people were dying from the virus? Yes. But the percentages were extremely small. I believed after a couple months that even Trump, in his private moments, was sorry he declared the national emergency. He may have panicked or listened to the wrong advice, and everyone fell in line. And even Trump eventually said the cure cannot be worse than the symptom. But it was. And for how long? States' Governors took Trumps lead on lockdowns and some seemed to enjoy their newfound power. If a Governor did not go far enough, a mayor might step in to put his or her own stamp of lockdown on his or her city. Every afternoon at approximately 5:00 pm, President Trump would address the nation with a Coronavirus update. This continued for many weeks. He was accompanied by the country's top infectious disease doctors, Anthony Fauci and Deborah Birx. Dr. Fauci was the most pessimistic and depressing man I have ever heard speak in my life. It sure seemed to me he enjoyed people's misery. He also enjoyed his new found stardom. I feel certain President Trump also regretted introducing the nation to Dr. Fauci. After four to six weeks of what originally was intended to be a two-week mitigation or lockdown, the protestors finally came out. It was mostly the conservative groups that were protesting. The liberal news media was aghast that the protestors were not social distancing and some were not wearing protective masks.

How to catch Coronavirus or how to avoid it changed weekly. At first Doctor Fauci said you should not wear a mask unless you have the disease. Later, everyone should wear a mask. At first you should stay indoors. Later, fresh air was good for you. It was thought

Coronavirus would die out in the heat of summer but it was starting to spread in Florida and temperatures were in their normal mid-eighties there. There was other conflicting news about COVID depending on the week. My feelings were simple. If you are sick, stay home. If you have immune deficiencies, which we were told COVID thrived upon, stay home. If you are just scared, stay home. The biggest difference between this pandemic and the Hong Kong flu of '68–'69 was our 24-hour news cycle and endless availability of information on cable news and I-phones. By the end of the summer, if no one ever told you about Coronavirus, you would never have heard of Coronavirus. Because I never knew anyone who had Coronavirus.

I found ways to keep busy during the initial periods of lockdown. Work was all done by phone and email. My employer instituted daily 3:00 pm educational zoom calls which became a welcome diversion. During the early days of the lockdown, I read a couple of books. 'Three Days in Moscow' was a good read about Ronald Reagan. Then I read a book called 'The Carnoustie Story' by Donald Ford about Carnoustie Golf Club in Scotland which was quite interesting.

In early May our Indiana Governor Holcomb put out a five-stage plan to reopen the State. Before this we always heard about the light at the end of the tunnel. Meanwhile, I was still looking for the tunnel. His five-stage plan did give me hope. Things would open slowly and we would plan to be back to normal by July 4th. I thought we could all live with that. For now, we looked like China with many if not most people walking around with masks on. I never could figure out what people were so afraid of while walking around outdoors. It appeared that cities and states run by liberals were enjoying the lockdowns the most. They thought it made President Trump look bad and it gave them power. Somehow, it really did turn into a political virus. Blue states suffered with strict lockdowns. Red states opened as safely as possible and many of them thrived. The Democrat Governor in Michigan may have been the worst but that was a hotly contested title. She would not allow people to buy gardening supplies or mow their lawns. No boats were allowed on the water for fishing. In many states people were not allowed to play tennis because you had to touch tennis balls that had been in others' hands. Recreational golf was spared in most states but they would not allow rakes in bunkers. The flagstick had to be left in the hole. There was no flagstick-tending. Styrofoam or some other gadget was installed in the cup so you did not have to put your hand in the hole. There was no 'drinking water' on the course and everyone had to either walk or take a cart on their own. Explain to me how that is protecting my health? Just kidding, save it. We had officially lost our minds. Stupidity and lack of common sense had no bounds.

As things were becoming relatively tolerable in Indiana, on May 25th a killing took place in Minneapolis that set us back to the riots of the 6ixties. A police officer, Derek Chauvin, with three cop accomplices, allegedly suffocated a black man named George Floyd to death by holding him to the pavement with a knee on his neck. It was seen on national TV as there are cameras everywhere these days. It was one of the most disgusting things I had ever seen. The death was blamed on a drug overdose by some. Minnesota fired the officers immediately but it took three days for them to arrest the lead cop, and another week to charge his cohorts. It took one day for the riots to start. First in Minneapolis and then in nearly every large city in the country. Atlanta, New York, L.A., Louisville, Seattle, Miami, Oakland, Denver, and even at home in Indianapolis. All the protesters wanted Justice for George. Anarchy was on the move led by BLM or Black Lives Matter. I was not old enough in the 6ixties to care about the riots or to pay much attention to them, but I watched these on TV and they went on night after night after night. It was 1968 all over again, only the participants were different. I suppose every generation must experience this mayhem for themselves. Some news people referred to them as peaceful protests. But as I watched, I saw mostly riots. Was everyone rioting? No. In my mind when protesters are cheering on the rioters and watching to see what is going to happen next, and taking video, those people are rioters. Protests typically include marching with signs and chanting slogans. There is normally a goal in mind, some demands you are seeking from authority or government. You start from one designated area to another designated area and then listen to a speech or two. This was not that. This was downtown windows and stores being destroyed with bricks and fires. Store after store being looted. It was five finger discount day in many cities. Cop cars were set ablaze. It was happening in dozens of cities from coast to coast. And make no mistake, these rioters were having a very good time. To make matters about as intolerable as they could be, the mayors, the people in charge, allowed it to happen. The cops were basically told to stand down, unlike Chicago during the 1968 Democrat National Convention. Anarchy was the flavor of the day. I believe it is safe to say that every city being demolished had one common theme. They were run by liberals. But why allow this in your city?

When the hundreds of right-wing protestors came out against the continued lockdowns, you would hear complaints from the main stream media about lack of masking and social distancing. When the thousands came out in cities across America for the George Floyd protests, (riots) no one said a word about social distancing. In fact, I heard this remark on the news, "social injustice matters more than social distancing." Some of the rioters wore masks but it was not to protect them and their neighbor from a virus but to protect their identity from the authority. I wondered how the Floyd protests being in the middle of many weeks of lockdowns and the weather turning nice did not help bring more people out. They were mad about more than Floyd, a man none of them knew.

Early on the protesters (rioters) demanded "Justice for George." But when the arrests of the police officers were made, that was not enough. They wanted a conviction. Convictions take months. How long would this one take? The trial did not begin until late March of the following year. If the conviction is not what the protesters want, or heaven forbid the killer(s) is exonerated, batten the hatches. Mercifully, Officer Chauvin was found guilty of all charges ten months after the incident and long after the destruction of countless properties.

During a St. Louis protest, (riot) an older black cop, Captain Dorn, was murdered by gunshot and lay dead in the middle of the street. No one wanted any justice for that poor guy. And no memorial was forthcoming for Dorn like the three memorials for Mr. Floyd. Murders of black men only mattered if they met a political narrative of the left. Officer Dorn did not meet the criteria. He was a cop first. Eventually cities were being placed under curfew to quell the evening mayhem but protesters found that as a minor inconvenience in many places. Much of the country was coming out of a lockdown, some states still in lockdown mode, and then some had to put up with a curfew. That Freedom thing had a good run but it was being tested like never before. Again, that is the way I saw it. And three months into the virus ordeal, there was not one person I knew that contracted the virus. That was great but I believe it showed how overboard we had gone. As all this was going on from March 12th, there was a Presidential election coming up in November but it was hardly talked about in the news.

May 29th was the day my daughter Christy and I were scheduled to leave for Dublin, Ireland. Of course, my critically acclaimed and finely tuned plans were not to be. If there is a piece of good news, it is I did receive a full refund for airline tickets, golf, and hotel deposits. I wrote Christy a check for her airfare as it was part of her 2019 Christmas gift. The parties responsible for the cancellation will never be forgiven. I, like 'Pai Mei', was what you might call, inconsolable. The pursuit of happiness depends on many things and two of them are Freedom, and Law & Order. We had limited amounts of both.

The George Floyd show seemed to be a never-ending news event. It was not going away. Cities began calling to defund the police. Wouldn't that be nice? Eliminating police forces would be the end of a humane society as we know it. As Warden Norton told Andy Dufresne in 'The Shawshank Redemption,' "there's only three ways to spend the taxpayer's hard-earned money when it comes to prisons. More walls, more bars, more guards." That is exactly what I felt we needed. Finally, on Tuesday June 9th, George Floyd was laid to rest near his mother in Houston, Tx. The funeral and procession were broadcast on nearly every TV station. The procession looked like a page out of 'Tay Bridge.'

Another period of tearing down Confederate statues took place all over the country. After the 2015 demolitions, I did not know there were any left. It was an orgy of destruction the likes we have never seen. No public or private property was safe. It got to the point where the vandals did not even know what they were mad about. A statue of Ulysses S Grant was toppled down. The man won the civil war for the Union which in turn freed the slaves. Even statues of Abraham Lincoln were not safe. This man was the great emancipator. He should be a hero to all. The mob appeared to do whatever someone told them to do. The anarchists reminded me of a conversation between Wyatt Earp and the dying Doc Holliday in the movie Tombstone as they were discussing the ill-tempered Johnny Ringo.

> Wyatt: "What makes a man like Ringo, Doc, what makes him do the things he does?"
> Doc: "A man like Ringo got a great empty hole right through the middle of him. He can never kill enough, or steal enough, or inflict enough pain to ever fill it."
> Wyatt: "What does he need?"
> Doc: "Revenge"
> Wyatt: "For what?"
> Doc: "Being born."

That is what the rioters wanted without even knowing it. Revenge for being born.

House Speaker Nancy Pelosi got busy having pictures taken off the House walls of Speakers from bygone eras who were known to have connections with the Confederacy. History and its people were not safe. Politicians with a D in front of their name seemed to be safe. R was the new 'Scarlet Letter'. Being a Democrat means never having to say you are sorry. I call it 'Liberal Privilege.' It got so bad that the left now went after food product. Logos from Aunt Jemima pancake goods, Mrs. Butterworth's syrups, Land O Lakes butter, and Uncle

Ben's rice were destined for the ash bin. They have been around since I have been around but suddenly, they're deemed racist? Also attacked was the great film Gone with the Wind. The Washington Redskins football team was forced to change their teams' name. Eventually, Dr. Seuss children's books were under attack. Mr. Potato Head lost his masculinity and became a gender-neutral potato toy.

The late Kate Smith, known as the Songbird of the South, an advocate of racial tolerance, and famous for her rendition of God Bless America has been cancelled. Since 911 her rendition of God Bless America was played at New York Yankee games during the seventh inning stretch. No more. Kate, who famously sang God Bless America in lieu of our National Anthem at Philadelphia Flyer playoff games during their Broad Street Bully days had a statue erected in her honor outside the Philadelphia Spectrum. Now, gone. Liberals were on a warpath of cancel culture. No, I really did not understand. Nothing remotely associated with race or gender was safe today. Even our nation's flag which all children used to pledge allegiance to in my grade school days is now deemed a racist or white supremacy symbol by some. This can only fracture race relations more in my opinion. I believe that before President Obama took office we were as close as we had ever been or might ever be to being a color-blind society. However, it seems to not be in some politicians' best interest to allow you to believe that measured racial progress had been achieved. It could cost them an election. Racial division or the appearance of it must continue for the benefit of perpetual political gains of the left, while masking a high level of contempt for it.

During this entire period of anarchy, the standard bearer of the Democrat Party and presumptive Presidential nominee of their party was mute. Hiding in his basement doing his Claude Rains imitation because he cannot string two sentences together without fouling up. He had no ideas of his own. People deserved to know Joe Biden's thoughts.

A new mid-summer surge of Coronavirus came mostly from southern States. Florida, Texas, Arizona, and Southern California were growing their Coronavirus cases. So much for the early thought that the heat of summer would put the virus in recession. It was thought at one time that our youth would lead us out of the problem but the millennials were now being blamed for its spread. Meanwhile, Sweden who went the herd immunity route was nearly clear of the virus. Yes, they have a much smaller population but I liked their game plan.

On July 6th a man I have never met died (not of Coronavirus) who has given me so much pleasure over the years. I started enjoying his work in the 6ixties though at the time I had no idea who he was nor did I care. His name is Ennio Morricone. He is the great Italian composer and conductor for many scores on movies. He was a mainstay on Clint Eastwood spaghetti westerns such as Fistful of Dollars, For a Few Dollars More, and The Good, The Bad, & The Ugly. All movies I love. He worked with Quentin Tarantino on The Hateful Eight, Kill Bill, and Django Unchained. I love these movies and the score and soundtrack are integral parts of these movies' enjoyment. In 2007 Mr. Morricone received an honorary Oscar for his contributions to the art of film music. In 2016 he received the Oscar for his score on Tarantino's Hateful Eight. Ennio is now gone but his music will live forever. I am certain we will hear his music in future movies, TV shows, and TV commercials.

A week later, long-time Congressman, civil rights leader, and friend of Martin Luther King Jr., John Lewis died at the age of 80. This was a great man of bravery, courage, and commitment. He was in the middle of the fray as a young man back in the 6ixties on the Edmund Pettus bridge in Selma, Alabama. He became the first black man to lie in State at the Capitol Rotunda. He had a great funeral held at Ebenezer Baptist Church in Atlanta, Georgia. The same church where Martin Luther King Jr. was a pastor. Three President's attended and spoke at the funeral. President's Clinton, Bush 43, and Obama. President Obama's speech became more political than a eulogy. He continued to stoke the fires of racial division in this country. Mr. Lewis and America deserved better.

On July 27th, Indiana took a step back from the Governor's 5 stage plan to reopen the economy by mandating masks again throughout the state. Governor Holcomb called it stage 4.5. The light I was searching for at the end of the tunnel in May was now closing tighter than a sphincter muscle. No light, no tunnel, no hope. Meanwhile, nightly protests in Portland, Oregon had reached 60 days and counting. Did the Portland mayor even consider a curfew? No way. These liberals enjoyed seeing properties destroyed. I never understood why.

The PGA tour was now back on TV for its 8th straight week without fan attendance. As one who watches a lot of golf on TV, lack of fan attendance made no difference to me. The game is the same. It was good watching golf again. Baseball, basketball, and hockey were all making a comeback. Baseball did have issues as the Florida Marlins team found about 15 team members who contracted the virus after a mere two games. This caused cancellations not only by the Marlins club but by the team that was supposed to play where the Marlins just were. Other teams such as St. Louis were also having Covid issues. Basketball and hockey seemed to be having success playing in their 'bubbles.' All games were being played in just a couple locations and teams were staying together with no travel. Of course, there were no fans at these games. I was not convinced any of these leagues would finish what they started, but they did. Fall football did not seem possible with fans and doubtful without fans. In August it was announced that the Big 10 was cancelling football for the season. The Pac-10 soon followed. It would only be a matter of time before other conferences followed suit. However, President Trump stepped in and convinced league commissioner's that the games could be safely played. Eventually, we had some college football and the NFL season went mostly unscathed but without fans in most stadiums.

Playing golf and now watching golf and playoff hockey on TV was the only normal thing going on in my life at this time. Thank God for my weekly golf games. I did not seem to be playing my best golf this year but I always looked forward to getting out. Seems like something had changed in my game and it just might be that age is catching up with me. Or my desire for improvement through change was not paying the dividends I hoped for. I had certainly lost my consistency.

In early August it was announced that Indiana hit a daily record high for Coronavirus cases. That was a real headscratcher. In April very few people were wearing masks and cases were light but worrisome to those in charge. In May and June more people were wearing masks voluntarily and cases were slowly rising. By July most stores would not allow anyone to enter without a mask. In late July Indiana's Governor announced that masks were mandatory in all indoor public spaces, except when you were eating or drinking. By late July you were hard pressed to go anywhere without seeing everyone masked up. Now here we are in August, virtually the entire population muzzled up like a character out of a Bazooka Joe comic strip and cases are hitting an all-time high. Something is clearly not measuring up. Should we not at least question whether masks work? I did. And I still knew no one with the virus. That would change in six months.

I mentioned earlier that there was a Presidential election going on. It was hard to know because the Democrat candidate, Joe Biden, seldom came out of his basement to speak. He campaigned less than the great General of the 6ixties. The eighteen 6ixties. Ulysses S Grant was known as a light campaigner. But today Biden announced his VP running mate. He did not come out and announce his selection with the usual fanfare this type of news deserves. He simply put out a memo. His selection was Kamala Harris, junior Senator from California. Kamala is female, born to an Indian mother and Jamaican father yet she identifies as African-American. Yes, these days you can identify as whatever you like. A full fifty-seven years after the black leader Martin Luther King Jr. dreamed of a day where his people would be judged by the content of their character and not by the color of their skin, Kamala Harris was selected on two qualifications. She was female and she was a person of color. She may have been fully qualified but Biden had announced long ago that he would select a female of color. I do not think that is what Marin Luther King Jr. had in mind. Still, it is a step forward.

In late August, one more police shooting of a black man in Kenosha, Wisconsin took place. What in the hell is going on? Jacob Blake was shot in the back seven times at point blank range. He survived his injuries but with crippling results. I would think pointing a loaded pistol at an unarmed suspect would be enough to quiet a disturbance. But no. It was thought Jacob was reaching for or had a knife on his possession or in his vehicle. Unless he's Ed Ames, (Mingo) who famously displayed his talents as an axe thrower on the Tonight Show in 1965, I believe the man holding a pistol would always have a superior advantage, without firing the weapon. Something very wrong was going on. I will not call it racism, but I will certainly call it wrong. That brings police shootings of black people to at least four this year that have been in the national spotlight, causing disruption of normal life. Other shootings not previously mentioned included Breonna Taylor in Louisville and Rayshard Brooks in Atlanta. I continually prayed for normalcy of life but it did not seem within reach. Kenosha, with the help of Black Lives Matter, was looted and burned for days. During the Kenosha riots, two men lost their lives to gunfire. Fifteen months later, the shooter was found not guilty on all charges due to self-defense. I had an issue either with the verdict, or the charges brought up.

On the last day of my 66th year. Supreme Court Associate Justice Ruth Bader Ginsburg died at the age of 87. Justice Ginsburg served on the high court for 27 years and was an advocate of gender equality and women's rights. With a national election only six weeks away, the battle was on to replace her seat before the election.

And then there was one. On this same day, September 18th, 2020 my oldest brother Michael retired from his forty-nine years of work in the plumbing industry. His retirement announcement and letter to his customers and industry friends was an achievement in first class farewells. This industry has been in our family since before I was born. My grandfather, father, mother, and all my seven siblings have taken a turn at earning a paycheck from the industry that 'Protects the Health of the Nation.' Many of us at the same time and place. This business of plumbing, plumbing supplies, and plumbing manufacturing, was pivotal in raising all of us and our descendants up a notch or two on the socio-economic scale. As a full-time employee at Mueller Industries, I am the last to be privileged to work in such a fine industry.

The age of 66 came in with as much promise as any year since my upper teens. Life was comfortable. Whatever my heart desired was within reach. We added a granddaughter to the family. Everyone in our family was seemingly healthy. My golf game was in decent shape. My sports team was winning. Three things changed it all.

> One – President Trump's speech on March 12th, 2020
> about Coronavirus.
> Two – George Floyds murder on May 25th.
> Three – Recent news learned that my wife Ginger
> was diagnosed with Parkinson's.

I never considered things could go so bad so fast as what transpired this year. Not in a country as great as the United States. Unfortunately, I did not see year 67 starting out much better. We were still all wearing masks that did not appear to be improving anything. I feel like I had visited the threshold of hell and I did not like it one bit. Most businesses in Indiana were open now but with onerous restrictions. There were still quarantines in place for international travel and even for some travel within our own borders. I was amazed at how nonchalantly many people seemed to take the new restrictions. It was like asking for a Coke in a restaurant and they tell you they have Pepsi products. The response usually being, "that'd be fine." The restrictions we were living under were much more serious than Coke vs. Pepsi. I had concluded it was not our safety the politicians were trying to protect. It was our Freedom they were trying to revoke. It was a political power play and my opponent was winning. Again, that is the way I saw it.

60 – John and Marty ready for the Old Course

63 – Marty centering sons and nephews, L-R Zack, Jason, John, Steve, Brandon, and Danny at Kavanaugh family Christmas

64 – Calgary bar before game

64 – Kevin, Tim, Mike, & 81 at Old Head

65 – Kevin, Marty, Tim, & Mike admiring the results from our Ireland golf trip. Christmas party 2018

65 – Christy and Marty on Swilcan Bridge, St Andrews

66 – Marty, Brian, (with flugelhorn) Mike,
and Steve prior to Notre Dame game

67 – Christy and I at Dunluce Castle, Northern Ireland

68 – Kinsley feels the excitement only Mickey can bring

68 – Christmas Day 2021. Sitting – James, Kennedy, Kinsley, Ginger. Standing – John, Casey, Kaley, Jason, Christy, Abby, Marty

68 – Hristo & Marty entering the Bear Trap. PGA National

65 – 18th hole at Carnoustie

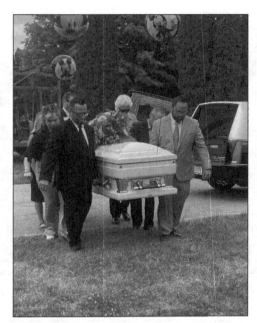

69 – John & Jason lead Mom's final walk

Christmas 2022. The Contest. John, Jason, and Abby

69 – Marty pointing to Lucy in the Sky for John

69 – Marty at young Tom Morris gravesite

67

9-19-2020 to 9-18-2021

It is Saturday, September 19th, 2020. I am 67 years old today. It really is hard to believe. Sometimes I may feel like it but do I act like it? The jury is deliberating. I basically did very little on this day and it was everything I thought it could be. The Virus had cancelled the US Open golf tournament in June and was re-scheduled to be played on this weekend. I watched a lot of golf on TV and the Stanley Cup Final started tonight between Dallas and Tampa. US Open golf and the Stanley Cup Final on my birthday. That was a great way to spend a birthday and I hope it never happens again under these conditions. I will figure out a way to make the most of this Covid affected year and it is going to start out strong.

I am playing in a three-day golf outing in northern Indiana beginning Tuesday September 22nd with my brother Michael and a group from our Sunday golf league. The group of four to twelve golfers on any given day of the four-day trip stay in a home on beautiful Lake George which straddles Northern Indiana and Southern Michigan. I have been on this trip a few times before and I have always chosen to stay at a nearby hotel. The added privacy leaves more room for those staying at the house and gives me a better opportunity at a proper night's rest. On this particular year of the Covid, a couple other fellows also chose to stay at a hotel. I actually stayed at a bed & breakfast in Angola, In., which is within ten minutes of the lake house and very convenient.

The purpose of the trip is golf, fellowship, fun, food, & drink. I played golf on three of the four days of the trip playing different courses, all beautiful. This was my replacement for missing out on my golf trip to Northern Ireland back in May. Not exactly Portrush but we all had a great time and the weather was personally ordered by the Chamber of Commerce. I shot the exact same score on different courses each day. 83. And I thought I had lost my consistency. I hit some of the most spectacular shots of my golf year bu of course found my share of difficulties.

About a week prior to leaving for this trip I ran across an add on Facebook for Pinehurst Golf Resort in North Carolina. It has always been on my mind to play there some day so I filled out an itinerary just to see what more I could learn. It was not my intent to run off to Pinehurst but I wanted to stay on their mailing list for a future time I might go. Once you fill out a form like that, they are like a dog on a bone. A few days after filling out my faux itinerary with October dates, I received a call from the Pinehurst sales staff. I knew they had responded to me by email, but I had not read it yet. I told the caller I would look at the email and see what they had in mind and I would get back with them. On the way up to Lake George I decided to call Pinehurst back and look at a trip in earnest. During our conversation, I was told that their rates drop after October 29th and now they had my full attention. Who knew what might happen in 2021? We were about to embark on the 13th consecutive most important election for our country since I have been voting and Covid still held a stranglehold on many areas of the country. International travel continued to be at a standstill. At this point in my life, I had more money than time so I decided to pull the trigger and book a short two-night, two-day solo stay for early November. Included in the trip was a tee time on the famed Pinehurst #2. It is good to have things to look forward to.

On October 6th I went down to our Florida condo for a short 6ix day stay. Ginger stayed back home as she was not quite up to the travel. She has been battling Parkinson's and has had other health issues develop that would soon come to a head. After my return, my wife Ginger's medical issues were coming full force. She was scheduled to have brain surgery for a benign tumor. They called it a craniotomy and it sounded like no fun. The surgery was set for October 23rd. The kids knew what was going on but I did not tell any other family members until she was successfully out of surgery. They knew there were issues but had no idea to what extent. I did not want people calling her saying, "you'll be in our prayers," "I'll be thinking of you," or "good luck". In other words, I did not want to give her added reasons to worry or have concern. I believed it was the right decision as she showed superior bravery. After surgery was complete, the doctor called it a major success but she looked deathly. It was as sad a moment as I have had in my life since my dad died thirty-two years ago. The next day in ICU was not much better as she was talking gibberish. She slowly came out of the anesthesia but spent four nights in ICU. This was followed by an additional 4 nights in a regular hospital room and nearly 3 weeks in a rehab facility to work on physical and occupational rehabilitation. The doctors' original pre-surgery expectations were home by day four after surgery. It was not the only time a doctor would over promise and under deliver. Our daughter Christy spent two weeks in town during the hospitalization and I named her 'manager of family medical affairs.' I continued my duties as President in charge of finance, travel, and domestic concerns.

On October 26th, Justice Amy Coney Barrett was voted to the Supreme Court, replacing the recently deceased Justice Ginsburg. Amy is a female, Catholic, pro-life, conservative. That type of person is one of the liberals' worst nightmares. They don't understand how a person of that type can exist. Though her qualifications were unquestioned, and she went through the gauntlet of Senatorial interrogation without missing a beat, not a single partisan Democrat Senator could find the temerity to vote in the affirmative. She passed the Senate vote by the Republican majority in place. The ultra-liberal Ginsburg had passed in 1993 by a 96-3 vote. Times have changed and it is not good for our country. The main stream media barely covered Barrett's swearing in ceremony and one news outlet left it out entirely. Simply shameful.

Today is Halloween and 233 days since the Presidents' night-time Coronavirus nationally televised speech. Why was 233 days interesting to me? In 1945, 233 days after landing at Normandy on June 6th, 1944, the Allies won the Battle of the Bulge in the Ardennes

Forest paving the way for an Allied victory. Many brave young men lost their lives fighting a much more serious battle for freedom. Meanwhile, our freedoms here continue to erode. The cure for Covid continues to be much worse than the symptom. The medical profession under President Trump's 'warp speed' vaccine initiative, have made great strides in therapeutics and a vaccine seems to be coming very soon. But in today's USA, many people including the Democrat candidate for President continue to cower in their homes or mask up if they dare to brave the outside world. Many businesses are still not open or could not survive, never to open again. I refer to them as Covid casualties. When I take my daily exercise maskless walks in the neighborhood and oncoming walkers are approaching, they always step off the sidewalk onto the street until I pass. They've all bought in. Did they think they could catch Covid telepathically?

November 3rd was election day. I had promised myself not to stay up all night and watch the returns as I would leave for my Pinehurst trip the following morning. By the time I hit the sack there was nothing concrete to report. When I awoke at 2:00 am, I turned the TV on to see that Trump was looking very good in all the states that seemed to matter. I did not vote for the man for personal reasons but I did not vote for Biden either. I did vote however. I was not going to sit it out. A vote for the incompetent Biden and his team with the socialist and green agenda seemed anti-American to me. The problem I have with democrat politicians is many will campaign as moderate, singular-minded independent Americans but they will almost always vote as a monolithic ultra-liberal group. A vote for Trump was like voting for an unseemly man with great ideas and a staunch advocate for the American people, but not a gentlemanly Presidential figure of dignity worthy of representing our country. His coarse language coupled with disrespectful and sometimes incendiary comments would not allow me to pull his lever. I am reminded at this time of a story I heard and liked back in the 1980's while at a sales meeting in the plumbing industry. The short version goes like this......

A gentleman was seen opening a door for a 'lady of ill repute' in their small southern town. A friend noticed and mentioned to him that people generally have nothing to do with that woman. The man forcefully replied, "I don't open the door for a lady because she's a lady, for she may or may not be a lady. I open the door for a lady because **I'm** a gentleman." Our 45th President was not representative of that gentleman in my eyes and I would not offer him my vote. I am seldom accused of applying the standards of that story to my own life but I like the story just the same. Though I did not vote for Trump or his opponent, I did see him to be the clear-cut superior choice that was offered to America and Americans at this time in history. Politics is an ugly business but should still be accomplished in a civil manner.

Later this morning, Trump's lead was shrinking. Some states had paused counting, and some districts brought in bags of Biden votes in the dark of night like Attorney Gailey calling on the postmaster to prove that Kris Kringle was indeed Santa Claus. Lawsuits and recounts would ensue but Joe Biden who had long ago lost his fastball pitched a perfect game with no speeches, no appearances, no ideas. He hid from sight well and quite simply; he was not Trump. It was said that everyone either voted for or against Trump. No one voted **for** Biden. However, Biden would become our nation's 46th President and first 'mail order' Commander in Chief.

The non-politician experiment of Donald Trump would come to an end. We would elect Biden's 'Lieutenant Dike' over Trump's 'Lieutenant Colonel Ronald Speirs.' I preferred the bravery and leadership of Speirs. I believe many voters traded in their Freedom, for Free. Trump did in his four years what he said he would do. Troop reduction overseas, military support, wall addition, tax reduction, improved trade deals, peace through strength, and America first. Following through on your campaign promises is a novelty in today's political arena. His legacy may be the addition of replacing three justices on the Supreme Court. His transparency as President was unmatched. He answered all questions daily from the media. And he enjoyed sparring with them. It is his honesty that helped do him in. People do not like the truth because it is oftentimes very ugly and offensive. People may be aware of their shortcomings, but they do not want to hear it. I too have been accused of speaking an unvarnished truth at times. President Trumps' accomplishments however were beneficial to all Americans. He had a four-year term of international peace. Income was on the rise while unemployment was only for the unemployable. The Coronavirus pandemic hit in early 2020 through no apparent fault of our elected officials. Trump attacked it with vigor and his 'Operation Warp Speed' with therapeutics and vaccines would be a success. It was said that nearly half of Democrat voters had never heard the term 'Operation Warp Speed.' That is how the dishonest mainstream media work. Nary a story gets mentioned that make a Republican President or the opposition party look good. It is not the lies the media tells but the truths they withhold. There is no point in letting the truth get in the way of a good story when you can easily dance around the periphery of that truth, or avoid it altogether. There were times the main stream media would not televise a Trump speech or press conference because they did not want their audience to hear what he had to say. I don't believe they trusted the acumen of their viewing audience. If I could tell a non-supporter one thing about Trump it would be, he loved America and Americans. He had our best interests at heart. He expected America to abide by its laws. He wanted every Americans life to be better and safer, but he expected each of us to pitch in pulling on the rope, ***if able***. I feel most conservatives think that way. I believe shutting down the economy for the virus was his grave error. But just as Carlo Rizzi had to answer for Santino, Trump eventually had to answer for Coronavirus.

I was not sorry Trump would be gone. I am sorry we cannot find common ground to continually improve all lives. Some politicians want to find the lowest common denominator amongst us and set policy based on those findings. We do not seem to compromise anymore. I am sorry we cannot do better than a lifetime politician with virtually no accomplishments like Joe Biden. However, we salute the rank, not the man. I wished him well.

During a portion of Ginger's three-week rehabilitation stay, I did take my solo trip to Pinehurst while our daughter Christy stayed at our home to tend to rehabilitation center visits with its strict and limited visiting hours. Pinehurst is known as the cradle of American golf. The trip included two rounds of golf. One at the famed #2 course and one at the Centennial Course or #8. I arrived by lunchtime on Thursday Nov 5th. After checking in at The Manor Inn, I went next door to the more opulent and historical Carolina Hotel to look around. A beautiful property and I checked out their gift shop and the 'Ryder Cup' Restaurant. The halls of the hotel had historic golf pictures covering every available space and from multiple decades. Leaving the Carolina, I went to the main golf clubhouse where 6ix of the courses play from. I ate lunch on the veranda behind the 18th green of #2. Number 2 is a famous Donald Ross designed course known for its turtle backed green designs. Slightly misplayed balls can roll off in every direction. Many championships including Ryder Cups and US Opens have been contested on #2. Eating lunch and looking directly at the close by 18th green, I could immediately see why it might be so difficult. I took special note of the bunker fronting the right half of the green. After lunch I hit some balls and putted on the humongous practice green with 'Putter Boy' looking on. I followed that up with some window shopping in town and a light dinner. I turned in early for the day.

Friday morning started with a full breakfast at the Carolina Hotel. The halls and foyer were surprisingly decorated for Christmas overnight as it looked completely different than my visit the previous day. November 6th sounded early to be putting out Christmas décor but it was lovely to see. I arrived early for my 9:10 tee time with a game that has found some form late in the season. I checked in, loosened up on the range, and moseyed over near the first tee where they had an additional practice putting green and a separate pitching green. I played with a single, Jay, who was a young flat-belly from central Pa. He was a low handicapper who played from the back tees. The back tees not to be confused with the US Open tees. He reminded me of a younger version of my brother Tim. He also brought along his beautiful non-playing wife Shaina who walked along and enjoyed the 74-degree day and added to the beauty of the land. Jay and I shared Adam as a caddie who was very happy that I hit 11 of 14 fairways and never once had to look for my golf ball. I am what I would call an easy loop. Joining our fourball was Anthony and Mack who had Derek as their caddie. We made for a comfortable foursome and enjoyed fine rounds of golf. The grain on the greens was so pronounced it had the effect of an illusion at times from a fairway view. Trusting your yardage and executing your shot was a must. Every time someone's ball started to roll off the diabolical Donald Ross greens, Derek would say, "welcome to Pinehurst," or "Donald Ross says hello." There was no malice in his comments. We all enjoyed his comedic commentary. Instead of 'greens in regulation' they might track greens 'visited'. My most difficult shot of the day was right of the 18th green. There is a bunker fronting the green and many people eating lunch outdoors sitting directly behind the green. When I was eating lunch the day before, I knew I did not want a front bunker shot with tables of people directly in my line. I am a decent bunker player, but I did not need that. In fact, had I found that bunker, I would have pulled it out. I used extra club on my approach to 18 but it sailed wide right though pin high. My now difficult shot required an uphill sand wedge from a flat tight lie, over a bunker, with a few dozen onlookers but none in line of sight. I pulled it off well but could not convert the follow up twelve-foot par putt. Low handicapper Jay sank a 25' birdie putt to enthusiastic applause from the onlooking 'gallery'. A fine way to finish his three-birdie round. I did not keep his score but I would estimate a fine mid to upper seventies round.

Over-all I found Pinehurst #2 easy to play but difficult to score. I expect most courses are easy to play when you keep your ball close to the fairway. I was pleased with my 87. I had my picture taken next to the statue of Payne Stewart. Payne was honored with the statue posthumously for his 1999 US Open win at #2. My brothers and I also had our picture taken with a Payne Stewart statue in Ireland at the Waterville Links. Waterville had honored Payne as one of their own after he made a couple of stops at Waterville prior to British Open play. That evening after a shower I went in to town for dinner and a few beers. I enjoyed French onion soup and a juicy thick burger. That is as good as it needs to be for me. And of course, my three Stella Artois.

The following morning after another fine breakfast at the Carolina, I headed out to the #8 course, or the Centennial course as they call it. It was built in 1995, 100 years after the original course. The three-ball I was paired with had hired a fore caddie, Lawrence. We all had carts, me in an individual cart. The three-ball included possibly the slowest player I have ever been around. On multiple occasions he was away on the green but putted last, such was his tempo. I do believe it was more painful for his buddies than it was for me. Again, I was hitting fairway after fairway. All told I hit 12 of 14 fairways on this round. On the back side I did what I have never done before. Three consecutive birdies and two of the putts were from inside of one foot. My final tally was 80. After the round, Lawrence the fore caddie, removed his cap and adjusted his before unseen long afro. I told him he looked like ex Indiana Pacers great Darnell Hillman. Of course, he had no idea whom I was referring to. The group shook hands or fist pumped and I was off. I continued with my plan that included driving straight home after leaving the course at 2:15 pm. I hit the highways hard for me and arrived home at 11:35, just a few minutes after Notre Dame outlasted Clemson in overtime. Much of the football game I listened to on the radio.

Ginger did finally come home from the rehab hospital on November 19th. She had thankfully improved to the point where she would not need a wheelchair, just a walker, and hopefully temporarily. In her slowing condition I started referring to her affectionately as 'Granny.' She bristled at the word every time she heard it which only meant it must continue. November 19th is the day we had tickets to go to Florida for our annual Thanksgiving trip. Under the circumstances, we delayed the trip until mid-December. Many of my brothers and sisters were kind enough to bring a meal over to us on various evenings after her return home. Varieties of chicken was very popular, oftentimes mixed in with a pasta. Salads and fresh breads were quite welcome. Brownies were a hit for dessert and my sister Mo made a dynamite carrot cake. The food however, was not the star of the show. Having siblings and their spouse over for a quiet hour or so of meaningful conversation is what we will remember years from now. It was all much appreciated.

Meanwhile, as the year headed toward the holidays, the virus continued to grow at an alarming rate. Liberal Governors and Mayors were back in full lockdown mode trying to limit the number of guests you may have for Thanksgiving or Christmas. **In your own home!** Republican Governors were in semi lockdown mode in many of their states. I continued to call BS. The common flu was amid pitching a shutout. No cases anywhere? Yet no one seemed to question it. Coronavirus had huge implications on daily life, all negative. Democrats or liberals were more in the scared to death category while Republicans or conservatives were more in the cautious but take personal responsibility column. I never knew what made liberals so afraid. I was pretty sure Democrat politicians wanted you to be afraid to cede more control to them. When and if Covid ends, I expect historical stories surrounding this time frame will be prefaced as pre-covid or post-covid just like BC and AD. I do pray for everyone's health and safety, but more so a large dose of common sense.

Ginger and I did finally enjoy nine December days in Florida and we hit the weather perfectly. Highs between 70 & 80 with cooling evening temperatures. I was able to enjoy a round of golf with my Miami cousin Larry Kavanaugh. We had never played together and we had a terrific time at Valencia golf club in Naples, Fl. followed up with a pair of beers each.

Drug company Pfizer went to market with their Covid vaccine on 12-13-2020. Moderna would soon follow but it looks like we still have a long way to go before a semblance of normal life returns. The holidays came and went but with less flair of past holidays. Instead of the annual Kavanaugh Christmas gala scheduled to be held this year at the home of brother Brian and his wife Robin, a handful of my siblings and spouses partied at Brian's house for a quiet evening of drinks and hors d'oeuvres. That did not excuse them of their expected obligation now delayed until 2021. Instead of my immediate family going out for a nice dinner on an evening prior to Christmas, the group came to our home for beef tenderloin and plenty of fixings the weekend before. Ginger and I had our normal Christmas day breakfast for the immediate family. Everyone received the usual amounts of gifts, followed by a peaceful day at home. I did receive one extraordinary gift from my daughter Christy. It is called a Skylight which shows treasured rotating photos on an 8 x 10 video screen. She had it all set up with over 100 pictures and I can add any picture I desire simply by emailing it to the Skylight. It looks like years of memories and enjoyment.

The 2020 sports season was unconventional to say the least. Due to the virus, The US Open for golf was contested in September as opposed to June, with no fans. The annual rite of Spring known as The Masters was also played with no fans but in November. The winners, Bryson DeChambeau at the Open and Dustin Johnson at Augusta did not mind. The Stanley Cup was awarded to The Tampa Bay Lightning in September and the NBA title to Lebron's LA Lakers in October. Retired Laker great Kobe Bryant perished in a helicopter crash earlier in the year. The baseball season was shortened by nearly two-thirds but ended in late October as usual. With the baseball playoff expanded to 16 teams due to the Covid shortened season, we ended up with the two teams with the best regular season records playing in the World Series. The Dodgers of LA bested the Tampa Bay Rays in 6 games. Only the Super Bowl was played in its scheduled time period. MY Kansas City Chiefs won their first title in 50 years beating the San Francisco 49ers 31-20. The game was played during its normal calendar slot, the first Sunday in February, five weeks before the Coronavirus nightmare.

Due to Covid, the movie scene was shuttered and I could not select a best movie for the year 2020. In fact, the Woke mob seemed to take over Hollywood's future and each new movie that I did see was worse than the one before. Many new productions were shown on pay TV channels only, not the silver screen. As a professional movie-goer, I could not even count those as real movies. The Academy Awards permanently changed the rules for awards qualifications. It's embarrassing. My years long pastime of theater going officially came to an end. Maybe someday it will return.

The 2020 calendar year ended and everyone seemed grateful for that. Hope springs eternal. I simply did not see where 2021 would be an improvement. At least the first 75 days of 2020 were outstanding. That could not be said for the first 75 days of 2021 and until we see our freedom returned in all its glory, the jury is out for 2021 and possibly beyond. I knew 2021 could not start out great because most of the country was still muzzled up with the virus and many businesses were on lockdown or diminished occupancy. I was happy to see that the Teflon stock market was still in record high territory.

A stain hit the nation on January 6th, 2021. Two weeks before President-Elect Biden would take office, President Trump held a rally in Washington DC to throngs of his supporters. Trump continued his assault on the honesty of the election and he may have had a point, but the writing was on the wall and he caused issues with his rhetoric. After his 1:00 pm speech concluded, the crowd dispersed but many of his supporters headed to the Capitol building where Congress was doing the official business of confirming November's vote. The at first peaceful crowd partially turned into an unruly mob which forced Congress to head for the tunnels of safety and eventually a few hundred or maybe a thousand Trump supporters broke through the gates of undermanned and unprepared security and breeched the Capitol Building. Many simply walked through open doors. Their game plan once inside was not clear but none were known to be carrying weapons. Politicians who had previously called for defunding the police were now looking for protection from the badge. It is funny how that works. The Capitol property suffered light damage compared to the 2020 summer bloodbaths throughout America but it was described on many news outlets as the apocalypse. Unfortunately, many Trump supporters did not get the message that he was the 'law and order' President. If Trump had designs of a Grover Cleveland like return to the Presidency, it may have perished on January 6th, 2021.

I spent inauguration week in Florida with Ginger and played two rounds of golf with brother Kevin at Tiburon Golf Club in Naples. It was nine solid days of retirement training and there was nothing not to like about it. Ginger was moving around seemingly fully recovered from her recent surgery and it was a welcome sight to see. She had already abandoned her walker. But like a duck paddling beneath calm waters, unseen health issues were brewing.

As for the inauguration? The mainstream media gushed over our freshly minted Commander-In-Chief. It is as if they had been living in a four-year blackout but now the sun rose and the lights were shining brightly over the hill. Glinda was floating in from the north to a now very colorful political landscape. Our newly sworn in President gave a bland inaugural speech about unity and being a President for **ALL** the people, but shortly after the ceremony he was off to the oval office to sign a passel of divisive executive orders unlike any of his forty-five predecessors. With a few strokes of a pen, President Biden immediately dismissed his words of unity. 70 million Trump voters and half the electorate were deemed nonessential. Some of these executive orders were job killers and others would cause northbound human traffic jams at our suddenly unsecure southern border. It was interesting to observe that with thousands of migrants soon to be crammed into close, unclean holding pens, Dr. Fauci was mute about one of his favorite cautionary tales, a "Covid super-spreader". There is no doubt that these EO's were the new administration's first efforts at weakening America.

And so, the four-year term begins by the pessimistic man who so eloquently announced that a dark winter would be upon us. We survived apologetic, divisive, and the father of the current Cold Civil War, Obama. They survived the crude, distasteful, yet successful Trump. This too shall hopefully pass with a flag still flying with the same meaning as its original intent. At a time where we could all use a kinder, gentler nation as George HW Bush once suggested, it did not look like it would come under our new President. However, I did wish the current administration all the best.

Two days after the Biden inauguration, Hammerin' Hank Aaron passed away. The hall of fame baseball legend out of Mobile, Alabama played in Milwaukee and Atlanta and was 86 years old. I played and watched a lot of baseball in my youth and Hank was one of our favorites. We might select Hank to emulate in a back yard game of home run derby back in the 6ixties. Most people I know tuned in to the TV the night in 1974 when he smashed his record-breaking 715th home run against the Dodgers Al Downing, besting Babe Ruth's long-standing record. The same Al Downing my brothers and I saw pitch in Yankee Stadium in 1963.

Through this Covid period of fear, turmoil, and unrest, I now knew of one person who contracted Covid that had difficulty with the dreaded disease. When I heard this news four weeks ago, I prayed for my friend, but my thoughts of the pandemic and how it had been handled remained resolute and steadfast. Today, March 6th 2021, Steve Richards passed away. I worked with Steve at Plumbers Supply for fifteen years and through all the 1980's. In fact, I hired Steve in 1977 after he received a tip from my wife that we were hiring. Steve and my wife Ginger were working together at a grocery store at the time. Steve was hired as a warehouseman but over the years became one of the most respected men in our industry and a gem for Plumbers Supply. Be it a simple toilet, or water heater issue, he had your solution. He became skilled in water pumps, valves, boilers, radiant heat, and many technical products that do not come easy for many in our industry. He worked hard, studied the product, and I believe had an innate understanding of mechanics. When an associate stumbled onto a difficult task, Steve became the go-to guy. He was the best hire I ever made in my twenty years at Plumbers Supply. He earned tremendous respect in our industry culminating in the Esprit de Corps (spirit of the troops) award presented to him by our local plumbing association in 2018. The honor being a tribute to his spirit, service, loyalty, and support in our industry. As previously mentioned, our father was a part of the inaugural Esprit de Corps class in the early 2000's and brother Michael, was awarded the honor in 2015.

Steve was one of the funniest guys I knew. We got along great from day one and he was a true friend to me and most of my brothers and sisters at some point in time, especially brother Mike whom he worked with at Plumbers Supply for over forty years until Mike's recent retirement. I recall being at Steve's wedding years ago with an aisle seat and giving him a clandestine 'low five' as he and his bride retreated down the aisle at the conclusion of the ceremony. He was a golf partner of mine at the Plumbers Supply golf outing in 2020. He was a terrible golfer and enjoyed every stroke. Better golfers were happy to have him in their group, such was his disposition and company. Toward the end of last year, my wife and I invited him to join us for lunch at a popular restaurant across the street from Plumbers Supply where he worked. We reminisced and had a wonderful time having no idea that trouble for him was lurking around the corner. My friend Steve, our family's friend Steve, will be sorely missed. He was the oldest of six boys and two girls and one of the Green Bay Packer faithful. He left behind a wife and twelve-year old son. As fast as we developed a vaccine for the virus, it was a couple months too late for my dearly departed friend.

Here we are. March 12th 2021. It is the one-year anniversary of the infamous Covid speech by President Trump. Like the 1963 JFK assassination or the 1966 tanker fire in front of my grade school, or 911, it is an event I will never forget the date or where I was when it took place. It is the topic, along with riots, that dominated the news every day for the past year. With numbers of newly infected and dying currently receding nationally, there finally appeared to be a glimmer of hope in our future. Albeit a future painted with a more austere palette than the kaleidoscopic colors of our past. President Biden gave a solemn speech a few weeks ago about our country's 500,000th Covid death. Flags were temporarily lowered to half-staff. His gloom and pessimism could not go unnoticed. President Biden addressed the nation today on national TV. I am certain people like me, expected a positive forward-looking message but true to his previous form, he was, if I can borrow a 50-year-old phrase, a "nattering nabob of negativism". Fifty days into his Presidency, the 78-year-old man looked like a guy who could not wait for his 1,461-day term to end. He simply was not physically or mentally up to the arduous task, witnessed by his recent attempt at the ascending version of the 'triple lindy' on the steps leading up to Air Force One. With millions being vaccinated daily, many states opening up, fear subsiding for many of us, we deserved better.

In the past year we have mitigated, constantly masked, maintained some distancing, and now we were registering for and receiving Covid vaccines at breakneck pace. It was time for a return on our investment in health and safety by reinstituting our choice of a free social life. I received my vaccinations but not as much for my health but for international travel insurance. I feared there would be a day that if you did not have proof of a Covid vaccine, your travel and freedoms may stay as limited as they were today. My fears proved to be correct.

Many public schools around the country were still not open. Our youth had suffered mentally with a lack of social contact and education and very few who can make the difference cared enough. Least of all the teacher's unions who were holding our children's education hostage in many major cities. Is it possible the left is so sinister that they know a less intelligent future population will be more dependent and can be more easily taken advantage of in the future? Sadly, I could not rule that out. Children need schooling for more than standard education. They need structure, discipline, and a social setting amongst their peers.

Unfortunately, many states were still locked down. Liberty and the pursuit of untethered happiness was still on hiatus. People who feel they have not lost their freedoms have set a low bar for life. Common sense leadership in too many states was difficult to be found. There was not a day gone by in recent months that I did not think about international travel, physical ability to be able to travel internationally, and general mortality. Not what I would call a healthy outlook but that is the way it was. I felt I may be running out of time to accomplish the things I desire. We lived the past year at the threshold of hell. I wish our government would quit concerning themselves with my health. I always thought that when the government was supposed to protect us from enemies foreign and domestic, they were talking about people and armies. Not some virus that seemed manageable from the beginning and less and less dangerous to me with every passing month. Health is important but not very useful without freedom. To me there is a difference between safety and health. It is a sad situation when I think I am smarter than most politicians elected to office. I thought it every day during this Covid period. I would say, "I can fix many of the nation's problems, I just can't get the votes." I am certain most people believe their elected officials are smart people. Please never confuse educated with smart. I never have. The Covid period in my mind would not be over until we return to a pre-covid society. Any restrictions on freedom since March 12th, 2020 would be considered a limitation on our liberties.

The first quarter of 2021 was not a total loss. I was able to travel to Florida twice during the first quarter of 2021 and enjoy some beautiful weather, good restaurants, and excellent golf. The Florida Governor was doing things right and with promising results. I am certain I have gotten as much out of the last twelve months as anyone possibly could under our dire conditions. I was thankful for that, but still unsatisfied. I have flown to Florida for remote work and leisure several times since the original Covid speech. I ate at restaurants where possible, visited people when able, and been to the hospital for my wife's health issues dozens of times. Yet, I have fortunately stayed Covid free. I would say it is considerably safer out there than most people would dare believe. Certainly, better than the news will report. If vaccines continue to be administered as they have been, and with a third vaccine from Johnson & Johnson recently approved, there may indeed be light at the end of this long tunnel. For the first time in a year, I had guarded hope. If only Biden and other leadership can stay out of our way.

In May while I was on another short trip to Florida, golf star Phil Mickelson beat the odds and father time. Less than four weeks short of his 51st birthday, he beat the field at the PGA on Kiawah Island's Ocean Course. It was the ever-popular Phil's sixth major championship and the pro Phil crowd could not have been happier. He became the oldest man to ever win a golfing major. Two weeks later, 46-year-old Helio Castroneves won his record tying fourth Indy 500 in exciting fashion and put on a celebration for the ages. The old guys in sports were getting it done.

Vice-President Harris, who was placed in charge of our southern border crisis, finally made a trip to the Texas border on June 25th. It only took her 93 days since she was put in charge of the situation. It became a ceremonial visit. She visited hundreds of miles from where the real action was taking place. She blamed the previous administration, solved nothing, and simply put on a political show. Again, I am reminded of a previous President who once said that the worst words to hear from a government official is, "I'm from the government and I'm here to help." The border crisis was clearly by design and would continue to worsen. Some days the border looked like an invasion. It was like Woodstock of 1969 only these people were not going back home.

Meanwhile, the pandemic did seem to be lightening up. Many things were looking a lot more normal. Ireland and the U.K. had recently announced that it would be open to US visitors beginning July 19th. They referred to the date as National Freedom Day. You don't declare a National Freedom Day unless you had lost your freedom. Immediately I went to work on re-scheduling my golf trip that had been postponed in May of 2020. After much research and at times receiving conflicting answers, I pulled a Speaker Nancy Pelosi when she once said, "you have to pass the bill, to see what's in the bill." I decided I had to go to Europe, to see if I could go to Europe. I set my new date for a September 3rd departure. Airline tickets for my daughter Christy and I were purchased on Father's Day.

In July, Ginger and I took two of our grand-daughters down to Florida for a summer getaway. Thirteen-year-old Kaley brought her friend Julie along for the trip. Julie had never seen a palm tree or the ocean. Her amazement and excitement were thrilling to watch. Hurricane Elsa or tropical storm Elsa caused minor issues during the trip. We have had plenty of experience with storms over these many years that we have had a condo in Florida. Charley came through in 2004 followed by the great hurricane year of 2005. I was there just before, during, or just after all of them. Katrina, Rita, and Wilma. Grand-daughter Abby and daughter Christy were with us in 2012 when tropical storm Debby paid a visit. Hurricane Irma came in 2017 and probably did more damage in our immediate Fort Myers area than any before or since. That is until Ian came calling in 2022. We have never (knock on wood) suffered any serious property damage directly from a storm. I never considered our experience with storms as bad luck but rather a testament to how many times we have had the good fortune to visit the Gulf Coast.

Shortly after our return, Jeff Bezos, the richest man in the world, went into space with three crew members on his much-anticipated space trip using his Blue Origin Aerospace company. I had not followed the news of his adventure but it was covered live on TV and radio as the crew took launch. I thought at least he would circumnavigate the earth. Not even close. The over-hyped trip was a tremendous achievement in engineering but lasted less than 15 minutes. It was basically a billionaire's carnival ride. A very fast and cool carnival ride.

This was followed by the Tokyo Olympics that had been delayed a year due to Covid. I was surprised they were not cancelled altogether. There were still no fans allowed for any of the events. There were no special acts of athletic heroism to report on. Winning athletes appeared to covet their medals like any other Olympiad.

In mid-August, Afghanistan fell to Taliban rule shortly after the US announced August 31st as a date to pull out all our troops. A war fought for twenty years was lost in a matter of weeks. As a reminder, this is the war that was brought on due to the events of 911. We allowed due to questionable decisions our enemy to keep billions of dollars in defense equipment. The President kept adding one disaster after another to his plate. It seems the issues piling up were more than one man can create in eight months and certainly more than he could handle. Maybe if he continues throwing Socialist money at his citizens that will pre-occupy them. The main focus of this administration seems to be; racial division, class division, socialism, green energy, and woke-ism. Biden claimed at one point that he inherited the Afghan problem. He also inherited a secure border, energy independence, and a Covid vaccine. He kept the vaccine. He just could not properly place the credit. Between August 17th and August 24th, Biden gave three televised speeches. The speeches were anticipated to be about Afghanistan, but were not. He carried on about Covid vaccinations, his 3.5 trillion-dollar 'build back better' spending bills, and some on Afghanistan. Twice he walked away from the podium taking no questions. One time he fielded three questions from pre-determined news people. The man is simply not up to the task. And then he is off to his Delaware beach home. President Trump enjoyed his tete a tete with the press. It was an oral duel. He relished the engagement. Whether you liked his answers or not, he was quick with them. No notes. He had total awareness of every situation. Our current President finds it difficult to recall the names of his Cabinet without checking on his cheat sheet.

Today is August 24th. The only thing I really have on my mind is my golfing trip now just 10 days away barring unforeseen negative developments. As Ellis Boyd (Red) Redding said, "I'm so excited I can barely sit still or hold a thought in my head." A news flash comes across my I-phone. Charlie Watts, aka the 'Wonder of Wembley' is dead. The drummer for the Rolling Stones, my favorite rock group, has been the drummer and heartbeat for the greatest rock n roll band since 1963. There was a time during the Stones long association that if there was ever a disagreement amongst the boys, the answer was, "go ask Charlie." Charlie was the epitome of cool. I fell in love with the Stones at an early age and I vividly recall banging on my own snare drum, imitating Charlie to the opening of Paint It Black. I played that song after hearing the news and later that day put in a DVD of a Stones concert in honor of Charlie. The man was 80 years old. He had a great life and he and the band made my life more enjoyable. I saw them four times in concert. In 1972, I was standing in the very front with my hand atop the 6ix-foot high stage.

Two days later, a horrific explosion outside the Kabul, Afghanistan Airport followed by gunfire killed 13 American soldiers and scores of Afghan citizens. There had not been any U.S. casualties in Afghanistan since February of 2020. A new group called Isis-K accepted the blame. For the fourth time in 10 days President Biden came out for a daytime speech. Our President said he was 'instructed' to call on a certain journalist first. Instructed? Who is running our country? Few actually think it is Biden. The man had few answers and looked defeated, one time placing his head down on folded hands seemingly trying to bite his hands or bite his lip while thinking about how he can answer these questions. He knew who was responsible for the lives lost. The only time Isis or Taliban ever seemed to be brought up during the Trump Administration was to talk about them being on the run or suffering defeat. The last plane with U.S. soldiers left Afghanistan on August 30th, 2021.

A new variant of coronavirus called Delta had been slowly picking up steam in the last few weeks. We will never get rid of this thing completely. We must learn to live with it. Masks were making an unwelcome return in many areas. Our President decided to go back on his May 13th announcement that masks would no longer be necessary. Schools were mostly going back to the mask, yet finally with in person learning. Between the Delta variant and issues in Afghanistan, I was counting down the days for my golf trip. I will never believe it will happen until I have actually returned. There was nothing easy about this trip. Passports, masks, vaccination cards, negative tests, etc. I had even written an email to my Congresswoman for information in case I encountered difficulty. And now hurricane Ida was rumbling up the east coast possibly putting a damper on the Newark Airport, home of our outbound terminal. It was reported that Ida was causing flooding issues at some of our northeast airports. Planning this trip was like running through the hedge maze in 'The Shining'. However, on September 11, 2021 at 9:00 pm, my daughter and I made a triumphant and joyful return home from Northern Ireland and The Republic of Ireland. Here is the way it went down.

After painstaking preparation and a year and a quarter after our initial trip plans, my daughter Christy and I were off to Dublin. Wheels up from Newark on September 3rd, 2021, 7:16 pm. Arrival by United Airlines was on schedule at 7:00 am and we started off so good that my golf bag made it to baggage claim before we did. After retrieving the balance of our grip, we picked up our rental car. First stop; Belfast. 'The Troubles' that had started in the late 6ixties was mostly a distant memory and we saw no signs of turmoil from the past. We rolled in to the beautiful Titanic Museum with its unique silver-clad shimmering facade in Belfast and received a terrific educational experience. We also toured a local market Christy had read about. After our short stay we then drove off to the Bushmills Inn in Bushmills, Northern Ireland for lunch. Bushmills was highly touted by brother Tim based on his experience on a trip a few years ago. We were not disappointed. Our home for the next four nights would be the Atlantic Portrush Hotel hard off the Atlantic coast at the northern tip of Northern Ireland. A gorgeous panoramic view of the ocean was in plain sight from our fourth-floor room. A light dinner and drink were followed by a night of turning in early.

Sunday morning, I was off to my first of three rounds on Ulster's Causeway Coast. First test was the strand course at Portstewart Golf Club. I was graciously greeted at the clubhouse and learned I would be playing as a single along with my caddie, Michael. I would always prefer to join a two or three ball but very happy to be playing. It was a windy but dry day and I would find Portstewart to be an arduous test. The wind was stiff enough that there was no point trying to wear a hat. The first tee was a beautiful sight with the beach down below to my right and the town further in the distance. One would be excused if he took the time to take in the beauty before the daunting opening tee shot to the sliver of fairway below between the threatening dunes. The tee shot reminded me of our tee ball at the narrow fourth hole at Lahinch in 2018. Occasionally during my round, I would run across 'dugouts' carved into the dunes with built in benches to protect players caught off guard from unsuspecting weather. It would become shelter from the storm. Boy, if those dugouts could tell stories. My total of 87 for the day was neither rewarding nor disappointing. Michael was a treat to spend the day with. He never assumed a 'gimmie' putt no matter how close my ball was to the cup. I found no bunkers on the day but Michael did lose my bag into a bunker on #15. He used a trolley and without the brake on, the wind blew the cart and bag to the bunker below. (I had a similar incident with a trolley in 2022.) He felt embarrassed but no damage done. While golfing, Christy, a non-golfer, took in the town of Portrush. That afternoon we visited the Dunluce Castle. The Dunluce ruins has gained popularity recently serving as a backdrop for the popular TV show, Game of Thrones. While touring I tried to imagine the people and the times of the area in the 1600's. The wealthy in their expensive clothing. The women and men cooking and caring for the grounds. The children of servants in their play areas. You can see whatever your imagination allows. Though a ruins, we thoroughly enjoyed our visit.

We returned to the Bushmills Inn for dinner that evening. Extremely polite people and proud of their wheaten bread. The sea bass was delicious coupled with a bottle of wine. Cheers! After dinner we headed down to the popular Harbor Bar in Portrush for a proper nightcap. This is a bar that golfer Darren Clarke likes to frequent. Somehow, we got engaged in a discussion with an English couple who asked me who shot JFK and my opinions on Trump v Biden. I obliged them with my unvarnished facts and opinions.

Monday, I had the only afternoon tee time of the week. It was possibly my most anticipated round of the trip. Today play would take me to Royal Portrush Dunluce Links, home of the 2019 British Open won by Irishman Shane Lowery. After breakfast we headed out for some sightseeing including the Giants Causeway and the Carrick a Rede rope bridge. Awesome and beautiful sights, both.

The weather at Royal Portrush was perfect. Calm breezes, overcast dry skies, and 70 degrees. I joined a three-ball from Pittsburgh and my caddie Collin. All four of us had our own caddy. You could not help but look out toward the first fairway from the opening tee box and gaze to the left at the area where hometown favorite Rory McIlroy hit his opening tee ball left and out of bounds during the 2019 Open. I started Par, Par and scored a birdie on the eighth and nearly again on the ninth. A 39 on the outward nine was most pleasing. I stopped for a photo on the 5th green with the White Rocks Beach below and text a picture to brother Michael wishing him a happy birthday on this September 6th. A hiccup or two on the inward nine ended up giving me a still very satisfying 81 on the day. Portrush was a magnificent course in perfect condition. We enjoyed dinner that evening at the highly recommended 'Tides' restaurant in the town of Portrush. After dinner we drove to the nearby Portstewart course. I wanted to show Christy the view of the magnificent opening hole. I also hoped to buy a souvenir that I overlooked from my list the day before. The gift shop was closed but after taking in the view and a photo, we stayed for a drink in their still open restaurant. Cheers! That evening we had additional drinks in our hotel bar while watching the Euro women fend off the Americans on the final day of Solheim Cup action back in the states.

Tuesday's golf was scheduled at the Castlerock Mussenden Course. I played with a delightful group of 7 from Wales. We played as two fourballs. They were playing a money game and asked if I would join in. They got my handicap and I had no idea how they were keeping score on the bet, I just played. I had no caddie this day and we would all pull a trolley for the round. After-round pints were had on a sunny rooftop bar at the club. Cheers! A ceremony of sorts had the team 'captains' comparing cards while a third player scored the difference, hole by hole. As I was about to put my beer money on the table, in unison the group shouted my money down. Apparently, I was their guest for the day. Some say the Welsh are more tight-fisted than the Scots. I did not see that to be the case. I do believe I helped our team win £10 a man. An embarrassing double bogey on the home hole after a perfect drive found me with a total of 88 on this sunny, pleasant day. I found Castlerock to be a strong test. Sight lines for play were oftentimes difficult to discern on my first time through. The boys from Wales helped point out the line of play as this was not their first visit to Castlerock. It was my great fortune to join the gentlemen from Wales.

Christy spent the day at the Spa in the nearby town of Coleraine. After golf I picked the refreshed Christy up but not before I took an occasion to visit the Mussenden Temple near the golf course, which is a popular tourist attraction perched on the cliffs overlooking Downhill Strand beaches. This week was opening week of school in Northern Ireland and I noticed every child from primary school through high school wearing a uniform. All the schools wore uniforms. I asked questions about it and this is the norm for public schools in the country. They look so much better than our kids at home. I have little doubt that their attention in class is on point and that they probably are receiving a better education than many of our students at home. They certainly looked smarter. Once again, I stopped at Portstewart to see about purchasing my omitted £3 golf ball souvenir and this time I was successful. On the way back to the car, a lady from the office rushed up and stopped me in the parking lot. She overheard that I had played there two days ago and presented me with a nice souvenir pewter bag tag. What a nice gesture. That evening we had dinner at our hotel followed by dessert at a nearby café.

Wednesday we were up early for departure to Newcastle, Northern Ireland where we would stay at the Burrendale Hotel for two nights. I dropped Christy off at the majestic Slieve Donard Hotel where she had a nearly full day of pampering scheduled in their ample Spa. (Christy enjoys the Spas). The Slieve Donard was our first choice for our stay but they were booked solid. I must say the Burrendale was a first-rate property and with a Spa of their own. After dropping Christy off, I was fast off to Ardglass Golf Club in Downpatrick, about 20 miles up the road. Ardglass boasts the oldest clubhouse in the world, built in 1405, though not built originally as a golf clubhouse. The Ardglass property offered a view of the Irish Sea on every hole on this sunny 70-degree day. It was a magnificent breathtaking links with some of the most beautifully scenic elevated Par 3's ever designed. I played as a single again today with young caddie Matthew. I believe we overread some putts but he was a fine caddie. I opened with four straight pars including an up and down from heavy rough and a sand save. I missed 5 birdie putts inside of twelve feet and still scored a 77 on the par 70 layout, my lowest round ever in Europe. The course was not manicured to championship conditions but the property and views were first rate. Behind the green of the short downhill 18th par 4 were 24 flagpoles representing various countries. It was a beautiful sight and finish to a fine round.

We ate dinner that evening at the highly recommended Villa Vinci in the town of Newcastle. The meals were perfect and the wine was smooth and relaxing. Cheers! That evening prior to turning in we both took our covid test, a requirement for re-entry to the States. We were both thankfully negative as predicted and relieved that that requirement was behind us. It is an anxiety mind trip that I could do without.

Thursday morning, I set off for Royal County Down which was a mile drive down the street from our hotel. Brother Tim, who is a scratch player, claims RCD to be the finest golf course in the world and oftentimes garners that ranking amongst those who rank courses for a living. Christy shopped in town and had her hair done while I played golf. Christy is a terrific non golfing traveling companion. She finds plenty of things to do, has the wherewithal to do it, and enjoys exploring new places and things. This is the one thing in her life where I will boast that she is low maintenance. I would play as a two ball today with an older gentleman named Tom who turned out to be quite the interesting person. We both had caddies, my man's name was Mark. I started off with an uncharacteristic unforced error (a chubby pitch) on the opening par 5 hole which cost me a bogey. Blind shots were commonplace on this links. This was the firmest links course I would play this week and Portrush was fairly firm. On the downwind holes the breeze blew from 5 o'clock, my favorite wind. The inward holes blew from 11 o'clock, an unfavorable wind for my game. Starting out in shirt sleeves was short lived as fog began rolling in from the Irish Sea about the 4th hole bringing a sudden chill to the air. On the short 130-yard par 3 seventh, fog made it difficult to even see the green from the tee box. I finished the front nine with a satisfying 41. By the back nine, the fog mostly cleared up. While chatting up my playing companion throughout the round I learned Tom was from Boston. He was in and still works in commercial real estate. He was a Bruins hockey fan, a definite positive for me as they are my favorite franchise in all of sport. He mentioned he had billeted young Bruin players back in the day to help them get acclimated to the city and the world of professional hockey. One of his young billets was #1 overall draft pick Joe Thornton back in 1997. He later showed me a picture of himself skating with his young grandson. Not to be outdone, I showed him a similar picture with me and my grandson wearing his Boston Bruins warmup outfit. Tom had an affiliation with Notre Dame and asked about my Notre Dame connections due to my Notre Dame name tag on my golf bag. I had no connections but love playing the Notre Dame course annually. He also mentioned he was a member of The Country Club in Brookline, Mass. He owned a home on the course and had recently purchased a second home, the home once belonging to Francis Ouimet near the 17th green. Ouimet famously won the 1913 US Open at Brookline as an amateur while living in that house. The Country Club hosted the 1999 Ryder Cup matches and would host the 2022 US Open. (Won by Matt Fitzpatrick)

On the back nine I really hit my stride. The first 5 holes playing down wind I started out par, par, birdie, par, par. We then headed into the wind toward the clubhouse with the Mountains of Mourne in the near distance. Surprisingly I hit terrific tee balls into the breeze on both 15 & 16 and went bogey, par. I was even on the back through the first seven holes. A bogey on 17 did not bother me but I fairly fell apart on #18. I will not call it a choke. Just a difficult tight hole into the strong breeze. I found my only bunkers of the day on 18 and took a double bogey. It was my only double of the day for an inward 39 and a total of 80. No regrets. It was indeed a fine test of golf and enjoyable walk. The fog may have obscured some of the course's beauty, but it enhanced its mystique.

After golf I met Christy in the clubhouse for lunch. She had already ordered when I arrived. I asked Tom to join us when he came up and he obliged us. When Christy picked up the tab for the table, (she and I usually trade off on meal tabs) Tom protested and was quite embarrassed but I assured him it was okay. I mentioned to my brother Kevin who works just outside the Boston city limits and who has played The Country Club, about the gentleman I played with. Three days later after I got home Kevin asked me if I knew the man's last name. I had written it down on my scorecard (Tom Hynes) and Kevin began doing some forensic work. He texted me a picture and asked if that was who I played with. The man in the picture looked similar but maybe 25 years younger. He then sent a picture of another man who also looked similar, but older. You could see a family resemblance in both photos. Then he struck the perfect note. I said, "that's him." It appears Tom was from the Upper Crust of The Cradle of Liberty. The man Christy and I guessed to be 74 years old was a fit 82. His uncle had a ten-year run as mayor of Boston 60-70 years ago. There is a convention center in the city named after their family. The man was clearly well heeled. No wonder he was embarrassed that we paid for his lunch. He was a delight to play with and an excellent guest at our lunch table. I wish I had known more about him during our short time together. Tom was meeting up with other golfers in the days to come.

The following morning, we drove closer to Dublin for my last round of golf. As the schedule presented itself, Christy joined me at the County Louth Golf Club aka Baltray and hung out near the clubhouse while I played only nine holes. Well, I played ten holes due to the proximity of the parking lot. I did this to enable us to spend more time in the Dublin City Center in the late afternoon and evening on our final day. County Louth is where Shane Lowery (2019 Open winner) won the Irish Open as an amateur in 2009. My nine-hole score of 44 was of no consequence. I played with a member Paul who had a very similar game to mine. After golf and before heading to Dublin, we checked in at the Grand Hotel in Malahide which was a convenient twenty-minute drive to the airport.

After unpacking and familiarizing ourselves with our surroundings, we took a cab to the Dublin City Center. City double-decker buses were everywhere. I have never seen so many buses in one area. Our primary destinations were the Temple Bar and Graffton Street Shops. The area was amazing and included Trinity University. Streets and sidewalks were packed with people. Shoppers in all directions were carrying bags as if it were the week before Christmas. Endless narrow streets and alleys housed bars and shops as far as you could see. We spent a few hours in the area including a drink at the ultra-busy Temple Bar. Cheers! Dinner was had at the Dakota. Christy enjoyed some light shopping of her own. Returning to our hotel meant an end to a fabulous week. We did everything we planned on and then some. We enjoyed comfortable temperatures all week and were never bothered by rain. Our return trip was as smooth as it could be. Most of the world was still on Covid hangover. On arrival to the airport there was no one in line to check bags in front of us. Customs was a piece of cake. We could have slept in another hour at least. On the flight home I had a chance to watch three movies. One I had never seen before and oftentimes is ranked as the greatest movie of all time. Citizen Kane. Greatest? No chance, but I enjoyed it. Now I know what Rosebud is all about. We were back home at 9:00 pm on September 11th. All that is left is a lifetime of memories. My passport does indeed still work although other time-consuming and anxiety laced machinations must also take place. It is time to plan the next overseas golfing excursion. The quest to play links golf is my passion and the idea is never far from my mind.

My 67th year would end on another high note as my high school class of 1971 celebrated our 50-year reunion on September 18th, 2021. I remained one of a few 67-year old's if only by a day. The event was hosted at the home of Jill Willey, partner of my friend and classmate Mike Bussell. They live just two miles down the street from me so I had a home court advantage. The outdoor evening event found comfortable temperatures. Some of the usual suspects were surprisingly absent from the event. Others were present that I had not seen in years. Many never show up for what I am sure are a multitude of reasons. And it is surprising to me how many no longer live in Indiana. Me? I loved my grade school and high school days.

231

I have fond memories of my classmates and old friends. Especially those who I went to both grade school and high school with. I think about them often. We share an invisible and unbreakable bond that I feel a strong attachment to and should be celebrated.

One classmate I would like to have seen was Linda Colville nee Kelley. She was the smartest girl in grade school and valedictorian at our high school. As kids, we had absolutely nothing in common socially. I connected with her a few years ago on Facebook so I knew a little bit about what she was up to. She was not going to make the reunion as she lives in Colorado so a few days before the reunion, I called her. Not exactly sure how I got her phone number. We talked for a half hour. Based on where she lived during grade school, (she was two blocks closer to the school) we must have walked home to school together nearly every day for eight years. She was probably in front of the line while I was reliably lollygagging toward the rear. I am so glad I got to speak with her. I purchased a painting from another old St Andrew and Chatard classmate, Vicki Rees nee Lane. She was the next smartest in school and Salutatorian at high school. Vicki is a regular at reunions. She lives in North Carolina and is a professional artist. I saw one of her paintings on Facebook and told her I would like to buy it. She brought it to the reunion. It was a painting of the Old Port Head lighthouse in Cape Elizabeth, Me. that Ginger and I admired so much five years ago while vacationing in Maine. It is the second painting I own from the talented Miss Vicki. We also own a colorful fish painting from her that hangs appropriately in our Florida condominium. I had a wonderful reunion evening.

After a year and a half of Covid restrictions, I can still count the number of known cases with complications on one hand. Meanwhile, serious issues like border security with unvaccinated and unvetted migrants go unheeded. Getting lazy people gainfully employed seems an impossible task based on the help wanted signs on nearly every retail door. At the 1961 Presidential inaugural address President Kennedy famously said, "Ask not what your country can do for you, ask what you can do for your country". That quote is currently being lived in reverse today by many. We have gone from an ask not society to a don't ask society. Inflation is soaring but denied or ignored. Crime is rampant and seems to be nearly encouraged or justified by the left. The perpetrators are sometimes said to be the victims of an unjust society. Liberal prosecutors refuse to do their job. The destruction of our social fabric can be seen unraveling on a weekly basis like the stitches of a well hit baseball by Roy Hobbs. There is a lack of basic manners and decency to fellow mankind in our society. The more 'progressive' society insists on becoming, the deeper we fall into social and moral chaos and depravity. Progressives should come with a warning label. Socialistic ideas appear to be alive and well in the Divided States of America with an inept President and a corrupt administration who seem to hate America and all the greatness that it stands for. With Trump we had peace and prosperity until Covid. But the man was unlikeable and the electorate took for granted that any old Joe could do the job. But not this old Joe. He is the true Trojan Horse of Troy. America as I knew it for 66 ½ years may be disappearing and the cold civil war continues.

Under the pall of Covid, I am certain I accomplished more in year 67 than most people. My life was good but we as a country should be doing so much better. I have convinced myself that this nation has seen equally difficult times in the past and not only survived but prospered. I must keep the faith that it will happen again. I pray for a return to sanity or what I would call, normalcy. Some day.

68

9-19-2021 to 9-18-2022

My 68th year started out much like my 67th ended, a golf trip. This time back to Pinehurst, North Carolina. In the spring of 2021, I was invited on this trip along with three other guys. With Ireland still in the dark, I jumped at the opportunity. This is probably a trip I might have declined had I known Ireland would happen, but I am sure glad I went. My bounty of good fortune continued to roll in. We would play six rounds as a foursome. I drove down with Bruce Johnson, leaving my house on Sunday afternoon September 26th as the US Ryder Cup team was waxing the outmanned European squad at Whistling Straits in Wisconsin. Meeting us on Monday at Tobacco Road Golf Club in Sanford, N.C. was Bill Cowell and Stu Tucker. As best as I can recall, this was the first time I had met Bruce. Stu is a fellow I know mostly through golf. Bill is a good friend I have known through the plumbing industry and golf leagues for many years. In a few days we would all know each other a little better. The oddity of this group is I was the oldest guy in it. I suppose I need to get used to that. The golf took us to Tobacco Road, Mid Pines, and Pine Needles, home of the 2022 Women's US Open. From there we would play Pinehurst #2, #4, & #8. Stu Tucker made all the arrangements and everything from the rooms, dining, courses, and weather were perfect. We each had cabins at Pine Needles for two nights followed by three nights at the majestic Carolina Hotel in Pinehurst. As a group we played competitive golf with all rounds for our group during the week scoring between 78 & 95. My six scores showed a low of 79 and a high of 89. Tobacco Road is a unique and fascinating course brought to life in the late 1990's. Mid-Pines and Pine Needles are older, traditional, tree-lined Carolina masterpieces. Everyone's most anticipated round would come at the famed Pinehurst #2. We had terrific young caddies at #2 in Topher and Ryan. I started out of the gate striping balls down the fairway. As is my habit at times, I tend to pick up my tee immediately after a well struck fairway-destined tee ball. I cannot see it roll out anyway. On the third hole, caddie Ryan says after my shot, "he doesn't even watch it, he knows it's good." After hole #7, Topher chimes in with, he's minus $250 to hit the fairway. In gambling parlance, that means the odds are good my ball will find the fairway. I do miss my share of fairways but usually not by much. The six-round trip with impeccable accommodations was enjoyed by all. My highlight was a pitch-in eagle on the Par 5 17th hole at Pinehurst #4. It was my only eagle of the 50 some round season.

With virtually everyone unmasked now in Indiana, Florida, and North Carolina save a few restaurant employees, it appeared I was living in a parallel universe to what the news was reporting in numerous cities or states. Many parts of America were still being hijacked by left wing idealogues. Total freedom and liberty we were deprived of in March of 2020 has still not been fully returned. Frankly, I am not convinced it ever will be. I will continue to navigate my opportunities the best I can as they arise. I welcomed my trip to and return home from Pinehurst.

While on the trip, Bruce clued me in to a golf book he thought I would enjoy called True Links. We talked in depth during our drive about my four previous trips to Scotland, Ireland, and Northern Ireland. Bruce had also played most of the Ireland courses I have played. Knowing my love for golf travel and links golf, Bruce was sure 'True Links' would be a hit with me. The book was written in 2010 by George Peper and Malcolm Campbell. I did order the book and please understand the authors' strict definition of 'True' Links.

1 – The course must be beside a river estuary.
2 – It must offer at least partial or occasional views of the sea.
3 – It must have few trees.

4 – It must have numerous bunkers.

5 – It should have nine holes that run out and back, the front heading to a far point and the back returning to the clubhouse, in the manner of the Old Course at St Andrews.

Even the authors admit that there may be a case for loosening the standards. With only 246 so-called True Links in the world, only four lay in the United States. Those would surprisingly be three at Bandon Dunes in Oregon plus Highland Links in Massachusetts. You might immediately protest for Pebble Beach in California yet the authors consider Pebble a clifftop course and not a links. I'm certain there are many others you traditionally refer to as a Links course. I would not argue. As it is I have played 23 True Links to date with many more on my wish list. The coffee table book was a joyous read with terrific pictures. I recommend it to any golf enthusiast.

On October 12th my wife Ginger went for her one-year brain scan and checkup. The Doc gave her two thumbs up. I would be lying if I did not say I was concerned before going to the visit. With what was to come in the following year, you might question if they missed something.

The following day I saw what I believed to be the feel-good story of the Covid period. William Shattner, aka Captain Kirk from the nineteen-6ixties Star Trek TV series went up on Jeff Bezos' billionaire's carnival ride. The 90-year-old Shattner, who looks to be at least twenty years younger, was overwhelmed by the experience. His sincere gratitude for the opportunity was shown by the tears on his face and the quiver in his voice as he spoke with Jeff Bezos after disembarking the capsule. His personal history as Captain Kirk on the starship Enterprise added to this fun appreciable story. It seemed the entire nation felt a part of his good fortune and gratitude. At the age of 90, I believe he gave hope to all senior citizens pondering their futures. And as Andy Dufresne once said, "hope is a good thing, maybe the best of things, and no good thing ever dies."

An additional trip that was put off a year due to Covid took place on October 19th. Our granddaughter Kinsley was a year past due on a promised trip to Disneyworld. Every child should have the opportunity to experience the wonder that Disney and Mickey can bring. Along for the trip with six-year-old Kinsley, was her thirteen-year-old sister Kaley, their mom and dad, her Aunt Christy, Grandma Ginger, and myself. We stayed at the same Bonnet Creek Hilton that we stayed at eight years ago when we took Kaley to Disneyworld for the first time. This time we stayed in a sparsely booked hotel apparently as a hangover to Covid and Disney's limit on the number of visitors to their parks daily. We arrived at Disney early in the morning and immediately set off for rides, characters, food, and fun. I rode along at the Haunted Mansion, Small World, and Pirates of the Caribbean. When the parade including Mickey and Minnie came by, those are the moments with young grandchildren that make these trips worthwhile at any price. Kinsley's face lit up exactly like we knew it would. I am sure I was the same way back in the 6ixties when as a young boy our family would travel to Riverside Park in Indianapolis and enjoy roller coaster rides like the Flash, the Thriller, and Wild Mouse. Ginger would burst into genuine tears of joy at the sight of her favorite Disney characters. In the late afternoon, Ginger, Christy, and I went back to the hotel for drinks and relaxation while the others stayed until the dark of night and enjoyed many additional rides, attractions, and terrific fireworks show. The highlight of the evening, I am told, was Tinkerbell ziplining from Cinderella's Castle over the crowd below while sprinkling her fairy dust. The entire trip, including a handful of days at our Ft Myers condo and trips to the beach was enjoyed by all. I am sure glad that Ginger had the opportunity to see Kinsley enjoy Disneyworld. This trip will never be forgotten.

In November, many of my siblings, spouses, and myself went to the theater to see the new movie 'Belfast.' It is about Belfast, Northern Ireland in the late 6ixties as 'The Troubles' were beginning. A few of us have been to Belfast, me recently, and others would like to go. Though the movie lacked blockbuster content, we universally enjoyed the movie and afternoon.

Ginger and I would spend Thanksgiving week in Florida at our condominium. As a nation, we began the 2021 holiday season on an ominous note. A holiday parade in Kenosha, Wi. just prior to Thanksgiving ended in tragedy as a man slammed his car into the unsuspecting merriment killing six people. Based on the drivers long list of priors, he should not have been allowed to breathe free air. (The driver of the car was convicted in the fall of 2022.) That was followed by the mob getting in some early Christmas 'shopping' as flash mob looters ransacked pricey stores in San Francisco, Chicago, and L.A. Stolen items included jewelry, luxury brand handbags, and tools. The thieves feel entitled, the authority allow them to believe it. That was closely followed by a new Covid variant called Omicron discovered in eight southern African countries that had people nervous around the globe. Omicron quickly made its way to Europe and it was knocking on the door of the U.S. On Thanksgiving Day, President Biden declared "America is back." I was not sold. We have a non-transparent administration with few answers' forthcoming. In fact, we were so far back that just a week after his "America is back" pronouncement, he tightened the screws on covid testing for international travel. Negative tests due 72 hours before return flights would now be required 24 hours prior to return from travel. A minor change but when does it stop? Testing is for the vaccinated and unvaccinated alike, unless of course you are a foreigner crossing the border illegally. New York and California were going back to the mask. Where is the benefit for the vaccinated? Does the damn thing work or not? It was hard to blame those who did not get the jab. There was no return on their investment. I was convinced that the Omicron variant that is known to be less virulent but possibly more contagious was this year's version of the seasonal flu. But our administration cannot retire the name Covid. It would lessen our fears and cede their power. They refer to it as a pandemic of the unvaccinated. It is more like a pandemic of the liberal mind. So, the restrictions and hysteria continue, particularly in the 'Blue' states. The great divide widens.

To cap off the early portion of the holiday season, another school shooting took place in Michigan, killing four students. If mayhem is not in your hometown yet, it is on its way. Why can't we stop some of this madness? Parents cower to Covid yet have little thought about sending their children to the uncertain safety of schools. Victims are picked at random and our government will not protect us. They want to act tough on gun violence yet they are soft on crime. America is unsafe. With many American cities looking like the wild west, I felt infinitely safer from Covid than I did from crime.

In early December my all-time favorite race driver passed. Al Unser died seven months after my second favorite driver died, Bobby Unser, his older brother. The Unser's are synonymous with Indy Car racing. Al won four Indy 500's while Bobby won three and Al's son, little Al won two. Big Al won Indy in both my Junior and Senior year of high school. Bobby won in my freshman year. As a close follower of the sport and event growing up, it is no wonder that I became an Unser fan. Al was a class act and I enjoyed following his career. I also enjoyed Bobby's commentary later during racing TV broadcasts. Bobby's winning car in 1968, the Rislone Special, became my all-time favorite Indy car. Al's Johnny Lightning Special in 1970 was a close second. Thanks for all the thrills.

Our annual family Christmas party which was sabotaged by Covid last year would be hosted by brother Brian and his wife Robin. They decided to make a double-header of the event. What were they thinking? There would be adults only on Saturday evening of December 18th and an all-hands-on deck affair for a Sunday brunch the following day. Both events were well attended with some expected lingering 'fear of Covid' holdouts. I truly enjoyed the adults only portion. We are a loud group without the help of the children. Both days had the traditional pinata and the food was outstanding. Brother Michael put together a great video of family holiday pictures mostly from the last twenty years which he videoed on TV. His efforts topped 250 photos. Since kids grow fast, sometimes you found yourself questioning who some of the people in the older pictures were. We all received a thumb drive to allow us to watch at home any time we like.

Christmas day 2021 in Indianapolis was unusually warm. Temperatures hovered around 60 degrees and there was an overnight rain that drenched Santa. All the gifts managed to stay dry. Off and on rain continued most of the day but none of the days' festivities were impaired. Our annual Christmas family breakfast and the opening of gifts was completed by noon. Afterward we had a nice family photo taken. The picture would become a keepsake for eternity. By 2:00 pm I equaled my previously set record by having the family Christmas tree undressed and hauled off to the recycling tree lot. The day ended with our Indianapolis Colts winning a primetime game at once one seeded Arizona. It was a somewhat surprising win by the Covid depleted roster of the Colts. Mild temperatures hung around for the remainder of the year. So much so that I got in a round of golf with son John on December 27th.

The 2021 sports season began with a couple of real surprises. The fact that Tom Brady won his seventh Super Bowl ring at the age of 43 was a surprise. The fact that he won it playing for the Tampa Bay Buccaneers was a real surprise. As the Celtics dominated my 6ixties, Tom Brady dominated my 60's. The Tampa Bay Lightning took their second consecutive Stanley Cup beating the dark horse Montreal Canadiens. For the first time in many years, I did not notice the presence of the traditional Stanley Cup Playoff beards. Most young men now wear a beard year-round.

In golf, the Land of the Rising Sun was never so proud as when Hideki Matsuyama became the first man from Japan to win a golfing major, getting the job done at Augusta. In a show of respect golf fans have never seen, Hideki's caddie faced the 18th fairway from the green and bowed to the course holding the 18th hole flagstick after the historic victory. The tournament had returned to its traditional spring time slot. Five weeks later, additional golfing magic had 50-year-old Phil Mickelson winning the PGA. Spaniard Jon Rahm took the US Open, besting a star-filled leaderboard. And young American superstar Colin Morikawa won the Claret Jug in the southeast of England at St. Georges. To round out the sporting calendar, The Milwaukee Bucks won the NBA title and Atlanta's Braves took the Fall Classic, fittingly, after losing the honor of host city of this years' all-star game to the Woke mob. 'Instant Karma' was never so quickly claimed.

The 2021 calendar year came to its merciful conclusion. I say this not because I had a bad year, I had a great year. However, as a nation, we are doing poorly in my opinion. Unlike the end of 2020, I did see 2022 being an improvement, but it was not going to happen immediately.

2022 began the same as many of the past twenty years. My employers national sales meeting. They are a lot more fun than they might sound. We all arrived at PGA National Resort in Palm Beach Gardens on January 5th for two days of meetings and an afternoon of scramble golf on the Fazio layout. By my count this is the sixth time our meetings took place at PGA National. Due to Mueller's (my employer) record breaking year, this year's meeting took on a different complexion. Spouses or significant others were invited. This is only the second time in my twenty-two meetings that spouses were invited to attend. Sadly, my wife Ginger did not make the trip due to her limited mobilities. She could still get around, but it was painfully slow and these large sprawling properties are a challenge for her. Last fall at Disneyworld we had rented her a wheelchair for faster and easier movement about the park. It is a shame she could not make it to our meetings. She would love it at PGA National. They have great restaurants, pool, and spa. The day of arrival there were no meetings, only drinks and dinner. Day two we all received Mueller's 'state of the company' address after morning breakfast and after lunch many of us hit the links for our traditional golf outing. The outing was played on the Tom Fazio layout. Non-golfers were free to enjoy the facilities as they saw fit and the weather was mid to upper seventies perfect. On the putting green prior to play I noticed from some distance an Asian girl practicing her putting with tees lined up for the perfect line and stroke. I wondered if she was an LPGA player but I did not bother her. During our round, on one of our two 'closest to the pin' holes, yours truly squeezed one to 7 feet 1 inch to win a prize. My award was something called a Bushnell Walkman. After our golf ended some four and a half hours later, the Asian girl was still putting. To the same hole. Now she had her mother with her and a carpenter's level on the green. They were taking nothing to chance. This time I had to interrupt them and as I got close, I realized she really was just a girl, probably about twelve years old. From my vantage point earlier in the day, I thought her to be nearer a twenty-year old. This girl was there for the Honda Junior Classic which would be played on Saturday and Sunday. There were three age brackets for girls and boys and they played on three of the PGA National courses. She had come to the Florida event from Vancouver, Canada. Quite a trip. I wished her well and was on my way.

The next morning our day long meetings started promptly at 8:30 after a full breakfast. Surprisingly, the most un-Mueller thing I have ever witnessed in my career at Mueller happened. We usually sit until we get saddle sores but at 10:30 a.m. we were released for the day. Released for the day until the awards dinner that evening at 7:00 pm. I was certain many in our young crowd would head to the pool and cabanas. Others would find never-ending drinks and relaxing laughter under the Florida sunshine. Since I did not pack a swim suit that I assumed I would never have occasion to use, I only had one thought. Can I get on the Jack Nicklaus Championship course where the pros play the annual Honda Classic PGA event? At first, I was told they were very busy but they could get me out at 2:30 pm. I turned that down flat as dark falls at 5:30. If you cannot play all 18 and especially the famed "Bear Trap" on holes 15, 16, & 17, what was the point? They were able to hook me up with a cart and a set of rental clubs for driving range access. I took him up on that and went to my room to change shoes, get my gloves, a couple of balls for putting and tees. Going down to my cart I decided to head back to the Pro Shop and tell them if there were any cancellations, to come get me at the range. At that time, he said he could get me out at 1:20. SOLD!

They hooked me up with a 16-year-old single male from Bulgaria who was also here to play in the Junior Classic. Young Hristo Yanakiev played as his mother Radka rode along in the cart watching the young hopeful. I later learned his younger brother was practicing on the Fazio course with his father. They were both in the states for a month playing various tournaments. Last week they were at Doral in Miami. Hristo played from the longer Pro type set up, me from my traditional white tee box. The kid was fantastic, long hitter, and a gentleman in every sense of the word. His manners and golf etiquette were impeccable and belied his age. He was rooting me on most of the day complimenting every good shot I struck. Myself, Hristo, and mother Radka talked much of the day. I learned there were only six courses in the small country of Bulgaria, though according to Radka they are all very nice. He was a sophomore in high school and would soon be looking at US colleges to further his golf career. He accompanied me for a photo in front of the large 'Bear' entering the 'Bear trap.' I navigated the Bear trap with par, bogey, par, and finished with a closing birdie on 18, my only birdie of the day. When the 20-foot putt found the hole, pretty Radka was applauding from the comfort of her cart. Hristo attacked me with a high five. Quite a finish, quite a day. I shot 84 and expect Hristo was closer to 76 or 77 from the much deeper tees. We met up with little brother and dad near the clubhouse after our round.

The following day was a travel only day for me and my fellow employees. With a mid-afternoon departure time, I saw Hristo off on the first tee of the championship course and wished him well. Prior to his tee time, Radka and I conversed for half an hour. If the youngster ever makes it on any tour, I hope I am around to follow his career. After I saw Hristo off, I moved over to the Fazio course where I learned the Tiger cub, Charlie Woods, was playing in the U12 version of the Classic. Based on his tee time, I would not have to go far. He would be coming in on #9 soon and headed back out on #10. It did not take long. Tiger was not on the property but his ex, Elin, soon walked past me near the 9th green. I would never have recognized her if I was not expecting her but when I saw her walk by, I knew. I watched Charlie putt out for par on nine and tee off on ten. He was playing in a three-ball and I am happy to report it just looked like any kid having a good time with kids his own age. They were tickled to find courtesy water and Gatorade waiting for them on the tenth tee. There was no entourage or security. The only bystanders for that short time besides myself was the parents or grandparents of the other two competitors, and Elin. I did however notice a photographer in the area. Sunday evening, I checked on Hristo's progress online and learned he finished 10th out of 72 after being in 2nd place after round one of the 36-hole event. I hope he was pleased.

The people I have met in my life by chance on golf courses has been extraordinary. I always considered myself the beneficiary. It becomes a surprising, yet integral part of every golfing excursion. During this week of meetings and golf I ran across people from Canada, Bulgaria, England, and Mexico. That includes Mueller employees. The point I took was that even with all the Covid nonsense, people are getting around. That was good for me to see. On this Saturday afternoon, I would be flying back to Indiana.

In February of 2022 the Beijing Winter Olympics came and went with little fanfare. Due to Covid restrictions and Communist China rule, athletes were cocooned in a 'closed loop' system with daily virus testing. Living conditions and food looked unpleasant. No international fans were allowed to attend and Chinese fans were allowed on a very limited and select basis. Empty arenas were the norm. Figure skating could have been competed in the Olympians home rinks and judged by zoom. Due to the time difference, very few events in this Olympiad were televised live. I never did see the downhill skiing event though I would have liked to. I did enjoy watching some curling. It is hard to explain and I am not looking to convert any detractors, but I like curling. The Olympics came and went peacefully but with little excitement. During the athletic fortnight I was able to plan and lock in another Scottish Golf Holiday. This one I would only have to wait a bit over three months. A departure date for Scotland was set for May 25th.

For some time now the Russian Army at the direction of their President, Vladimir Putin had been amassing their army at the border of neighboring Ukraine. It appeared an invasion was likely. Biden and his other allied leaders negotiated with the Russian strong man but he was undeterred. The Russian invasion began in earnest on February 24th. It appeared that plans of the attack had been on the mind of Russia's President for many years but its roots took a firm hold the day President Biden took office and shut down the Keystone pipe line. This was followed by our bungled departure from Afghanistan. Whether that was the impetus or not, it is difficult for me not to connect those dots. What Biden always referred to as Putin's War looked an awful lot like Biden's War to me. Putin saw a weakened America. The minor incursion that Biden publicly said was acceptable looked much more like a genocide. With a stronger leader at home in the U.S., Putin would be sitting comfortably in Moscow eating caviar, borscht, and sipping vodka. Peace through strength has proven to work.

The Russia v Ukraine battle would continue beyond the last words of this book. It is amazing how hardened we could become to the daily briefings of sorrow. In my world, life went on.

As I was in Florida at brother Kevin's house for a golf weekend the day Trump gave his life-altering Coronavirus speech, I was there again on February 24th, 2022 for another three-day golf weekend the day Russia invaded Ukraine. This golf trip was a family affair that also included brothers Mike & Brian. We enjoyed perfect weather and accommodations at Kevin's house along fairway #2 of the Tiburon Gold course in Naples, Fl. I played my normal game with scores of 84,87, & 87. The interesting thing about my play is that I had a total of three birdies for the weekend. All three came in succession in the middle of the 54-hole event. I birdied #'s 8, 9, & 10 in round two. It was the second time in recent years I had hat trick birdies. I accomplished the feat at Pinehurst on my 2020 trip. I have never considered myself to be a streaky player.

March 12th, 2022. Two years now from the crippling coronavirus speech. For the most part, Covid restrictions nationally had been abated in recent months. They initially asked for two weeks of mitigation. Two weeks! Yet they seemed to be on a never-ending search for government control. I oftentimes wondered how much life and freedom people were willing to grant to their government. I was never in the giving mood. Fear had clearly been the most effective tool in the government's arsenal. I remember a President once using the word fear twice in a very famous quote. They continue to remind us of new variants that are likely to pop up. A couple months ago the CDC Director, Dr. Walensky, admitted that 75% of Covid deaths were from people that had four or more comorbidities. Dying with Covid is a far cry from dying **from** Covid. A more recent report by Johns Hopkins University revealed that lockdowns did not work in curtailing Covid and reported that it saved virtually zero lives. Or 0.2%. Most media did not report on the Johns Hopkins study. Maybe science never was followed, based on the convenience of the administration removing all remaining mask mandates the day before President Biden's State of the Union address on March 1. How many lies had we been told over this dark period by Dr. Fauci, our Presidents, and others? How many truths have been withheld? I am reminded of a song from 1967 that goes, "when the truth is found to be lies, and all the joy within you dies".

We might someday conclude that all our mitigation efforts did nothing to curb covid. The virus after two years seemed to be the clear winner. It would leave when it is good and ready. Trust was hard to come by. We might consider changing our country's motto from e pluribus unum to caveat emptor or fidete, sed verificate. Biden promised to shut down the virus. He never had a chance, only a gullible electorate. As the two-year slog continued, it seemed that more and more talking heads on TV were finally parroting my comments that I made to anyone who would listen over the past two years. Especially comments about freedom which I had made from day one. If I only had their forum. We still have many freedoms, but not all that we had in 2019. We thought 911 negatively changed our world twenty years ago and it did. But I have no doubt that Coronavirus has changed it even more.

On March 30th and 31st I was making sales calls in Kentucky with an overnight stay. I was home by late afternoon on the 31st and everything was normal. Ginger and I had dinner at home which is not normal and we talked about our annual spring trip to Florida only five days away. Later in the evening as we were off to bed, I finished the day with the same line I have told Ginger on scores of occasions in the last few years. "Another day in the books."

Health is sometimes taken for granted when you and nearly everyone I know has been blessed with it most of our lives. Ginger was living with Parkinson's and moving slowly. Things seemed reasonably normal or I had just gotten used to it. One difference was she was driving less. In the past month she simply was not comfortable behind the wheel of a car. Maybe her body was telling her something. It is April 1st, 2022. This Friday morning, I was casually going over sales reports in my office. I heard a thud from the kitchen which is on the other side of the office wall. It sounded like a heavy book hitting the floor. I did not think much of it at first. There were no sounds of anguish. I did not know when I heard the sound that at that very instant, lives would be forever changed. After a minute I walked around the corner to see my wife lying on the floor. We have been here before. It was falls that led us to brain scans that eventually led us to her brain surgery. It was not immediately apparent to me that something was gravely wrong. Her speech was normal. She was alert. I thought maybe it was a relapse of sorts. She refused my help and assured me she would get up but wanted to regroup. A while later my son Jason and his wife Casey who works in nursing came over. I had called my daughter and told her of the incident. She called her brother who lives nearby. Casey immediately determined Ginger had suffered a stroke. Minutes later, the sirens could be heard entering the neighborhood. Ginger was off to the hospital. She spent a few days in the ICU before being transferred to a regular hospital room for a couple nights. Her memory and speech were fair to good. Her mobility on the left side was non-existent. This was followed by four prayerful weeks at the same acute Rehab Center she visited after her brain surgery in 2020. We then went back to the hospital for three days due to what they referred to as pneumonia and delirium. This was followed by five additional weeks at a sub-acute rehab facility. Seeing results or modest improvement was difficult. The waiting was indeed the hardest part as my loved one lie nearly in a state of suspended animation. Honest information from medical staffs was hard to come by. It would be 78 days from the date of the event, or June 17th, before she would come home again. Her condition was unimproved with a long road ahead. Insurance put an end to her non-improving Rehab stay. Our home had been set up with hospital equipment. My daughter Christy sacrificed so much of her time to be with her mother and I. My daughter-in-law Casey and her mother Theresa, both in the nursing business, were a godsend to me for the friendship, love, time, and care they gave to Ginger. These three were indeed the women in the arena and doer of deeds.

On April 7th, President Biden had his first choice for Supreme Court Justice approved by a 53-47 vote. Ketanji Brown Jackson would replace liberal justice Stephen Breyer at the end of his current term. The 53-47 vote was a larger margin than the two previous Justice votes but seemingly far closer than it should have been. I guess you must vote your conscience but everyone knew she would be confirmed. The days of overwhelming support for Justices is over. The cold civil war continues and it is rather sad. Elections matter but it should never be a 'my way or the highway' scenario. Biden, as expected, replaced a liberal Justice with a liberal Justice. I do not even understand why Justices are labeled as conservative or liberal. The logo of the courts is a blindfolded lady holding a set of scales, representing balance and fairness. We should expect neutrality. But I know better.

In May there were two more mass shootings in our country. In Buffalo, ten were shot dead at a grocery store. The shooter was later convicted and sentenced to life in prison without parole. A week later in Uvalde, Texas, 19 grade school students and 2 teachers were massacred. Meanwhile, the authorities cannot agree on sensible answers. I heard a good point from someone on the news. Before 1970, smoking was commonplace in this country. Public smoking was everywhere and no one thought a thing about it. We smoked in homes, business offices, grocery stores, on television shows, and it was nearly mandatory in bowling alleys and pool halls. We even smoked on airplanes. My first job in the 6ixties was at a grocery store. There was a cigarette ash can at the end of every aisle and some ash and butt receptacles affixed to grocery shelves. In 1965 Congress required all cigarette packs to carry a health warning. Eventually, TV advertising of cigarettes was banned. It took many more years but in the 21st century it became difficult to find a place, other than your home, to smoke indoors. Even bars went sans smoking. And it is all for the better. If we can get rid of cigarettes, we can reduce the usage of weapons in this country. Harsher penalties and sentencing (or worse) would be an easy start along with mandatory background checks. It seems after every one of these unfortunate incidents, people put the pieces of the puzzle together and conclude; we could see that coming. I am not totally opposed to jailing people on suspicion alone. I know that sounds far out and it is a slippery slope but that is the way I feel. Since we do not exactly have a fair and balanced judicial system, it is probably not the wisest of ideas. Additional shootings occurred shortly after. On July 4th at Highland Park, Illinois, seven were killed during an Independence Day parade. Thirteen days later three were killed at a food court in a mall just south of my hometown of Indianapolis. As I have said, if mayhem has not visited your area yet, it is on its way.

On Wednesday, May 25^{th,} I left for my solo Scotland golf trip that I booked back in January. My wife Ginger was still in the rehabilitation center from what was now a very serious stroke suffered on April 1. Our daughter Christy came home to look after things while I went off to recreate. I wished I was leaving under normal circumstances but that is not the hand we were dealt. The trip was mostly all prepaid and so I was off. Ginger was glad I was leaving to enjoy what she knows I love to do. The morning of my departure I received an email from the booking agent that one of the courses I was set to play was closed due to issues with the greens. The round was rescheduled for me at a very nice course I had previously played in 2014 when I was on my maiden European golf trip with my son John. I had no issue with the trade. The flights were all smooth and on schedule which is always a relief. I was met at the Edinburgh airport by Iain of the booking company and I upgraded my rental car. They entrusted me in a brand-new Mercedes sedan. The vehicle had three miles on it when I took the captains seat. My trip would start up north in Inverness, then go east to Aberdeen and south from there to St Andrews. Three cities, three nights in each. The countryside on my drive north to Inverness looked beautiful. Sheep on the hillsides and the gorse in full flower. I stopped for lunch at the Inverness golf club before checking home with my health minister for the days report. There were no changes and all was going as expected. My stay for the first three nights was at the Glen Mhor Hotel along the River Ness in Inverness. The water was moving pretty good on that river, just a stone's throw away from the narrow road fronting the property. My room was below my standards, very small, but nothing to be upset about. The shower was of a size you would not want to drop the soap. You may have to turn the water off and get out to have room to pick it back up. I had dinner on a rainy evening at the acclaimed Hootenanny Bar which was within walking distance as everything in town center was.

My first round of the trip would take me further north in the Highlands to Brora. On the way I stopped at two other courses for a looksee. The first stop was Tain, a course designed by Old Tom Morris. The second was highly acclaimed Royal Dornoch, also designed by Old Tom. I inquired about a tee time at Dornoch for later in the day but their booking for guests was full. Brora was an interesting course that I had been schooled on just a bit. It was not uncommon to find sheep and highland cows on the course, mostly on the perimeter. The greens had a single strand of wire about two feet off the ground encircling them to keep the livestock from straying onto the greens. None of the animals nor the wire bothered my play. The wind did however. Today would be the windiest day of my trip and in subsequent rounds, playing companions would talk about Friday's winds regardless of where in Scotland they may have played. I went off at Brora, a James Braid design, as a single which was disappointing. It would be my only single round of my nine-round trip. The lady in the Pro Shop was not aware of any caddy arrangements and since the first tee was open, she invited me to start my round while pushing a trolley. On the 7th hole looking out at Kintradwell Bay, it began to rain. On the 8th I decided to cover the gabardines and top with my rain suit. It rained moderately by Scottish standards for about two holes but I continued to play with the rain gear on. As I approached the 12th green, I pulled my putter and parked my trolley on the nearby elevated 13th Par 3 tee box. Walking to the green I saw in fear out of the corner of my eye my cart racing down the hill as if it was qualifying for the upcoming weekends Indy 500. The wind must have caught the bag perfectly as I had it pointed straight down breeze without the wheel brake applied. I should have learned something the previous year when my caddie at Portstewart lost my bag and cart into a bunker. At the bottom of the hill was a burn. In most cases the cart would topple over sideways before reaching the stream some thirty feet below. Not this good ole sturdy cart. I had no chance to catch up to it and I watched as it splashed into the water. By the time I got to the scene my bag is horizontally floating, but taking on water like the Titanic. Due to the width of the burn (maybe 6ix feet) and steep angle from land, I could not bend over and reach the bag. Fearless, I walked into the water unsure of its depth. I found out it was waist deep. I grabbed my bag with both arms and carried it out like John the Baptist saving a drowning lamb from the Sea of Galilee. The pull cart was not attached and nowhere to be found in the dark, murky waters. I immediately counted my clubs and found the number of 13 to be satisfactory. While attempting to dry off, regroup, and wring out my socks on the bench at the 13th tee, I realized that 14 is the proper number of clubs. After a recount, I did have only 13 clubs and my pitching wedge was gone into the abyss. Moments later my heart sank again as I remembered my wallet and I-phone were in the bag. They were both zipped in a pocket and survived with barely a few drops of water on them. You can imagine my relief. My scorecard was destroyed as it was in my pants pocket and the recreated scorecard made after my round was written with scores as best as I could remember. There were no players behind me and I had time to regroup. My trousers under my rain pants stayed mostly dry. I now realized that my waterproof golf shoes are only waterproof until the point of submersion. After putting out on 12, some fifteen minutes later, I went back to see if the wedge or pull cart might have surfaced but it was of no use. I then soldiered on, carrying my bag, and nearly birdied the short Par 3 thirteenth. Another two holes later I realized my rental car keys were also in the bag. They also survived followed by an exhale of relief. After the 18th hole, which was a very difficult uphill par 3, I took a circuitous route to the car park to avoid being seen by the golf staff. Might they have asked me where the pull cart was? I certainly was not forthcoming with any information on its whereabouts. Lunch and a beer in the clubhouse had me feeling fortunate about the ordeal. Heck, I even creased a smile. This day could have been a disaster of major proportions. Other than the 13th and 18th par three holes, I hardly remember the last six holes at Brora. There is a big difference between losing your valuables at a local municipal course ten miles up the road from home and losing them in the Highlands of Scotland. Today, I considered myself the luckiest man on the face of the earth. I could hear the feint sound of Argentinian Roberto De Vincenzo from 1968 whispering, "what a stupid I am". After my round and lunch, I visited the Dunrobin Castle which I found very enjoyable. That was followed with a visit to Glenmorangie Distillery which was conveniently on the way back to my hotel. There were no additional moments of anxiety during my trip.

My Saturday round would be played at Castle Stuart on the Moray Firth. Stuart has hosted multiple Scottish Opens in recent years and the course was impeccable. Today would also find good weather. I played with a two ball from Toronto and we got to talk about one of my favorite subjects, hockey. The large Scottish flag fronting the clubhouse in an odd position and nearly in the parking lot was purposely placed as a direct center line for the blind tee shot to the fairway of the 18th Par 5 hole. It turned out to be my best tee ball of the day. The red jacket with blue trim I wore today matched the clubs caddie jackets perfectly. After the round, I took a picture of me and the two caddies in our matching outfits. Reminiscent of when my son John had a matching jacket to the caddies at Kingsbarns in 2014. Lunch and drinks at the clubhouse were enjoyed with my new Canadian friends Chris and Jeff. Cheers! I shot 85.

On Sunday May 29th I would play at Nairn golf club, also on the Moray Firth. With a mid-afternoon tee time I took the morning hours to visit the Loch Ness area. The mythical sea serpent had spawned a cottage industry in the area of the Loch's. After that I visited Cawdor Castle which was close by Nairn Golf Club. I believe this to be the first time I ever stopped at two castles on the same trip but both were worthwhile. At Nairn, I was visited by more stiff winds and an angry sea. As I got out of the car in the parking lot you could feel the spray of the mist from the adjacent waters. The clubhouse, restaurant, and pro shop were very modern and American looking which surprised me. We began our round in rain but it turned reasonably pleasant after the fifth hole. The course was a genuine links with the first eight holes heading straight west with the firth directly on our right. The 8th green was the perfect spot for a group photo. I played with Sam Wallach while his wife Kelsey walked along as a spectator. They were on their Covid delayed honeymoon and along with my best caddie of the week David, we had a terrific afternoon. I said of Nairn, it under promised and over delivered. This course should be on everyone's list if traveling in the area. After golf I drove east to Aberdeen. Back home, Marcus Ericsson of Sweden was winning the Indy 500. I pulled in to my Aberdeen Hotel called the Malmaison. Now this was more my speed for a hotel. Ample room, easy parking, cozy bar with fireplace, and an excellent restaurant for both breakfast and dinners.

My first of three rounds on the Aberdeen leg of the trip would be at Royal Aberdeen. I played here in 2019 and looked forward to my return. I played with a two ball from the German speaking section of Switzerland; Pascal, and Pedro. They were both left-handed players. The weather started out a bit iffy but it quickly turned into a fine day. The Royal Aberdeen would be the firmest course on the trip and I loved it. It was probably my best ball striking round of the trip excluding an error on #10 which cost me a careless double bogey. After golf we enjoyed a beer in the warm and friendly clubhouse. Cheers! Then it was down the street for lunch at a course called Murcar. It was a planned excuse to visit additional venues. I talked at length with their very proud club pro by the name of Gary Forbes. Gary had been here thirty years and bragged about how great his lesser-known course was. After his heartfelt dissertation, I nearly felt guilty I was not playing it. He was also proud of his golfing family. He and his three brothers had an aggregate handicap of four at one time and his sister was an assistant captain at one of the early Solheim Cup events. A very proud golf man indeed. He presented me with a sleeve of 150th anniversary 'Open' golf balls which I thanked him for. Back home I also had a proud brother as I learned that brother Tim shot his age today at his home course.

Round two in Aberdeen or along the Aberdeenshire coast along the North Sea was played at Trump International. I was shocked at how few cars were in the parking lot. Possibly many golfers were dropped off at the classy course by chauffeured vans. The course was not empty but I expected an overflow crowd at the renowned property. This was one of the most amazing looking courses I have ever seen, and as you know by now, I have seen a few. Massive dunes covered in tall native green and golden fescue waving in the breeze. The course was carved in meticulously so that you could never see any hole on the course other than the one you were playing. Nor than could you see any other players. The walking paths from green to tee were manicured to perfection with perfectly mowed dark green grass. It looked like 18 Monet paintings. The clubhouse and bar area were ample, but not overblown. I started out very good and even took the jacket off early as the sun was warming. Weather can change fast in Scotland and on the 6th hole the skies darkened, the wind picked up, and rain followed. It rained fairly hard on holes 6 through 9 and my playing partner Jake from Colorado and I were plenty wet. Luckily it dried up after the ninth and the balance of the day was enjoyable. The wind even died down after the 12th. My caddie, Blair, took me up to the back tees on #18 for a photo high atop the North Sea. It was a majestic site with the Par 5 green 651 yards away and maybe 50 yards below. I parred the finale from my more appropriate tees at a still healthy 557 yards giving me a total of 86 on the day. I checked in back home daily as Christy was spending a lot of time at the rehab facility with her mother. She was doing her job both remotely and capably. There was no good news to report from the infirmary.

Wednesday June 1st took me a little further north up the coastline to Cruden Bay. This was my most anticipated round of my week simply based on all my pre-trip scrutinizing. It has been ranked as high as #52 in worldwide rankings. I was fortunate to play with two local members, Jack and Winkie, along with my young caddie Cameron. The weather was nice but the wind picked up on the final six inward holes. Cruden Bay had some interesting holes that are hard to explain. On one Par 4 your approach shot was like hitting a blind shot into a wok pan. If your ball was close either left or right, it would usually, but not always, end up on the green. They also had a drivable Par 4 even for me. I did hit the green on my drive and made a three-foot putt for birdie helping me to an 81 total. Our group went into the clubhouse for a pint after our round. Cheers! I enjoyed Cruden Bay and my golfing companions very much. I then drove to St Andrews, the highlight of any trip to Scotland. After checking into the Ardgowan Hotel less than a block away from the Old's 18th green, I walked to the Old to look around. The stands and yellow iconic scoreboard were already in place awaiting the 150th Open being played here in seven weeks. The massive souvenir tents were two of the largest buildings in town. I cannot imagine the amount of merchandise it will take to fill them. I was able to secure a round on the Old at 6:00 pm and I played with three students from the University. It was getting dark on 15 & 16, both of which I three-putt for bogey. It was simply too dark to play the final two holes and the group in front of us had not teed off on 17 yet. I carded two bogeys, packed it in and headed for the hotel a short walk away.

Thursday's afternoon round is the one that was changed due to greens issues but I started the day walking through the town of St Andrews and taking the opportunity for some pictures at the Swilcan Bridge with the claret jug that was on hand for the upcoming Open. I also went to St Andrews Cathedral Graveyard in hopes of visiting Old and Young Tom Morris' burial site but the cemetery was closed until final inspection of falling rock and debris from the ruins that had been reported a couple weeks prior. That was a disappointment for me as I have seen gravesite photos, particularly from a recent movie called Tommy's Honour. My round today originally scheduled for Dumbarnie Links was traded for Kingsbarns. Kingsbarns is played annually by the pros during the Alfred Dunhill Links Tournament. Another good weather day, I was fortunate to play with 81-year-old Fred, along with his children Roy and Emma. Roy and Emma looked a little younger than my kids. Fred lives in Liverpool while his kids were up from London. The trip was Fred's covid delayed 80th birthday present from his children. Other of their family members were back in town. In 2014, Kingsbarns was my highest score of the week. Today, my mostly solid play allowed me to shave 4 strokes off my 90 from 2014. My caddie David was excellent and gave me some great advice that I hope to help me in future years. We finished about 6:00 pm and I decided to have dinner in their beautiful dining area overlooking the 18th green. I enjoyed a nightcap at the Dunvegan, next door to the Ardgowan Hotel. Cheers!

My final round would give me another crack at Carnoustie. I played a solid round with a father son team from Glasgow and my caddie Mark. In 2019 when I played Carnoustie, my caddie suggested I use a fairway metal off the tee on #17 and play short of the meandering burn which left me too far away to reach the Par 4 in regulation. I was never happy about that. Also in 2019, playing 18 into a breeze and driving into light rough I was forced to lay up to the Barry burn, leaving me a 60-yard wedge for my third shot to the Par 4 finishing hole. Today hole 17 played down breeze. I decided I would use driver to carry the burn on my drive and my wind aided effort made it. My accomplishment however did not pay off as it found a penal bunker over the burn just left of the fairway. About three yards of cut and my drive would have bounded another 25 yards down the fairway. As it was, I had to pitch out sideways. My three-putt double bogey did not detract from my accomplishment off the tee. On 18, playing into the breeze, I hit a solid drive that found the fairway. Facing the stiff three club wind it was earlier determined that my maximum carry length off the fairway turf going in that direction was roughly 155 to 160 yards. My caddie Mark said the carry required for this shot was 158 yards. The green was another 25 yards beyond that. What happened next is what the pros would call deliberation and my friends at home would call slow play. I finally answered my own question when I told Mark, "If I go in the burn, drop, chip and two putt I will make a six. If I cross the burn, it is doubtful I would reach the green. I would probably pitch on and maybe make a four but more probable a five. But whether I make a four, five or six, it does not matter. I have had a great day." At that point it was easy, I was going for it. It was never a sure thing but I did cross that burn, just, and ended up rolling into the left front greenside bunker. The bunker shot was intimidating with a back flag and people lunching outdoors behind the green. It reminded me of Pinehurst. I did not attempt the proper shot for that length of bunker shot because of the diners present but we did put it on the green and two putt for bogey. Regardless of the score recorded, I will always be proud of my shots on those difficult finishing holes. My rounds for the week were eerily close. I carded scores of 82, 85, 83, 82, 86, 81, 86, 86, 85. That evening I passed my test to come home virus free.

As I drove back to the airport on Saturday morning and I crossed the Forth Bridge again, I thought of the Stones' song 'The Last Time.' Because this could be the last time. I don't know. Spoiler alert, it would not be the last time.

The joy I had on my solo trip was immense, but it was not lost on me that a trip shared is twice rewarded. The flight home was on schedule, it was June 4th, and it was good to be back home. I missed my wife who unfortunately had not shown any improvement from the day I left. I feared some difficult time ahead, possibly years.

A week after my return, our government lifted the covid testing for inbound travelers. Has freedom finally been restored after 822 days? The World Health Organization officially announced that the pandemic was over on May 5th, 2023. Roughly two years after I experienced a similar revelation. CDC Director Dr. Rochelle Walensky resigned shortly thereafter. What concerns me is I am convinced our government will manufacture reasons in the future to attempt to lock us down again. That is one of the reasons I feel a need to travel while I can. Responsible U.S. citizens have plenty on their minds. Their freedom should not be one of the topics.

My wife came home from the rehabilitation center on Friday, June 17th. She was not rehabilitated but the insurance company said, enough is enough. I was not upset with them. They had extended our benefits on multiple occasions. I was very concerned about our long-term future but I had been trying to mentally prepare myself for it. Our home was set up with all the necessary equipment to handle what would be required. The dining room became our hospital room. My daughter came home again to help and visit for Father's Day, June 19th. We held an open house for my wife Ginger on June 25th for family only. Originally, we thought a party but an open house was a better term based on her condition. It was a short morning brunch affair with about twelve of my siblings or their spouses, plus our kids and grandkids. I came up with the idea a month ago. I felt she deserved some love and attention. She had been through a lot. Ginger was weak but we had her in a chair for the event though she would rather have been allowed to stay in bed. Overall, it went very well and based on the following weeks unseen and unimagined events, I am so glad we did it. It was her last good day.

The following Monday, June 27th, Ginger had an appointment with a wound specialist. She had developed a bad wound on her backside in rehab from constant bedrest and lack of movement. That, I did fault the rehab center for. The size and depth of the wound was that of a hockey puck. Or so it was described to me. I had the good fortune to have never seen it. I had my 'women in the arena' help with the wet work along with daily in-home care. I cannot forget the first time a male, seasoned nurse came to the house to dress the wound. I believe it was June 20th. The look on his face spoke volumes. He was the one that recommended we see the specialist. The doctor suggested two things after seeing her, surgery, or hospice. Hospice is a scary word to me and it was not the first time we had heard it in the past month. I think of that word as a term of finality and I did not feel we were close to that. Neither Christy or I ever thought surgery would be a good idea. Things were getting worse quickly. After consultation including my daughter-in-law Casey, on Tuesday June 28^{th,} we did call in the hospice team and they made their initial visit the following day. We did not get a positive report. They gave her one to three weeks to live. It was truly unimaginable news to us. The kids and grandkids visited that evening. By June 30^{th,} Ginger was sleeping nearly 24 hours a day. It was a sad time. That evening Ginger said something to me. I could not hear her so I muted the TV, put my ear near her mouth and asked her to repeat it again. I still could not make out the faint words but I will bet it was something nice. Christy hung around the entire time and her bosses were gracious in their understanding. It was amazing how bad things had gotten so quickly, even in twelve-hour periods. Christy gave her medicine to ease any discomfort. On Friday July 1st, Christy and I went to the funeral home to prepare for arrangements that now seemed imminent. I began putting words to paper for an obituary. To lighten the mood of the obit slightly, I mentioned that her favorite meal was reservations. I wasn't lying. That evening about eight of us, some of my siblings and their spouses had a nice dinner together at a favorite local restaurant. I do not recall why it was arranged. Maybe it was just a holiday weekend. It was a fun evening and I never discussed Ginger's health issues. But as we were about to break up, I casually mentioned, "there may be a funeral next week." That was shocking news to them. Some had just seen Ginger on the 25th but others at dinner were not available that day. Ginger's health had fallen that far that quickly.

Hospice was out the following morning on July 2nd and we were now given the 12 hours to two-day warning. I immediately called my sister-in-law Linda to ask if she would do the eulogy. Believe me, it took a while for me to get the words out. A little after 10:00 pm that evening, Christy, and I kissed Ginger (who was asleep) goodnight and went to our respective bedrooms. About 30 minutes later I heard Christy get up and walking around which was very unusual for her. She is usually tucked away watching a show or movie on her I-phone. Soon thereafter she turned the hall light on and I knew what she was going to say before she spoke her first word. At 10:45 pm that evening, Saturday, July 2nd, Ginger was gone. I folded her arms and made the phone call to the hospice team and our other children. Hospice arrived within an hour. From our vantagepoint, it seemed like as peaceful an ending as one could have. I was so happy that it happened at home. It was a mere 93 days from the day of her now fateful fall due to a stroke and 17 days since her return home from rehab.

We had a nice visitation and funeral on July 6th just as Ginger always wanted. Some happy music, Christmas, and Disney tunes. Some balloons including Mickey Mouse balloons. Flowers and plants sent in from friends and family filled the room. There was a variety of mourners in for the calling from various walks of our life, past and present. Friends of many years, high school classmates, people from our neighborhood, people I work or had worked with, people from our many years in the hockey world when our children played hockey for so many winters, customers I currently call on, people from my golf league, and of course a host of family members. Her send-off went as well as I could have hoped. I spoke a few words thanking her for our good life followed by the Beatles tune 'Thank You Girl.' Our Granddaughter Abby spoke eloquently followed by the song 'Grandma's Love' by Mark Yamanaka. There was a lot of sniffling during that tune coming from the gathering behind me. I found that song while searching for the right music to play. I had never heard the song before but it was very fitting. Finally, my sister-in-law Linda gave the final tribute which was outstanding including a letter she read from our daughter Christy about her mother. That was followed by the song, 'All Love Can Be' by Charlotte Church and finally a piece of instrumental music, the theme song from the mini-series, 'The Thorn Birds.'

After the service we headed to the gravesite that was on the same property and a mere 200 yards from the funeral home where the service was held. The pallbearers chosen included our two sons, John, and Jason. Our two oldest granddaughters Abby and Kaley. And my two sisters' husbands, Mary's husband Tony and Maureen's husband Brad. Kaley had taken the passing of her grandmother harder than anyone as best as I could see. They were extremely close. I am certain that many years from now, she will take heart in knowing she had a major and honored role in her grandmother being laid to rest.

The cortege following the hearse tied the record for the shortest cortege ever. Zero cars. It was perfect. As mentioned, the gravesite was a mere two hundred yards away and we all walked to the final resting site in comfortable July weather. The balloons at the service were carried to the gravesite and released into the air in unison. I am certain Ginger would have liked that. It was a touching, memorable moment. My brother Mike and sister-in-law Linda had a group over for food and drink following the service.

I mentioned a few days later that the funeral was so well done that I had an inner peace about the entire event. In future weeks it seemed like a surreal situation. I knew it was true but it was hard to believe. It got very quiet and oftentimes lonely at home. We were not what I would call a publicly affectionate couple, but she was my best friend. I will face a major adjustment. We had plans for a Golden Anniversary event less than two years away. This writing will end on my 70th birthday but the final fourteen months will be lived in a way that I never considered. Widower was never a title I expected to hold. If a trip shared is twice rewarded, you can only imagine sharing forty-eight years with one person. My retirement will be put on the back burner as I need something to occupy my time. I now consider work to be an essential part of my wellness plan. I visited the gravesite every day I was in town and seeded and watered her plot daily until fall. By mid-October her resting place had the greenest grass in the city. I think about her every day.

Other deaths of people I have admired from afar close to this same time period included:

Mike Bossy on April 15th. One of my all-time favorite NHL hockey players who never wore a Bruins jersey.

The great Bruin killer Guy Lafleur died a week later. The flashy Quebecois with the flowing locks, nicknamed the Flower, scored over 50 goals and even more assists for 6ix straight seasons throughout the seventies.

Len Dawson died on August 24th. He was the quarterback and MVP of the Super Bowl IV champion Kansas City Chiefs, my all-time favorite team. Herb Kohler on September 3rd. Herb was the modern day patriarch and bold leader of the Kohler plumbing fixture company. Our family was a Kohler distributor for all our years in the plumbing wholesale world. He was an important man for our business and industry. He also owned the Old Course Hotel on the 17th fairway at St Andrews.

Queen Elizabeth II on September 8th. The lady had grace, duty, dignity, and discipline. She was born into privilege and spent a lifetime earning it. As my wife Ginger welcomed family into our home seven days before her passing, the Queen welcomed a new prime minister a mere two days before her passing. Liz Truss, the new PM, resigned six weeks later.

Loretta Lynn on October 4th. 'The Queen of Country Music.' I had my years of being a big country music fan and the Coal Miner's Daughter was a big part of it. I was a fan of both Queens.

What was the main difference between people who died in the 6ixties versus people who died in my 60's, except for my grandfather and a few icons? I was not old enough to understand or care in the 6ixties and most people who passed are not people I had a connection to. In my 60's it is common to lose people you loved, cheered for, was a big fan of, or admired. It becomes natural to consider your own mortality.

I left my 68th year with the U.S. seemingly in bad shape and certainly heading in the wrong direction. I found it difficult to agree with anything this administration did. I gave them a fair shot. They did absolutely nothing that helped me in my life, or anyone I know. We went from an America first administration to an America last administration. You had to wonder if the American dream is still attainable. A better question might be is the American dream still desired? Being a bum and expecting our government to take care of you has gained immense popularity in recent years. There has certainly been a shift in values.

We are led by a man who speaks weakly, struggles to come to grips with the truth, slurs his words, and walks gingerly. He is prone to go into angry tirades. I take that as a sign he knows he is a failure. The national debt soared under the weight of printed money. They love our open borders. The US may be the only country on earth that has no borders and does not know its own population. Drug issues with fentanyl coming across our southern border are killing children and adults daily. They had no answer for their self-created inflation including fuel and energy prices. Another non–bipartisan bill was recently passed called the Inflation Reduction Act. A stroke of marketing genius by the democratic party. The bill had nothing to do with reducing inflation but the uninformed public thought it sounded good. It was more inflationary green energy spending being shoved down our throat. We gave up energy independence for a green energy that is not ready for prime time, full time. Does the administration even understand where electricity and energy come from? Are they looking for utopia or dystopia? President Biden and his 'Bidenomics' 'War on Energy' is the core to our inflationary pain. California recently passed a law saying they would sell no gas-powered cars by 2035. During a recent heat wave in California that was sucking the state's energy supply, the Democrat Governor asked people not to charge their electric vehicles. You cannot make this stuff up. Interest rates are at their highest levels in years and still rising. Crime is off the charts and go unpunished making all major

American cities unsafe. They are fans of lawlessness and in fact seem to fuel it. The inmates are clearly running our asylum. They have no regard for the sanctity of life. If they do not care about life inside the womb, why would we think they care about life outside the womb. Homelessness goes unchecked and disrupts life in crowded public areas. Our supply chains are not up to speed with no answer forthcoming. They just want us to lower our expectations. We have an education problem due to their obligation to the teachers' unions and woke agenda. We continue to fall below other countries in education. We have gender identification issues. Pronouns are deemed as hate speech by some. We have employment issues. Unemployment is down yet nearly everyone is hiring. Our government has made it too easy on too many. Unemployment benefits were designed as a short-term life line, not a career path. Our stock market had finally had its Teflon shine scoured away. This is not the America I was raised in. I believe we may be closing in on the point of no return. I have named President Biden the Commander in Chaos.

Biden ran as the basement unifier but is the leader of the party of hate, the fabricator of stories and lies, and Divider in Chief #2. He really could care less about many citizens. He is more concerned about his antique car. We are living under a divisive and treasonous administration. He sold himself as a centrist but he has moved further left than anyone who has held the office. That was hard to do. It may not have mattered. People hated Donald Trump that much. The crises we face are not acknowledged by the administration because these are crises by design. The devious plan to change and weaken our country is slowly working. The real insurrection may be brewing from within. What I refer to as our cold civil war comes from polarizing ideology's which is doom for our country. I used to think all Americans wanted the same things but had vastly different ideas how to achieve those things. Now I am not convinced we want the same things at all. I feel that we have been divided by ideology in this country for many decades but we used to be able to compromise. Not anymore. The scary thing is that we could do worse. The liberals have a deep bench of America hating politicians. This is the hand we are dealt. I will endeavor to persevere.

How could I rate a year when you lose a spouse of forty-eight years? I had some great times as a 68-year-old, but overall, it was the saddest year of the nineteen I have written about.

69

9-19-2022 to 9-18-2023

My 69th birthday was nothing to celebrate. It was simply put, a sad day. I thought about Ginger. The fact is I was in life's unchartered territory. To make things a little more depressing, I watched quite a bit of Queen Elizabeth's funeral on TV today. It seemed fitting. Operation London Bridge began a week prior at Balmoral Castle in northern Scotland. I was in that area just four months ago. The event went from Balmoral and down to Dundee, across Tay Bridge and on to Edinburgh for a few days. I am very familiar with that part of the route. She was then taken to London, spent some time at Buckingham Palace before ending up at Windsor Castle. Hundreds of thousands and most likely millions poured onto the streets to get a glimpse of the cortege and pay respects. The planning and choreography were flawless. In my opinion, the Queen was the greatest female in my lifetime. I know a few other ladies that could come to mind, but I am going with the Queen. That evening I had a solo birthday dinner at Eddie Merlot's bar. Had Ginger been around, I know we would have eaten there, with reservations.

On September 28th, Hurricane Ian struck southwest Florida and basically wiped Fort Myers Beach off the map, along with Sanibel Island and many other places in that area. Many of the stores, bars, and restaurants we have frequented for the last twenty years were gone. I do not mean they are a shell of their former selves. I mean they are gone. Wiped out to sea, never to be seen again. I would not be surprised if a few bodies took the same route. It was an apocalyptic scene as I viewed it on TV. There were over 100 casualties, mostly in the Ft Myers Beach area. Our government's transportation of the future, electric cars, were inexplicably catching on fire. Sign me up for one of those. Our condominium, more inland, survived virtually untouched. I was finally able to go to the condo in mid–October to see for myself. I was amazed at how well the structures in our community held up. It does seem as though the past six months, except for my trip to Scotland, has been my version of semi–Annus Horribilis.

Halloween was upon us. My son Jason and his wife Casey are huge fans of the night of horror. Their house is decorated inside and out all month long. Neighbors drive by daily to see their decor and what is new each year. In 2015, Ginger and I had the idea to go to their house on Halloween evening and cook hot dogs on the grill out by the street. We gave hot dogs to all comers. Children, and adults alike. It was a smash hit handing out over 100 hot dogs. We had continued the tradition ever since and though I was not planning on doing it this year, Jason said the show must go on. And, so it did. Jason had the grill going by 5:30. His sister Christy was in town so she went over to help. I arrived about 6:00 pm to make sure they were doing it right. The thing I find most interesting about the event is Jason lives in a neighborhood that doubles as the cradle of diversity. White, Black, Hispanic, Latino, and Asians. Everybody gets along and in a very festive mood on Halloween. It is a night that renews my faith in humankind. It is good for my soul. If we can accomplish kumbaya in a mixed group of hundreds, we ought to be able to find a way to accomplish similar unity as a nation. Imagine. Imagine all the people, living life in peace.

With all the issues we currently face in our country, we had coming up what must have been the 'most important mid–term election of our lifetime.' Not many politicians fighting for their political life wanted to be seen with the unpopular sitting President. While he spent a lot of time hiding in Delaware, the Democrats trotted out the veterans committee in Barack Obama, Bill Clinton, Hilary Clinton, and others to 'save our democracy.' Biden continued to say democracy is on the ballot. I looked for her when I voted but did not see her listed. What Biden may not realize is that democracy **IS** the ballot. And the people had their say. Surprisingly, at least 50% of America appear to like an inept, corrupt, and opaque government.

The red wave or tsunami that even Democrats anticipated never materialized. The Democrats flipped the Republican Senate seat in Pennsylvania and held ground on all the others. That was enough to hand them back the Senate even before another Georgia runoff. The Senate went 51-49 blue. They did not win because of Biden. They won despite Biden. The congressional seats were expected to go blazing red as much as a 235-200 GOP edge. But the final result was a meager 222-212 win for the GOP. A shocking result. Our country is as divided as ever and our elected officials are not seeking harmony. Can a divided America stand and prosper? It would be nice if the persistent investigations would come to an end. I say it is time to look forward but I expect the abscess of corruption must first be addressed. However, that is a rabbit hole that may have no end.

For most of the last twenty-two years, Ginger and I would spend ten to twelve days at our Florida condo during the Thanksgiving holiday. It will always be referred to as **our** condo. Since we usually never spent more than nine days at a time there, and sometimes as few as three, Thanksgiving was our favorite week of the year. This year I was a solo act and spent the twelve days prior to Thanksgiving in Fort Myers. I would be home for the holiday. It did not take long on day one for me to know something, someone, very important was missing. I wondered what I would do for twelve days. I was already looking forward to playing golf with brother Kevin but that was six days away. The questions I asked myself; should I be here? Should I keep our little slice of paradise? The wheels were grinding.

The holidays began with a couple more mass shootings. One in Virginia at a Walmart and another in Colorado at a bar. These things are so common that it is hardly worth bringing up. It has become routine. As a nation we are almost desensitized to the events. A mass shooting has been described as four people shot, excluding the gunman. They say the United States averages more than one per day. Most don't even make the national news. I find it sickening.

The Christmas season of 2022 understandably had a perpetual pall on it for me. Christmas was Ginger's favorite time of year and it did not take much for a tear to develop in my eye. It could come from as simple a thing as seeing her favorite holiday food or hearing a song or seeing a clip from a favorite movie on TV. We both loved the movie 'The Holiday'. When Graham spells out why he has two little girls in his house to Amanda Woods during her surprise visit to his home, that is tough for me to hear. She asks if he is married? Possibly divorced? If you aren't familiar with the movie, he shakes his head no and spells out his situation in front of his little girls, W-I-D-O-W-E-R.

The season always seems to begin in earnest with the annual Kavanaugh family Christmas party. This year it was held on its earliest date ever, Saturday December 17th. My sister Mary and her husband Tony hosted this year. Mary being the youngest of the siblings, I believe this ends the fourth rotation of our parent's children carrying on the tradition of family Christmas. I know our parents would be very proud of us. Like last year, it was held as a double header. In the morning, Mary and Tony's daughter Auna, and her husband hosted the youngsters for a pancake breakfast with all the children wearing pajamas. As an added benevolent act, all the attendees were asked to bring a new pair of pajamas for a local worthy cause. I did not attend the morning event but I heard it was very well done.

That evening the adults headed to Mary & Tony's home for drinks, dinner, desserts, fun, and laughter. The home is spacious enough to comfortably hold the light crowd of thirty-four attendees. After what I referred to as the best dinner of the year starring prime rib and ham, most of us headed downstairs for drinks in their authentic custom-made Irish bar they have named 'Jimmy's', after our father. Tony's brother and stepdad also go by Jim or Jimmy. This bar is authentic Irish in every way from the pictures on the walls, an area for a band, stained glass, and bronze harp shaped handles on the red doors. Irish brands abound as they serve up Guinness, Smithwick's, Harp's beer, plus your favorite domestic brands. Plenty of Irish whiskey is also available. It was a lovely evening that lasted beyond the posted hours and the weather was good all day long.

An Alberta clipper roared into town on the 23rd and hung around through Christmas Day. This would be our first Christmas without

Ginger. The group photo from last Christmas is truly a keepsake. Myself, my kids, and grandkids had an exquisite meal at Eddie Merlot's on Christmas Eve. As usual, the entire group was over at our home Christmas morning for breakfast and the opening of gifts. There was somewhat of a contest over who received the best gift. My son Jason and his wife Casey easily got the best gift because as we have done in past years, their gift was a March trip to Boston to see two Bruins hockey games. I would be accompanying them. But the contest only included gifts that were under the tree. The three-person contest was on. John received the awesome looking new retro jersey of the Florida Panthers. When I was in Florida just before Thanksgiving, I saw a commercial advertising this beauty. The moment I laid eyes on it, I knew my material son would have to have it. Many months earlier I had bought my granddaughter Abby Taylor a Dave Taylor throwback L.A. Kings jersey. Dave was a star player for the LA Kings from 1977-1994. It is gold with purple trim with the royal crown crest on the chest. I thought it was cool and appropriate. Abby is not a hockey fan but I knew just where she could put it to good use. I don't anticipate ever seeing her wear it. My daughter Christy bought Jason a shadowbox frame which held a sweatshirt that his mother bought when Jason played in the 1997 Pee Wee hockey national tournament. Jason was one of the star players on the team I coached. A 2003 photo of Jason with his mother wearing the sweatshirt accompanied the framing. The photo was taken the night Jason went to senior prom. Jason considered the contest a 'no-contest' as he declared himself the clear-cut winner through moistened eyes. There were few dissenters though I really loved the Taylor jersey.

Early on Christmas afternoon my daughter Christy and I began our drive to a warmer climate. We arrived in Fort Myers, Florida at 2:00 pm the following day. We drove because I was going to stay south for a few weeks. And it is a good thing we drove. Southwest Airlines (our usual airline for flights to Fort Myers) had managerial incompetence of gargantuan proportions ruining 100's of thousands of people's holiday vacations. The transportation secretary had no answers other than to say the situation was a complete "meltdown."

The 2022 sports season of champions began in mid-February. The Los Angeles Rams beat the surprising Cincinnati Bengals with a last-minute touchdown. This concluded the most exciting set of playoff games the NFL has ever produced. No fewer than five of the thirteen playoff games were decided on the last play. The NBA title was won by Golden State and the Stanley Cup by the Colorado Avalanche ending the Tampa Lightnings' two-year reign. The 2022 World Series championship went to the Houston Astros. The 2022 golf season saw the majors won by Scottie Scheffler at The Masters, Justin Thomas in come from behind fashion at the PGA, and Matthew Fitzpatrick at the US Open played at The Country Club in Brookline, Mass. Fitzpatrick also won the US Amateur on the same course in 2013. Cameron Smith of Australia won the 150th British Open at the home of golf six weeks after my visit to St Andrews. Meanwhile a new Saudi backed golf league set sail under the name of LIV and headed by Greg Norman. The new league with its obscene amounts of guaranteed money had dominated much of the golf talk this year. Much of it was negative, depending on your slant. And on December 29th, Brazilian superstar footballer Pele' died. He won three world cups with Brazil, his first in 1958. He is the reason many soccer superstars wear the number 10 to this day. Growing up in a non-soccer country, we all knew who Pele' was, such was his international stardom.

The news cycle in 2023 began the same as the previous couple of years. Political corruption, cover-ups, and lies. Think classified documents, election interference, and bribes.

Mass shootings. Recently in California (2) and Michigan State University.
Another black man dies at the hands of policemen. This time in Memphis.
Spy balloons from China. Now we had open borders and open airspace.

An Ohio train derailment. A toxic plume. And an inept Transportation Secretary who had no answers.
A President devoid of empathy.

Some good news to start the year was my annual national sales meeting. For the first time in my 23 years at Mueller we held our meeting out west. Scottsdale, Arizona at the Phoenician Hotel to be exact. I looked forward to the change of venue. The only time I had ever been in Arizona was on a Mueller awards trip when we flew into the Grand Canyon by helicopter from Las Vegas for a champagne lunch. We flew in, looked at the muddy water, ate lunch, and flew out. The weather in Scottsdale was chillier than what we would have experienced in Florida but there were plenty of space heaters to keep the outdoor events comfortable. Jackets or sweaters came in handy for our annual golf outing. The surprise of the event is they gave everyone on the sales team a new I-pad computer. It was pre-loaded with all the Mueller apps necessary to conduct business at home or on the road. As a guy who has an electronic disability and already capable of doing everything necessary on my I-phone or lap top, I found it quite unnecessary. However, the generosity was not lost on me and in time I would surely adapt. Afterall, our company motto is 'be flexible and receptive to change.'

One other piece of delightful early year news, at least for me, is that my brother Tim gave me a book to read. As a few of us went to Tim and Noreen's house to watch some playoff football, he asked if I wanted a copy of a book. He had three or four copies as they were given to him. It was a book of golf stories and he did not sound too excited about it which made me not terribly excited about it. Later that evening, his wife Noreen mentioned it was golf stories mostly from Scotland and Northern Ireland. That sounded interesting since I have been there on five occasions. Eventually, while watching the football game, I opened the book to a random page and saw the words Royal Dornoch. As I was recently at Royal Dornoch, that had my full attention. The book's title is 'One for the Memory Banks' by Luke Reese. There were a lot of great golf stories that I could easily relate to, based on my overseas golf experiences. I read the book. Twice. Also, I booked a September 2023 golf trip to St Andrews and Liverpool. Hoylake, Royal Lytham, and Royal Birkdale are in my future. More things to look forward to.

As previously mentioned, we had a contest for the best Christmas gift this past holiday. And as I also mentioned, the clear winner was a trip to Boston to see the Bruins including myself with Jason and Casey. Today is March 9th and we are off. We stayed at my brother Kevin's apartment which sits beautifully on the harbor and is just a short one mile walk from the TD Garden. Even closer to many bars and restaurants we patronized. Day one began with a greeting from Kevin before he was off to his southern compound in Naples. We soon thereafter left for drinks at the Black Rose and The Greatest Bar. Game one tonight was against the Edmonton Oilers. The best player in the league, Connor McDavid, plays for Edmonton. Boston was on a ten-game win streak and owned the best record in the league, playing at an NHL record pace. The Bruins was coming off a four-day rest and I really expected them to pounce. They took a 2-0 lead into the 2nd period with goals from Marchand and Pastrnak but overall played a lackluster game. The Oilers were not much better but good enough taking a 3-2 come from behind win. I have mentioned before that I never judge a hockey trip on wins and losses but I must say, this was a disappointing loss.

The following day was mid-forties and sunny. There was no game today. We did something today that I have never done in all my trips to Boston and I could not tell you why. (I think this was my 15th visit) We walked the Freedom Trail. The Freedom Trail was approved in the 1950's by then Mayor John Hynes. It was his nephew I played golf with in 2021 at Royal County Down in Northern Ireland. We passed Faneuil Hall, Paul Revere's home, The Old North Church, Copps Hill Burying Ground, Bunker Hill, and walked onto the USS Constitution. Along the route we stopped for a drink at Fillipo's Ristorante. We engaged at depth with the manager and I felt bad we could not come back for dinner that day or the next as we had already made reservations elsewhere. The proud man convinced all of us that they had great food. If I get back, Fillipo's will be my first dinner stop. This evening we ate dinner at Cantina Italiano. Both are in Boston's North End.

The next day, Saturday, the Bruins played Original 6ix Detroit in a matinee. It is always special seeing an original 6ix matchup. We arrived early and had some food and drink at a new place next to the Garden called Banners. Banners has a forty-two-foot TV screen for patrons to view the game. Biggest restaurant screen I have ever seen. This game was the reverse of Thursday night's game. The Red Wings got off to a 2-0 lead before the Bruins kicked it into gear in period two. Captain Patrice Bergeron tallied a beauty in period two and the Bruins escaped with a 3-2 win. There was plenty of pressure and bouncing pucks in front of the capable Bruin netminder during the last few minutes of frantic action. It seemed to be a very emotional win for me. I really do love the Boston Bruins and you just never know when or if you might be back. Lower bowl seats for both games were outstanding. After the game we visited Stanza Dei Sigari's cigar bar below street level in the North End to buy our generous apartment dweller a small gift of appreciation. A drink at the Sail Loft preceded dinner at the Old Oyster House. There was never a lack of good food or drink during our stay. Other establishments patronized during our visit included Mike's Pastry Shop, Quincy Market, Bell in Hand Tavern, and others. This was possibly my best trip ever to Boston. Despite the loss on Thursday evening, everything was perfect. I think Jason and Casey agree. This is the first time I have ever been to Boston where I did not purchase a souvenir. I am flush with gear and memorabilia. With all my good fortune, I barely have room for the memories. Seven weeks later, the Bruins historic record-breaking season in wins and points came to a crashing and disappointing end with a first-round playoff loss at home against the Florida Panthers. The Bruins lost two home games in overtime including the series clincher in game seven.

March 27, 2023. Shortly after I began driving down the road, I turned the radio on. The first words I heard were 'school shooting'. I was immediately sick to my stomach. How bad would this one be? The shooting was at a pre-K thru grade 6 Christian School in Nashville, Tn. Three nine-year-olds dead along with three adult administrators. The shooter was courageously taken out by local police within fourteen minutes of the initial call coming in. The President came out a few hours after the event to make his comments. He began by making jokes about being his wife's husband and about chocolate chip ice cream. What was obviously a solemn moment, he was not up to the task. He seldom is.

On April 25th, President Biden announced his intention to run for President again in 2024. He was still concerned about the 'soul of the nation' and being able to 'finish the job'. 'Finish the Job' will be his campaign slogan. I might suggest, 'we have met the enemy and they are us.' The job he is referring to is green energy, Socialism and social engineering. Seventy percent of Americans including fifty percent of democrats hoped he would leave the job to someone else. They were hoping he might replicate the announcement President Johnson made in the 6ixties when he declared he would not accept his party's nomination. Biden did not make his announcement with the usual fanfare this type of news deserves but rather his team released a three-minute video complete with voiceover while most of the country was still asleep. He began his video with the word Freedom. The same Freedom we had been denied of during the Covid period. There was no vision for the future and no mention of past accomplishments. I expect this will be another basement campaign with few appearances and no debates. He has a reticence to debate because he can barely speak, cannot defend his policies, and has a lack of stamina.

After two and a half years of seemingly the most corrupt, anti-American, mentally bankrupt, inflation driving, divisive President in my lifetime or any I have read about in our great history, Biden still polls even in a virtual 2024 election poll against Donald J Trump. If this is the ticket that the American people are forced to vote on, it is clearly an indictment of our political system. In my poker playing days I had the option of folding my hand. This one must be played out by all of us. At this point in time the 2024 election shapes up to be a Biden / Trump rematch. A rematch election may come down to this simple question: do we hate Trump more than we love ourselves and our country? Possibly, just possibly, these two men will exit stage right and two better candidates will step forward and right the ship. It is easy for me to see why people would not vote for Trump. It is difficult for me to see how anyone would vote for Biden. Either way, it is sure to be an exciting campaign and I will endeavor to persevere. Our nation must endeavor to persevere.

On May 6th, King Charles was coronated in England. The grand event was televised on nearly every American channel. Later that day, another mass shooting at an outlet mall took place in Texas. Eight dead with more wounded and taken to the hospital. The news claims this to be the 199th mass shooting in the year 2023. As always, the politicians, citizens, and media send their thoughts and prayers. I am sick and tired of hearing about thoughts and prayers. Either take the measures necessary to reduce the threat or shut up. Yea, I get upset hearing about these events. The depth of my emotions cannot come through on these pages. We should not have to live with this daily threat. The Texas event gave Biden reason to order flags at half-staff once again. In the 6ixties, lowered flags were a rare event.

Mothers' Day of 2023 was the first since Ginger had passed so it was another tough day. The sorrow of the weekend was happily masked by our granddaughter Abby's college graduation. She worked very hard on it and we are all very proud of her. Her grandma would have enjoyed our dinner celebration at Ocean Prime. As sad as Mother's Day was, I found Father's Day weekend to be even more sad. A year ago, Ginger came home from the rehab center on June 17th. This year Father's Day was June 18th. It was hard not to reflect on the year that had passed. For as long as I could remember, Ginger always bought me very nice and upscale clothing items for Father's Day. Things I would never buy for myself. There would be no fufu bags waiting for me this year.

The traditional Kavanaugh Father's Day golf outing went on as always under comfortable June temperatures. We had thirteen players this year and I had a nice podium finish. My brother Tim and his wife Noreen hosted a post golf party and brother Michael presented everyone with his newly published 'Kavanaugh Family History' pictorial book that had pictures of family members as far back as the late 1800's.

In a moment of weakness and stupidity, I asked brother Michael to bring with him to the course a 3,000-piece Beatles themed jigsaw puzzle that he has owned for a few years. We both knew he owned it. We both knew he loved it. We both knew he would never tackle it. I told him I would take a swing at it. I completed the puzzle by the end of July, had it framed, and will surprise him with it at the family Christmas party later this year which he and his wife Linda are hosting. If an idle mind is the devil's workshop as our mom often said, he could not find me for the five weeks I spent working on that puzzle. I expect Mike will be extra surprised when he sees it because he will forget I even had it. I know it will be a big hit. I was never convinced I had all the right pieces until it was actually finished. What a relief and adrenaline rush that was to place the final piece in its rightful spot.

My 60's are quickly coming to an end. The July 4th holidays will always coincide with my wife's passing on July 2nd, 2022. It is amazing how fast time flies when you have an event to measure it against. This 4th of July it was hard to discern between fireworks and gunfire. At least seventeen shootings were recorded nationally led by Philadelphia, Fort Worth, and at home in Indianapolis. The Indy shooting occurred one block south of the Forest Manor baseball diamonds I played on as a kid in the 6ixties. We played often on summer days under the blanket of sunshine, safety, and happiness. My daughter Christy joined me over the holiday weekend to see Peter Noone and Herman's Hermits in concert at a small venue in Ft. Wayne, In. I admit to liking a lot of his songs and he sang them all. Even Christy was familiar with many of his tunes. He put on a good family friendly show.

Not long after the July holiday my favorite Boston Bruin, Patrice Bergeron, retired. He played only for the Bruins in his nineteen-year professional career. For those of you who don't follow the sport of hockey, I can say with no doubt that Bergeron was to the Bruins what Derek Jeter was to the Yankees or Peyton Manning to our Indianapolis Colts. He was a gentleman, a Pros Pro, and leader of men. His long time Bruin teammate, David Krejci retired a few weeks later. Both Patrice and David played over 1,000 regular season games for the Bruins and were Stanley Cup winning teammates in 2011. Congratulations to both.

In August, the town of Lahaina, Maui, Hawaii literally burned to the ground. Over 100 dead and hundreds more unaccounted for and presumed dead. The man who was elected President partly because of his empathetic nature was again well short of the mark. Twice when asked about the situation he replied, "no comment". When he finally flew to Hawaii nearly two weeks later, he wanted to compare the tragedy to a small kitchen fire he experienced in his home some years ago. In the past 6ix months he has ignored or disrespected Gold Star families from losses in Afghanistan, the town of East Palestine, Ohio after their train derailment containing hazardous materials, and now the State of Hawaii. The man cannot even handle the most basic of ceremonial functions without embarrassing the nation.

September 7th, 2023. I am off on another golf trip. This time flying into Edinburgh, Scotland and driving down to Liverpool, England for six rounds of golf on 'True Links' and British Open Rota venues. From Liverpool we would head back north for a couple of days in St Andrews. Three months ago, Christy decided to join me on the trip. It certainly reminds me of the traveling companionship my paternal grandfather had with his sister, our Great Aunt Margaret. They took many trips together back in the nineteen forties and fifties including abroad on the Queen Elizabeth and a 26-state automobile trip Grandpa titled in his diary, "A Trip of a Lifetime". Some photos from these trips including our grandmother were included in brother Mike's pictorial family history book. My plan for this trip first took root when the boys from Wales I played with in 2021 mentioned how great the courses are in England's Golf Coast.

United Airlines did us no favors on this trip. Our outbound from Chicago was cancelled due to an oil leak after we had boarded and we had to re-schedule through London as opposed to Edinburgh the following day to make things work out. It cost me my first scheduled round of golf at Wallasey. Our return trip still out of Edinburgh was delayed three hours due to fueling problems which caused connecting issues in Newark and delayed luggage in Indianapolis on the return trip. Having Christy by my side was like traveling with an experienced travel agent. Our ground travel agent (SGH Golf) who made all the golf, hotel, and rental car plans was amazing with their agility and efficiency, adjusting to our changing itinerary. During the entire ordeal, I displayed a calm which I am unaccustomed to.

Arrival in London a day late was smooth and we were on our way to Liverpool. It was a warm day. We cruised by The Cavern Club and enjoyed a walk along the Liverpool Albert Docks. We took the Mersey River Cruise which was quite enjoyable. In the depths of my mind this is a cruise I've thought about since hearing Gerry and the Pacemakers sing 'Ferry Cross the Mersey' in 1965. There were many other landmarks along the pier but none meant as much to me as seeing the statues of the Beatles. I had my picture taken with the boys and delighted in pointing skyward, showing John a glimpse of Lucy in the Sky. After relaxing drinks and a light snack, we were onward for the first of four overnight stays at the Grand Hotel in Lytham & St Annes. We arrived shortly after dark and enjoyed dinner at the Hotel.

Finally on Sunday morning I was off to Southport, England for my first round of golf at Southport & Ainsdale. Before hitting S&A, I stopped at nearby Royal Birkdale for a look around. I was not able to connect for a tee time at Birkdale. S&A hosted two of the earliest Ryder Cups in Europe. The historic club hosted in 1933 and 1937. After my solid round of 79, my caddy Martin gave me as good of a souvenir as I may ever have. He gave me his caddy bib that showed the Ryder Cup years and flags of the competing nations in the aforementioned Ryder Cups. God knows I have enough polos. We enjoyed a couple of pints together after the round. Cheers! It is the first time I ever shared a drink with my caddy. I bought a round and he reciprocated. We got on famously as if we had known each other for years. Back at the Hotel which is along the massive St Anne's beach, Christy enjoyed kite day. Hundreds of kites being flown and these were not your typical kites. Massive kites, nearly vehicle sized kites dotting the skyline along the beach. That evening we enjoyed dinner and drinks at Spago. Cheers!

The following morning, I would play my most anticipated round of the week at Royal Lytham & St Annes. Founded in 1886, the course was bestowed Royal status in 1926 just prior to Bobby Jones winning at Lytham to claim his first of three Open titles. The storied course where Seve Ballesteros won two Opens including his famous birdie from the car park. The course where Gary Player won while being forced to putt left-handed onto the 72nd green due to his ball being up against the clubhouse wall. The championship course that opens with a par 3 and where one hole later Ian Woosnam learned he had two drivers in his bag putting him over the 14-club limit. The ensuing penalty more than eliminated his opening hole birdie and lead. And the course where Adam Scott could not hold a solid lead down the stretch that led to Ernie Els second Open victory.

I played Lytham today with a couple of Aussie boys playing a 'reciprocal' round as they are members of Royal Melbourne. Paul and Justin. Justin was a dead ringer for Justin Rose's older brother if Rose had one. I agreed under no pressure to play the longer tees with the men from down under. We measured out at 6,731 yards, nearly a half mile beyond my comfort zone. After a few holes they knew I was up to the task. What they didn't know is that I was playing out of my mind starting with a tap in par at the opening 198-yard par 3 in a light rain that died out after the third hole. I rolled in a birdie two at the 188 yard sixth. My outward 40 on the par 35 was extremely rewarding. The inward nine of par 36 measured an additional 200 yards. My Stealth woods were up to the moment. I made up for my double bogey on #10 with another birdie on the shortish par 4 thirteenth. The next two par 4's was 436 yards down breeze and 455 back into it. On the 14th, two smashing shots left me on the rear fringe where I took two putts for par., I gave two more shots the full treatment on the 15th that left me about twelve feet short of the green but close enough to put the flat stick in my hand. Two putts later I had consecutive pars on holes of length I have no business playing on a daily basis. A light drizzle began again as we left the 17ᵗʰ green. The 393-yard par 4 finishing hole with the iconic clubhouse in the background is a beautiful sight. I've dreamt of this moment. Playing and finishing at Royal Lytham & St Annes. A mediocre flared tee ball left me 180 yards into the wind with a front flag to a narrow, well-bunkered opening from light rough. A flat-out laser was sent toward the home hole with my trusty Stealth 5 wood that landed fifteen feet from the cup. I had fairly impressed some boys including my caddy James with my fairway wood ball striking. I did not make that putt. The tap in par gave me a most satisfying total of 81 on the famed course that has 174 bunkers. I found two of them on the day. The Aussie boys had to abruptly head for the airport after our round and felt bad about not being able to join me for lunch and a pint in the beautiful clubhouse. They assured me that that is not the Aussie way. So, as it was, Cheers to me. Later that day I took Christy over to the course which was just down the street from our hotel for a look around. She was impressed with the beautiful surroundings. Who wouldn't be? The late afternoon took us both to the pool and hot tub, including my nap before dinner on the town of Lytham. What a day.

The following Tuesday morning I was off for my doubleheader rounds including Formby Golf Club and Hillside. Along the way I saw dozens of children walking unaccompanied to school. (Our kids at home can't make a two-block walk from home to the bus stop without parental support.) All of them in uniform. Boys with their ties cinched up neatly. I have no doubt the US of A is missing the boat on this uniform topic. Anyway, I found Formby to be a quiet, challenging club that had 18 holes encircling the ladies separate 18-hole layout. The grill room was modern and comforting with its green carpet and furnishings. It was at Formby where I met the famous John Parrot. Famous if you are from England. John is a former snooker world champion, quite a popular game in these parts. My round at Hillside started in rain but it didn't last long. I had a rare eagle putt attempt on the 482-yard fifth hole. My two-putt birdie was my only birdie of the day. I had scores of 82 and 83 on the two terrific layouts. The Royal Birkdale clubhouse was in plain view from the 17th tee of Hillside. The courses are virtually side by side. After a long day where Christy spent much of the day in the Grand Hotel Spa, we enjoyed a couple drinks at the ample Hotel bar. Cheers!

The following day would take me to Royal Liverpool, aka Hoylake. The club built in 1869 has the most beautiful clubhouse of any of the seven Open venues I have played. A three-story brick front covered in Ivy. A few pounds were immediately dropped off for souvenir purchases. I found the course to be as difficult as any of the Open venues I have played. I had difficulty finding fairways which is not my nature. The wind was up, the fairways well-bunkered, greens with Donald Ross type roll-offs, and thick heavy rough. I needed to be a better player today. The 2023 Open was played here just 7 weeks ago won by American Brian Harman. Unfortunately, I was playing as a single today with my young caddie Nick. The fortunate part, thanks to pro John Heggarty, he saved me about an hour and a half by starting me on the eighth hole, just ahead of a passel of four balls. Since I have never played the course, the routing had no effect on me. All I remember from the Open is they did not play the course in the same sequence that members play. The 17th short par three with the infinity green was controversial. And the pros did not like the in-course out of bounds to the right on #18 and #3. Both holes bordered the driving range, going in opposite directions. My score of 91 was not what I had hoped for but I have had plenty of strong scores on this side of the Atlantic. The highlights of my day came in succession with a green-side sand shot to one foot on the Par 4, 16th (my 9th) followed by my lone birdie on the controversial 17th. (my 10th). My caddie thought it was going in for an ace. The only thing I knew is I hit it well and on its intended line. As my head ascended the horizon and I observed the result, I found my ball had pitched about ten feet left of the hole and curled toward the pin with the aid of the left to right wind before settling three feet directly behind the hole. It is always nice to put a deuce on the scorecard. After my round Christy met me in the clubhouse for lunch before the long drive Home. To St Andrews.

It was dark when we arrived at the glorious Rusacks Hotel in St Andrews. Upon opening our room door, you could see it was nearly Presidential. The full beauty came into focus in the morning as we opened the heavy curtains of the three paneled bay windows onlooking the sun-kissed 18th and first fairways of the Old, the R&A, and all the history that surrounds it. I had no golf planned while in St Andrews. I have played the Old four times and though it's never enough, I wanted to take in the town and enjoy it to its fullest. I have said before that I could enjoy the town without having my golf clubs with me. I proved it to be a true assessment on these two days. Christy spent much of day one in the Kohler Spa at The Old Course Hotel. I was off to complete a quest that was unavailable to me on my last trip to St Andrews. I headed straight to the St Andrews Cathedral and burying grounds in search of Young Tommy Morris' grave. Tommy is a four-time Open champion who died at the age of 24. The quest was completed in short order. Surprisingly I was the only person on the grounds and I had to work on my cell phone selfie talents. Old Tom Morris (also a four-time Open champion) was right there with Tommy and eventually I ran across the grave of Old Tom's employer, Alan Robertson. Robertson is known as the first professional golfer. Some other sightseers eventually made their way to the grounds and I had a proper picture taken with me at the Tommy Morris shrine. With all the golf played this week, my two most coveted photos from our trip are me with the Beatles and with young Tommy. My day continued to St Andrews Castle and into the shopping district where I stopped for a pint at famed Keys Bar. After some light window shopping and watching students moving to and from the University, I had a solo lunch at the Dunvegan. I then spent an hour or so watching golfers out on #1 and in on #18 while awaiting Christy's completion of pampering at the Spa. Shortly after heading toward Christy's location, I ran across a guy I have known virtually my entire life. I ran into fellow Indianapolis native Paul Madden who was vacationing. Paul's parents are my God-parents.

His mother went to school with my mother and was the maid of honor at our parents' wedding. Paul's father was the long-time accountant for our father's business. Seeing Paul in front of the Old Course gift shop was shocking, but I recognized him immediately. The last time I saw him was probably at his fathers' funeral over five years ago. I finally met up with Christy shortly after 3:00 pm at The Jigger Inn for a drink and then headed to the top floor of The Old Course Hotel for additional drink and views of golfers down below. Cheers! Later, the two of us were down to the Swilcan Bridge for a photo opp. Our evening dinner was enjoyed on the top floor of the recently renovated Rusacks at their new high-end restaurant. Upon entering I realized what happened to many of the golf paintings that were down on the main floor during my last visit at Rusacks. Many of them were on the ceiling of the new restaurant. Additional paintings of golfing greats could be found at The Bridge Restaurant on the main floor where we ate our daily breakfast.

On our final day we strolled through town for additional shopping and sightseeing. When we returned to the Rusacks to retrieve our car we told the valet Room 218. He immediately commented that we had one of the best rooms in the Hotel. He knew. After discussion he told us we had the second-best room. The premier room is #116 which is the only room with a large balcony. From our room we could see the balcony of #116 just below us and to our left. So, our room was indeed nearly Presidential. I will never again see a tournament on TV from St Andrews without having the fondest of memories of the exact room we spent two nights in. Upon departure to our final stop at the Airport Hampton Inn, I planned to have lunch at Kingsbarns Golf Club. Not only do they have a fine restaurant and view of the course, this was John's favorite course from our 2014 trip and I wanted Christy to experience the property. I also wanted her to be able to rub her brother John's nose in her good fortune. After lunch we then visited the Crail Golfing Society where I played back in 2019. A final drive across the Forth Bridge would lead us toward the Edinburgh Airport. When we finally arrived home on Saturday, September 16th at 9:00 pm and we had our luggage the following day,

I considered the ordeal with United Airlines history. Christy would later pursue her pound of flesh.

In my 60's I had the good fortune to make six trips to The United Kingdom and The Republic of Ireland to play golf, the game and places I love. After returning from my 6ixth trip I got out my True Links golf book that my friend Bruce Johnson had recommended to me a couple years ago. The authors have the courses divided into sections. The first section they call the Crucible. There is only one course that fit that description which is the Old Course at St Andrews. The course where the game has its roots and its soul. I have had the pleasure to play it four times. The next section in order of importance is called the Icons. I have played 16 of the 25 Icon courses. I have played 5 of the 25 courses listed in the ensuing Classics section and eleven other links courses in Europe. All told I have played 42 rounds in the U.K. and Ireland and visited over a half dozen more. I will always have fond memories of the wonderful venues and the players and people I have had the pleasure to play with or meet beginning with the senior gentleman at Royal Troon and Sheena, owner of the Dunvegan. Others who have made my trips more enjoyable include but is not limited to:

> George from Swaziland at Troon's Portland Links.
> Mike at the Old helping me read the 17th green nearing darkness.
> Dan and Ryan from Wisconsin on the Old.
> Mike and Pete at Kingsbarns.
> Caddies Dominic and John at Waterville.
> Three brothers Brandon, Chris, and Jeff from Idaho at Carnoustie.
> Mark, Ryan, and Kenny at the Old on a drizzly evening.
> Adam, Greg, and Taka at North Berwick.
> Patrick, Dean, and Don from Pittsburgh at Royal Portrush.
> The generous gang of seven from Wales at Castlerock.

Tom Hynes from Boston at Royal County Down.
Chris and Jeff from Toronto at Castle Stuart.
Sam and Kelsey Wallach from Texas at Nairn.
Lefties Pascal and Pedro from Switzerland at Royal Aberdeen.
Gary Forbes, the Pro at Murcar.
Jack and Winkie at Cruden Bay
Fred, Roy, and Emma at Kingsbarns &
Paul & Justin from Melbourne at Royal Lytham.
But no memories will be as fond as the rounds played with my son John, especially at the Crucible and my brothers Mike, Tim, and Kevin in Ireland. Also, the time spent with my daughter Christy will leave her with a lifetime of good memories.

The following day, September 17th, I had planned for some time ending my fascinating decade in style. An Open House party and cookout at home including family, friends, and neighbors. Most of the arrangements were already in place before I departed for England. A strong turnout of 60 arrived for a delightful afternoon of food, drink, music, and laughter. A light drizzle could not dampen the mood. I could not think of a better way to end this decade for me.

It is September 18th, 2023. My brother Pat's 64th birthday. The last day of My 60's. 6ixty years ago today we would have celebrated Pat's birthday with a family meal, gifts, cake, and ice cream. I would be looking forward to my turn tomorrow and I was never cheated. Fifty-One years ago today, would be the last night I spent under my parent's roof. I moved out the following day at the age of 19. Today I cannot say I am excited about being 7eventy tomorrow. No other birthday ending in a zero bothered me like this one. They say it beats the alternative but let me know when you hear that from someone who has experienced the alternative. I feel good, my health appears to be good, and I look great, but 70 is a high bracket. Father time waits for no one. Retirement, which is still being mentally negotiated, was not supposed to be a solo act for me. I consider work as part of my wellness plan now. I think about Ginger every day. As I said before, I will endeavor to persevere.

Through this point of the year the world of sports crowned MY Kansas City Chiefs again as Super Bowl Champions back in February. On consecutive days in June, the NBA crowned the Denver Nuggets as champions while the NHL crowned the Vegas Golden Knights. Both titles were the first for each franchise. Jon Rahm won the Masters on his countryman Seve's birthday. LIV stalwart Brooks Koepka won the PGA for his fifth major title. The World Series is yet to be contested.

In sports they say the harder you work, the luckier you get or that luck is the residue of hard work. That may sum up a good portion of my life. I worked hard and I got lucky. I realize I have been blessed with good fortune in my life spearheaded by good parenting. Our ancestors lived different lives than my generation as our descendants will live different lives than us. I hope they and future generations have the same opportunities as I was afforded.

The country I will depart from someday is much different from the one I was raised in. I will leave it for you to decide which is better. I do wish everyone would have the opportunity at as good an education as I was offered. A real education including reading, writing, arithmetic, history, geography, science, and a dose of discipline. An education using books, pens, paper, and your mind.

There are many differences in the two decades we looked at but also there are similarities. Starting at St Andrew and ending in St Andrews was purely coincidental and my good fortune. Maybe the biggest personal difference from My 6ixties and My 60's could be something that was seldom mentioned but happened organically. In My 6ixties, loved ones worried about, looked after, provided for, and took care of me. In my 60's, I did the same and will continue to do the same for my loved ones. It was my good fortune to live the 6ixties twice. One of those who loved me (and us) was our father. Born in 1928, he was only able to live the 6ixties once. He never saw 60.

Afterword

"That kid's long gone, and this old man is all that's left. I got to live with that."
Ellis Boyd Redding, The Shawshank Redemption

"What I wouldn't give for.... twenty more years."
Hyman Roth, The Godfather, Part II

"We all have it coming kid"
William Munny, The Unforgiven

"There are places I'll remember
All my life though some have changed
Some forever, not for better
Some have gone and some remain
All these places have their moments
With lovers and friends, I still can recall
Some are dead and some are living
In my life, I've loved them all."
The Beatles

Index

Printed in the United States
by Baker & Taylor Publisher Services